Scripting in Java

Integrating with Groovy and JavaScript

Kishori Sharan

Apress®

Scripting in Java: Integrating with Groovy and JavaScript

ISBN-13 (pbk): 978-1-4842-0714-7

ISBN-13 (electronic): 978-1-4842-0713-0

Managing Director: Welmoed Spahr
Lead Editor: Steve Anglin
Technical Reviewers: Vinay Kumar and Massimo Nardone
Editorial Board: Steve Anglin, Mark Beckner, Gary Cornell, Louise Corrigan, Jim DeWolf,
    Jonathan Gennick, Robert Hutchinson, Michelle Lowman, James Markham,
    Matthew Moodie, Jeff Olson, Jeffrey Pepper, Douglas Pundick, Ben Renow-Clarke,
    Gwenan Spearing, Matt Wade, Steve Weiss
Coordinating Editor: Kevin Walter
Copy Editor: Laura Lawrie
Compositor: SPi Global
Indexer: SPi Global
Artist: SPi Global
Cover Designer: Anna Ishchenko

Distributed to the book trade worldwide by Springer Science+Business Media New York, 233 Spring Street, 6th Floor, New York, NY 10013. Phone 1-800-SPRINGER, fax (201) 348-4505, e-mail orders-ny@springer-sbm.com, or visit www.springeronline.com. Apress Media, LLC is a California LLC and the sole member (owner) is Springer Science + Business Media Finance Inc (SSBM Finance Inc). SSBM Finance Inc is a **Delaware** corporation.

For information on translations, please e-mail rights@apress.com, or visit www.apress.com.

Apress and friends of ED books may be purchased in bulk for academic, corporate, or promotional use. eBook versions and licenses are also available for most titles. For more information, reference our Special Bulk Sales–eBook Licensing web page at www.apress.com/bulk-sales.

Any source code or other supplementary material referenced by the author in this text is available to readers at www.apress.com. For detailed information about how to locate your book's source code, go to www.apress.com/source-code/.

To my wife, Ellen

Contents at a Glance

Contents

About the Author

Kishori Sharan is a Senior Software Consultant. He holds a Master of Science degree in Computer Information Systems from Troy State University in Montgomery, Alabama. He is a Sun Certified Java Programmer and Sybase Certified PowerBuilder Developer Professional. He specializes in developing enterprise applications using Java SE, Java EE, PowerBuilder, and Oracle database. He has been working in the software industry for over 17 years. He has helped several clients migrate legacy applications to the web. He loves writing technical books in his free time. He maintains his website at www.jdojo.com, where he posts blogs on Java and JavaFX.

About the Technical Reviewers

Vinay Kumar is a Technology Evangelist. He has extensive experience of more than seven years in designing and implementing large-scale projects in enterprise technologies in various consulting and system integration companies. His passion helped him achieve certifications in Oracle ADF, Webcenter Portal, and Java. Experience and in-depth knowledge has helped him evolve into a focused domain expert and a well-known technical blogger. He loves to spend his time mentoring and writing technical blogs, publishing white papers, and maintaining a dedicated education channel at YouTube for ADF/Webcenter. Vinay has contributed to the Java/Oracle ADF/Webcenter Community by publishing over 250 technical articles on his personal blog, Techartifact. com. He was awarded an Oracle ACE in June 2014. You can follow him at @vinaykuma201 or in.linkedin.com/in/vinaykumar2.

Massimo Nardone holds a Master of Science degree in Computing Science from the University of Salerno, Italy. He worked as a PCI QSA and Senior Lead IT Security/Cloud/SCADA Architect for many years and currently works as Security, Cloud, and SCADA Lead IT Architect for Hewlett Packard Finland. He has more than 20 years of work experience in IT, including in security, SCADA, cloud computing, IT infrastructure, mobile security, and WWW technology areas for both national and international projects. Massimo has worked as a project manager, Cloud/SCADA Lead IT Architect, software engineer, research engineer, chief security architect, and software specialist. He was a visiting lecturer and supervisor for exercises at the Networking Laboratory of the Helsinki University of Technology (Aalto University). He programmed and has taught how to program with Perl, PHP, Java, VB, Python, C/C++, and MySQL. He is the author of *Beginning PHP and MySQL* (Apress, 2014) and *Pro Android Games* (Apress, 2015).

He holds four international patents (PKI, SIP, SAML and Proxy areas). This book is dedicated to Pia, Luna, Leo, and Neve, who are the beautiful reasons for his life.

Acknowledgments

I would like to thank my friend Richard Castillo for his hard work in reading my initial draft of the book and weeding out several mistakes. Richard was instrumental in running all the examples and pointing out errors.

I would like to thank my family members and friends for their encouragement and support for writing this book: my elder brothers, Janki Sharan and Dr. Sita Sharan; my sister and brother-in-law, Ratna and Abhay; my nephews Babalu, Dabalu, Gaurav, ZSaurav, and Chitranjan; my friends Shivashankar Ravindranath, Kannan Somasekar, Mahbub Choudhury, Biju Nair, Srinivas Kakkera, Anil Kumar Singh, Chris Coley, Willie Baptiste, Rahul Jain, Larry Brewster, Greg Langham, Ram Atmakuri, LaTondra Okeke, Rahul Nagpal, Ravi Datla, Prakash Chandra, and many more friends not mentioned here.

My sincere thanks are due to the wonderful team at Apress for their support during the publication of this book. Thanks to Kevin Walter, the Senior Coordinating Editor, for providing excellent support and for being exceptionally patient with me during the editing process. Thanks to Matthew Moodie, Vinay Kumar, and Massimo Nardone for their technical insights and feedback during the technical editing process. Last but not least, my sincere thanks to Steve Anglin, the Lead Editor at Apress, for taking the initiative for the publication of this book.

Introduction

When I wrote the three volumes of *Harnessing Java 7* in 2012, I did not include a chapter on the Java Scripting API because of the limited space that I had for each volume. Note the phrase "Java Scripting," which uses two separate words: "Java" and "Scripting." "JavaScript" is the name of a scripting language, which has nothing to do with the Java programming language, whereas the phrase "Java Scripting API" is the Java API that lets Java applications interact with scripting languages.

In the first release, I had titled this book *Harnessing Scripting in Java*, and it covered only the Java Scripting API and Rhino script engine. The release did not cover the JavaScript language. JDK 8 ships with a lightweight high-performance JavaScript engine called Nashorn, which replaces the Rhino engine that shipped with JDK7. This book covers the JavaScript language completely with comprehensive coverage of the Nashorn engine.

Learning the Java Scripting API, which was introduced in Java 6, is not essential for all Java developers, although it is important and very useful if you are familiar with scripting languages such as Rhino JavaScript, Groovy, Jython, JRuby, and so on and want to take advantage of those scripting languages in Java applications.

I started learning the Java Scripting API by reading some online blogs and articles; they were helpful, but not quite comprehensive in giving me a clear and complete picture of how the Java Scripting API helps Java applications interact with scripting languages. My next step in the learning process was reading the specification for JSR-223, Scripting for the Java Platform Specification, along with the Java API documentation for the `javax.script` package. Reading the JSR-233 specification gave me a complete picture of the Java Scripting API; however, I was not ready to write this book. I was still missing some pieces of the puzzle. Therefore, I decided to read the source code for the classes in the `javax.script` package. I also read the source code for some scripting languages. Finally, in the process of learning the API, I developed a simple scripting engine, which I named JKScript. Finally, I read the ECMAScript 5.1 specification to get a complete picture of the JavaScript language itself. The main difficulty that I faced in writing this book was getting the information on the Nashorn engine and its features. A Wiki is maintained at `https://wiki.openjdk.java.net/display/Nashorn/Main`, which provides information about the Nashorn engine in bits and pieces. Tying them together in this book with cohesive examples was a challenge.

It is my sincere hope that readers will enjoy this book and benefit from it.

Structure of the Book

This book contains 13 chapters: Each chapter introduces a new topic from the Java Scripting API and the JavaScript language. Each chapter makes use of the material covered in the previous chapters.

Chapter 1, Getting Started, introduces you to the Java Scripting API and demonstrates how to write your first Java program to execute a script written in Nashorn. It walks through the steps that are needed to download and install other scripting languages such as Groovy, Jython, and JRuby. Finally, this chapter takes a brief tour of the classes and interfaces contained in the `javax.script` package, describing their usages and relationship with other classes.

Chapter 2, Executing Scripts, shows how to execute a script, which is stored in a file. It also demonstrates how to pass parameters from a Java application to a scripting engine, and vice versa.

Chapter 3, Passing Parameter to Scripts, discusses advanced techniques and all the internal setups that are involved in passing parameters between a Java application and a scripting engine. It starts with a detailed description of the terms binding, scope, and script context. Later, it explains in detail with several illustrations how bindings, scope, and script context work together in the Java Scripting API. Each explanation is paired with a snippet of code, a complete program, or both. The chapter ends with a program that shows how to redirect outputs from a script to a file.

Chapter 4, Writing Scripts in Nashorn, covers the JavaScript language in great detail as described in the ECMAScript 5.1 specification that is supported by the Nashorn engine.

Chapter 5, Procedures and Compiled Scripts, explains how to invoke top-level procedures, functions, and object-level methods written in a scripting language from a Java application. It explains how to compile scripts in intermediate form, if supported by the scripting engine, and execute them repeatedly.

Chapter 6, Using Java in Nashorn, explains how to use features and constructs of the Java programming language inside scripting languages. The Java features discussed are importing Java classes, creating Java objects, using Java overloaded methods, implementing Java interfaces, and so on.

Chapter 7, Collections, explains untyped and typed arrays in Nashorn. It also explains how to use Java collection classes such as `java.util.Set` and `java.util.Map` in Nashorn.

Chapter 8, Implementing a Script Engine, discusses the steps needed to implement a new script engine. It explains all classes and interfaces in the Java Scripting API that are involved in creating a new script engine. It walks through the deployment setup that makes a script engine autodiscoverable by a script engine manager. In the process, it creates a simple script engine, which we call JKScript, which is capable of executing an arithmetic expression.

Chapter 9, The jrunscript Command-Line Shell, explains how to use the `jrunscript` command-line shell to execute script using different scripting engines.

Chapter 10, The jjs Command-Line Tool, explains how to use the `jjs` command-line tool to execute Nashorn scripts in different modes. It walks through the syntax and the options for the command-line tool. Several examples are provided to illustrate the usage of the shell.

Chapter 11, Using JavaFX in Nashorn, explains how to write and run JavaFX programs using the jjs command-line tool.

Chapter 12, Java APIs for Nashorn, covers the Java classes and interfaces that can be used to work with JavaScript objects in Java programs.

Chapter 13, Debugging, Tracing, and Profiling Scripts, explains the debugging support in NetBeans 8.0 for debugging Nashorn scripts. It also explains how to trace and profile Nashorn scripts.

Audience

This book is designed to be useful for anyone who wants to learn the Java Scripting API in Java and Nashorn JavaScript. A basic knowledge of Java is required to use this book. Although it would be helpful to have a prior knowledge of a scripting language such as Rhino JavaScript, Groovy, JRuby, Jython, and so on, it is not required.

Examples contained in this book are written in Nashorn JavaScript. Examples are deliberately kept simple and short so that readers can understand them without any prior experience with a scripting language. If you do not have experience working with a scripting language, you need to read the book chapter-by-chapter sequentially.

Source Code and Errata

Source code and errata for this book may be downloaded from www.apress.com/source-code.

Questions and Comments

Please direct all your questions and comments for the author to ksharan@jdojo.com.

■ ■ ■

CHAPTER 1

Getting Started

In this chapter, you will learn:

- What scripting in Java is
- How to execute your first script from Java
- How to use other scripting languages such as JRuby, Jython from Java
- javax.script API
- How script engines are discovered and instantiated

What Is Scripting in Java?

Some believe that the Java Virtual Machine (JVM) can execute programs written only in the Java programming language. However, that is not true. The JVM executes language-neutral bytecode. It can execute programs written in any programming language, if the program can be compiled into Java bytecode.

A *scripting language* is a programming language that provides you with the ability to write *scripts* that are evaluated (or interpreted) by a runtime environment called a *script engine* (or an interpreter). A script is a sequence of characters that is written using the syntax of a scripting language and used as the source for a program executed by an interpreter. The interpreter parses the scripts, produces intermediate code, which is an internal representation of the program, and executes the intermediate code. The interpreter stores the variables used in a script in data structures called *symbol tables.*

Typically, unlike in a compiled programming language, the source code (called a script) in a scripting language is not compiled but is interpreted at runtime. However, scripts written in some scripting languages may be compiled into Java bytecode that can be run by the JVM.

Java 6 added scripting support to the Java platform that lets a Java application execute scripts written in scripting languages such as Rhino JavaScript, Groovy, Jython, JRuby, Nashorn JavaScript, and so on. Two-way communication is supported. It also lets scripts access Java objects created by the host application. The Java runtime and a scripting language runtime can communicate and make use of each other's features.

Support for scripting languages in Java comes through the Java Scripting API. All classes and interfaces in the Java Scripting API are in the javax.script package.

Using a scripting language in a Java application provides several advantages:

- Most scripting languages are dynamically typed, which makes it simpler to write programs.

- They provide a quicker way to develop and test small applications.

- Customization by end users is possible.

- A scripting language may provide domain-specific features that are not available in Java.

Scripting languages have some disadvantages as well. For example, dynamic typing is good to write simpler code; however, it turns into a disadvantage when a type is interpreted incorrectly and you have to spend a lot of time debugging it.

Scripting support in Java lets you take advantage of both worlds: it allows you to use the Java programming language for developing statically typed, scalable, and high-performance parts of the application and use a scripting language that fits the domain-specific needs for other parts.

I will use the term *script engine* frequently in this book. A *script engine* is a software component that executes programs written in a particular scripting language. Typically, but not necessarily, a script engine is an implementation of an interpreter for a scripting language. Interpreters for several scripting languages have been implemented in Java. They expose programming interfaces so a Java program may interact with them.

JDK 7 was cobundled with a script engine called Rhino JavaScript. JDK 8 replaced the Rhino JavaScript engine with a lightweight, faster script engine called Nashorn JavaScript. This book discusses Nashorn JavaScript, not Rhino JavaScript. Please visit www.mozilla.org/rhino for more details on Rhino JavaScript documentation. If you want to migrate programs written with Rhino JavaScript to Nashorn, please visit the *Rhino Migration Guide* at https://wiki.openjdk.java.net/display/Nashorn/Rhino+Migration+Guide. If you are interested in using Rhino JavaScript with JDK 8, visit the page at https://wiki.openjdk.java.net/display/Nashorn/Using+Rhino+JSR-223+engine+with+JDK8.

Java includes a command-line shell called jrunscript that can be used to run scripts in an interactive mode or a batch mode. The jrunscript shell is scripting-language-neutral; the default language is Rhino JavaScript in JDK 7 and Nashorn in JDK 8. I will discuss the jrunscript shell in detail in Chapter 9. JDK 8 includes another command-line tool called jjs that invokes the Nashorn engine and offers Nashorn-specific command-line options. If you are using Nashorn, you should use the jjs command-line tool over jrunscript. I will discuss the jjs command-line tool in Chapter 10.

Java can execute scripts in any scripting language that provides an implementation for a script engine. For example, Java can execute scripts written in Nashorn JavaScript, Rhino JavaScript, Groovy, Jython, JRuby, and so on. Examples in this book use Nashorn JavaScript language.

In this book, the terms "Nashorn," "Nashorn Engine," "Nashorn JavaScript," "Nashorn JavaScript Engine," "Nashorn Scripting Language," and "JavaScript" have been used synonymously.

The Nashorn scripting engine can be invoked in two ways:

- By embedding the engine in the JVM

- By using the jjs command-line tool

In this chapter, I will discuss both ways of using the Nashorn script engine.

Executing Your First Script

In this section, you will use Nashorn to print a message on the standard output. You will access the Nashorn engine from Java code. The same steps can be used to print a message using any other scripting languages, with one difference: you will need to use the scripting language-specific code to print the message. You need to perform three steps to run a script in Java:

- Create a script engine manager.

- Get an instance of a script engine from the script engine manager.

- Call the eval() method of the script engine to execute a script.

A script engine manager is an instance of the ScriptEngineManager class. You can create a script engine, like so:

```
// Create a script engine manager
ScriptEngineManager manager = new ScriptEngineManager();
```

An instance of the ScriptEngine interface represents a script engine in a Java program. The getEngineByName(String engineShortName) method of a ScriptEngineManager is used to get an instance of a script engine. To get an instance of the Nashorn engine, use JavaScript as the short name of the engine as shown:

```
// Get the reference of a Nashorn engine
ScriptEngine engine = manager.getEngineByName("JavaScript");
```

■ **Tip** The short name of a script engine is case-sensitive. Sometimes a script engine has multiple short names. Nashorn engine has the following short names: nashorn, Nashorn, js, JS, JavaScript, javascript, ECMAScript, ecmascript. You can use any of the short names of an engine to get its instance using the getEngineByName() method of the ScriptEngineManager class.

In Nashorn, the print() function prints a message on the standard output and a string literal is a sequence of characters enclosed in single or double quotes. The following snippet of code stores a script in a String object that prints Hello Scripting! on the standard output:

```
// Store a Nashorn script in a string
String script = "print('Hello Scripting!')";
```

If you want to use double quotes to enclose the string literal in Nashorn, the statement will look as shown:

```
// Store a Nashorn script in a string
String script = "print(\"Hello Scripting!\")";
```

To execute the script, you need to pass it to the eval() method of the script engine. A script engine may throw a ScriptException when it runs a script. For this reason, you need to handle this exception when you call the eval() method of the ScriptEngine. The following snippet of code executes the script stored in the script variable:

```
try {
        engine.eval(script);
}
catch (ScriptException e) {
        e.printStackTrace();
}
```

Listing 1-1 contains the complete code for the program to print a message on the standard output.

Listing 1-1. Printing a Message on the Standard Output Using Nashorn

```
// HelloScripting.java
package com.jdojo.script;

import javax.script.ScriptEngine;
import javax.script.ScriptEngineManager;
import javax.script.ScriptException;

public class HelloScripting {
        public static void main(String[] args) {
                // Create a script engine manager
                ScriptEngineManager manager = new ScriptEngineManager();

                // Obtain a Nashorn script engine from the manager
                ScriptEngine engine = manager.getEngineByName("JavaScript");

                // Store the script in a String
                String script = "print('Hello Scripting!')";
```

```
        try {
                // Execute the script
                engine.eval(script);
        }
        catch (ScriptException e) {
                e.printStackTrace();
        }
    }
}
```

Hello Scripting!

Using the jjs Command-line Tool

In the previous section, you saw how use the Nashorn scripting engine from the Java programs. In this section, I will show you how to perform the same task using the jjs command-line tool. The tool is stored in the JDK_HOME\bin and JRE_HOME\bin directories. For example, if you have installed JDK8 in C:\java8 directory on Windows, the path for the jjs tool will be C:\java8\bin\jjs.exe. The jjs tool can be used to execute Nashorn script in a file or execute scripts interactively.

The following is an invocation of the jjs tool on a Windows command-prompt. The script is entered and executed. You can use quit() or exit() function to exit the jjs tool:

```
C:\>jjs
jjs> print('Hello Scripting!');
Hello Scripting!

jjs> quit()

C:\>
```

You may get the following error executing the jjs command:

```
'jjs' is not recognized as an internal or external command, operable program
or batch file.
```

The error indicates that the command prompt was not able to locate the jjs tool. In this case, you can either enter the full path of the jjs tool or add the directory containing the too in the system PATH.

Consider the code listed in Listing 1-2. It is Nashorn code that uses the print() function to print a message on the standard output. The code is saved in a file named helloscripting.js.

Listing 1-2: The Contents of the helloscripting.js File

```
// helloscripting.js

// Print a message on the standard output
print('Hello Scripting!');
```

The following command executes the script stored in the `helloscripting.js` file assuming that the file is stored in the current directory:

```
C:\>jjs helloscripting.js
Hello Scripting!

C:\>
```

If this command gives you an error similar to the following, it means that the command was not able to find the specified file and you need to specify the full path of the helloscritping.js file:

```
java.io.FileNotFoundException: C:\helloscripting.js (The system cannot find
the file specified)
```

The `jjs` command-line tool is a big topic and I will devote a complete chapter to it. I will discuss it in detail in Chapter 10.

Printing Text in Nashorn

Nashorn provides you three functions to print text on the standard output:

- The `print()` function
- The `printf()` function
- The `echo()` function

The `print()` function is a varargs function. You can pass any number of arguments to it. It converts its arguments to string and prints them separating them by a space. At the end, it prints a new line. The following two invocations of the `print()` function are the same:

```
print("Hello", "World!"); // Prints Hello World!
print("Hello World!");     // Prints Hello World!
```

The `printf()` function is used to use the printf-style formatted printing. It is the same as invoking the Java method `System.out.printf()`:

```
printf("%d + %d = %d", 10, 20, 10 + 20); // Prints 10 + 20 = 30
```

The echo() function is the same as the print() function, except that it works only in scripting mode. Scripting mode is discussed in Chapter 10.

Using Other Scripting Languages

It is very simple to use a scripting language, other than Nashorn, in a Java program. You need to perform only one task before you can use a script engine: include the JAR files for a particular script engine in your application CLASSPATH. Implementers of script engines provide those JAR files.

Java uses a discovery mechanism to list all script engines whose JAR files have been included in the application CLASSPATH. An instance of the ScriptEngineFactory interface is used to create and describe a script engine. The provider of a script engine provides an implementation for the ScriptEngineFactory interface. The getEngineFactories() method of the ScriptEngineManager returns a List<ScriptEngineFactory> of all available script engines factories. The getScriptEngine() method of the ScriptEngineFactory returns an instance of the ScriptEngine. Several other methods of the factory return metadata about the engine.

Table 1-1 lists details on how to install script engines before you can use them in your Java application. The list of websites and instructions are valid at the time of this writing; they may become invalid at the time of reading. However, they show you how a script engine for a scripting language is installed. If you are interested in using Nashorn, you do not need to install anything on your machine. Nashorn is available in JDK 8.

Table 1-1. *Installation Details for Installing Some Script Engines*

Script Engine	Version	Website	Installation Instructions
Groovy	2.3	groovy.codehaus.org	Download the installation file for Groovy; it's a ZIP file. Unzip it. Look for a JAR file named groovy-all-2.0.0-rc-2.jar in the embeddable folder. Add this JAR file to the CLASSPATH.
Jython	2.5.3	www.jython.org	Download the Jython installer file that is a JAR file. Extract the jython.jar file and add it to the CLASSPATH.
JRuby	1.7.13	www.jruby.org	Download the JRuby installation file. You have an option to download a ZIP file. Unzip it. In the lib folder, you will find a jruby.jar file that you need to include in the CLASSPATH.

Listing 1-3 shows how to print details of all available script engines. The output shows that the script engine for Groovy, Jython, and JRuby are available. They are available because I have added the JAR files for their engines to the CLASSPATH on my machine. This program is helpful when you have included the JAR files for a script engine in the CLASSPATH and you want to know the short name of the script engine. You may get a different output when you run the program.

Listing 1-3. Listing All Available Script Engines

```java
// ListingAllEngines.java
package com.jdojo.script;

import java.util.List;
import javax.script.ScriptEngineFactory;
import javax.script.ScriptEngineManager;

public class ListingAllEngines {
        public static void main(String[] args) {
                ScriptEngineManager manager = new ScriptEngineManager();

                // Get the list of all available engines
                List<ScriptEngineFactory> list = manager.
                getEngineFactories();

                // Print the details of each engine
                for (ScriptEngineFactory f : list) {
                        System.out.println("Engine Name:" +
                        f.getEngineName());
                        System.out.println("Engine Version:" +
                                f.getEngineVersion());
                        System.out.println("Language Name:" +
                        f.getLanguageName());
                        System.out.println("Language Version:" +
                        f.getLanguageVersion());
                        System.out.println("Engine Short Names:" +
                        f.getNames());
                        System.out.println("Mime Types:" +
                        f.getMimeTypes());
                        System.out.println("--------------------------");
                }
        }
}
```

```
Engine Name:jython
Engine Version:2.5.3
Language Name:python
```

```
Language Version:2.5
Engine Short Names:[python, jython]
Mime Types:[text/python, application/python, text/x-python,
application/x-python]
---------------------------
Engine Name:JSR 223 JRuby Engine
Engine Version:1.7.0.preview1
Language Name:ruby
Language Version:jruby 1.7.0.preview1
Engine Short Names:[ruby, jruby]
Mime Types:[application/x-ruby]
---------------------------
Engine Name:Groovy Scripting Engine
Engine Version:2.0
Language Name:Groovy
Language Version:2.0.0-rc-2
Engine Short Names:[groovy, Groovy]
Mime Types:[application/x-groovy]
---------------------------
Engine Name:Oracle Nashorn
Engine Version:1.8.0_05
Language Name:ECMAScript
Language Version:ECMA - 262 Edition 5.1
Engine Short Names:[nashorn, Nashorn, js, JS, JavaScript, javascript,
ECMAScript, ecmascript]
Mime Types:[application/javascript, application/ecmascript, text/javascript,
text/ecmascript]
---------------------------
```

Listing 1-4 shows how to print a message on the standard output using JavaScript, Groovy, Jython, and JRuby. If a script engine is not available, the program prints a message to that effect.

Listing 1-4. Printing a Message on the Standard Output Using Different Scripting Languages

```java
// HelloEngines.java
package com.jdojo.script;

import javax.script.ScriptEngine;
import javax.script.ScriptEngineManager;
import javax.script.ScriptException;

public class HelloEngines {
```

```
        public static void main(String[] args) {
                // Get the script engine manager
                ScriptEngineManager manager = new ScriptEngineManager();

                // Try executing scripts in Nashorn, Groovy, Jython, and JRuby
                execute(manager, "JavaScript", "print('Hello JavaScript')");
                execute(manager, "Groovy", "println('Hello Groovy')");
                execute(manager, "jython", "print 'Hello Jython'");
                execute(manager, "jruby", "puts('Hello JRuby')");
        }

        public static void execute(ScriptEngineManager manager,
                                   String engineName,
                                   String script) {

                // Try getting the engine
                ScriptEngine engine = manager.getEngineByName(engineName);
                if (engine == null) {
                        System.out.println(engineName + " is not available.");
                        return;
                }

                // If we get here, it means we have the engine installed.
                // So, run the script
                try {
                        engine.eval(script);
                }
                catch (ScriptException e) {
                        e.printStackTrace();
                }
        }
}
```

```
Hello JavaScript
Hello Groovy
Hello Jython
Hello JRuby
```

Sometimes you may want to play with a scripting language just for fun, and you do not know the syntax that is used to print a message on the standard output. The ScriptEngineFactory class contains a method named getOutputStatement(String toDisplay) that you can use to find the syntax for printing text on the standard output. The following snippet of code shows how to get the syntax for Nashorn:

```
// Get the script engine factory for Nashorn
ScriptEngineManager manager = new ScriptEngineManager();
ScriptEngine engine = manager.getEngineByName("JavaScript");
ScriptEngineFactory factory = engine.getFactory();

// Get the script
String script = factory.getOutputStatement("\"Hello JavaScript\"");
System.out.println("Syntax: " + script);

// Evaluate the script
engine.eval(script);
```

```
Syntax: print("Hello JavaScript")
Hello JavaScript
```

For other scripting languages, use their engine factories to get the syntax.

Exploring the javax.script Package

The Java Scripting API in Java consists of a small number of classes and interfaces. They are in the javax.script package. This chapter contains a brief description of classes and interfaces in this package. I will discuss their usage in subsequent chapters. Figure 1-1 shows the class diagram for the classes and interfaces in the Java Scripting API.

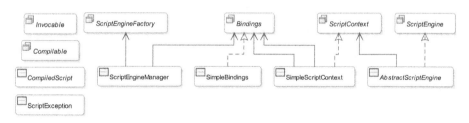

Figure 1-1. *The class diagram for classes and interfaces in the Java Scripting API*

The ScriptEngine and ScriptEngineFactory Interfaces

The ScriptEngine interface is the main interface of the Java Scripting API whose instances facilitate the execution of scripts written in a particular scripting language.

11

The implementer of the ScriptEngine interface also provides an implementation of the ScriptEngineFactory interface. A ScriptEngineFactory performs two tasks:

- It creates instances of the script engine.

- It provides information about the script engine such as engine name, version, language, and so on.

The AbstractScriptEngine Class

The AbstractScriptEngine class is an abstract class. It provides a partial implementation for the ScriptEngine interface. You will not use this class directly unless you are implementing a script engine.

The ScriptEngineManager Class

The ScriptEngineManager class provides a discovery and instantiation mechanism for script engines. It also maintains a mapping of key-value pairs as an instance of the Bindings interface storing state that is shared by all script engines that it creates.

The Compilable Interface and the CompiledScript Class

The Compilable interface may optionally be implemented by a script engine that allows compiling scripts for their repeated execution without recompilation.

The CompiledScript class is an abstract class. It is extended by the providers of a script engine. It stores a script in a compiled form, which may be executed repeatedly without recompilation. Note that using a ScriptEngine to execute a script repeatedly causes the script to recompile every time, thus slowing down the performance.

A script engine is not required to support script compilation. It must implement the Compilable interface if it supports script compilation.

The Invocable Interface

The Invocable interface may optionally be implemented by a script engine that may allow invoking procedures, functions, and methods in scripts that have been compiled previously.

The Bindings Interface and the SimpleBindings Class

An instance of a class that implements the Bindings interface is a mapping of key-value pairs with a restriction that a key must be non-null, non-empty String. It extends the java.util.Map interface. The SimpleBindings class is an implementation of the Bindings interface.

The ScriptContext Interface and the SimpleScriptContext Class

An instance of the ScriptContext interface acts as a bridge between the Java host application and the script engine. It is used to pass the execution context of the Java host application to the script engine. The script engine may use the context information while executing a script. A script engine may store its state in an instance of a class that implements the ScriptContext interface, which may be accessible to the Java host application.

The SimpleScriptContext class is an implementation of the ScriptContext interface.

The ScriptException Class

The ScriptException class is an exception class. A script engine throws a ScriptException if an error occurs during the execution, compilation, or invocation of a script. The class contains three useful methods called getLineNumber(), getColumnNumber(), and getFileName(). These methods report the line number, the column number, and the file name of the script in which the error occurs. The ScriptException class overrides the getMessage() method of the Throwable class and includes the line number, column number, and the file name in the message that it returns.

Discovering and Instantiating ScriptEngines

You can create a script engine using a ScriptEngineFactory or ScriptEngineManager. Who is actually responsible for creating a script engine: ScriptEngineFactory, ScriptEngineManager, or both? The short answer is that a ScriptEngineFactory is always responsible for creating instances of a script engine. The next question is "What is the role of a ScriptEngineManager?"

A ScriptEngineManager uses the service provider mechanism to locate all available script engine factories. It searches all JAR files in the CLASSPATH and other standard directories. It looks for a resource file, which is a text file named javax. script.ScriptEngineFactory under a directory named META-INF/services. The resource file consists of the fully qualified names of the classes implementing the ScriptEngineFactory interface. Each class name is specified in a separate line. The file may include comments that start with a # character. A sample resource file may have the following contents that include class names for two script engine factories:

```
#Java Kishori Script Engine Factory class
com.jdojo.script.JKScriptEngineFactory

#Another factory class
com.jdojo.script.FunScriptFactory
```

A ScriptEngineManager locates and instantiates all available ScriptEngineFactory classes. You can get a list of instances of all factory classes using the getEngineFactories() method of the ScriptEngineManager class. When you call a method of the manager to get a script engine based on a criterion such as the getEngineByName(String shortName) method to get an engine by name, the manager searches all factories for that criterion and returns the matching script engine reference. If no factories are able to provide a matching engine, the manager returns null. Please refer to Listing 1-3 for more details on listing all available factories and describing script engines that they can create.

Now you know that a ScriptEngineManager does not create instances of a script engine. Rather, it queries all available factories and passes the reference of a script engine created by the factory back to the caller.

To make the discussion complete, let's add a twist to the ways a script engine can be created. You can create an instance of a script engine in three ways:

- Instantiate the script engine class directly.

- Instantiate the script engine factory class directly and call its getScriptEngine() method.

- Use one of the getEngineByXxx() methods of the ScriptEngineManager class.

It is advised to use the ScriptEngineManager class to get instances of a script engine. This method allows all engines created by the same manager to share a state that is a set of key-value pairs stored as an instance of the Bindings interface. The ScriptEngineManager instance stores this state.

■ **Tip** It is possible to have more than one instance of the ScriptEngineManager class in an application. In that case, each ScriptEngineManager instance maintains a state common to all engines that it creates. That is, if two engines are obtained by two different instances of the ScriptEngineManager class, those engines will not share a common state maintained by their managers unless you make it happen programmatically.

Summary

A scripting language is a programming language that provides you the ability to write scripts that are evaluated (or interpreted) by a runtime environment called a script engine (or an interpreter). A script is a sequence of characters that is written using the syntax of a scripting language and used as the source for a program executed by an interpreter. The Java Scripting API allows you to execute scripts written in any scripting language that can be compiled to Java bytecode from the Java application. JDK 6 and 7 shipped with a script engine called Rhino JavaScript engine. In JDK 8, the Rhino JavaScript engine has been replaced with a script engine called Nashorn.

Nashorn engine can be used in two ways; it can be embedded into the JVM and invoked from the Java programs directly or it can be invoked from a command prompt using the jjs command-line tool.

Nashorn provides three functions to print text on the standard output: print(), printf(), and echo(). The print() function takes a variable number of arguments; it prints all arguments separating them with a space and at the end, prints a new line. The printf() function prints formatted text; it works the same way the printf-style formatting works in the Java programming language. The echo() function is works the same way the print() function works, except that the former is available only when Nashorn engine is invoked in scripting mode.

Scripts are executed using a script engine that is an instance of the ScriptEngine interface. The implementer of the ScriptEngine interface also provides an implementation of the ScriptEngineFactory interface whose job is to create instances of the script engine and provide details about the script engine. The ScriptEngineManager class provides a discovery and instantiation mechanism for script engines. A ScriptManager maintains a mapping of key-value pairs as an instance of the Bindings interface that is shared by all script engines that it creates.

CHAPTER 2

■ ■ ■

Executing Scripts

In this chapter, you will learn:

- How to use the eval() method of ScriptEngine to execute scripts
- How to pass parameters from Java code to Nashorn engine
- How to pass parameters from Nashorn engine to Java

Using the eval() Method

A ScriptEngine can execute a script in a String and a Reader. Using a Reader, you can execute a script stored on the network or in a file. One of the following versions of the eval() method of the ScriptEngine interface is used to execute a script:

- Object eval(String script)
- Object eval(Reader reader)
- Object eval(String script, Bindings bindings)
- Object eval(Reader reader, Bindings bindings)
- Object eval(String script, ScriptContext context)
- Object eval(Reader reader, ScriptContext context)

The first argument of the eval() method is the source of the script. The second argument lets you pass information from the host application to the script engine that can be used during the execution of the script.

In Chapter 1, you saw how to use a String object to execute a script using the first version of the eval() method. In this chapter, you will store your script in a file and use a Reader object as the source of the script, which will use the second version of the eval() method. The next section discusses the other four versions of the eval() method. Typically, a script file is given a .js extension.

Listing 2-1 shows the contents of a file named helloscript.js. It contains only one statement in Nashorn that prints a message on the standard output.

Listing 2-1. The Contents of the helloscript.js File

```
// helloscript.js

// Print a message
print('Hello from JavaScript!');
```

Listing 2-2 contains the Java program that executes the script stored in the helloscript.js file, which should be stored in the current directory. If the script file is not found, the program prints the full path of the helloscript.js file where it is expected. If you have trouble executing the script file, try using the absolute path in the main() method such as C:\scripts\helloscript.js on Windows, assuming that the helloscript.js file is saved in the C:\scripts directory.

Listing 2-2. Executing a Script Stored in a File

```
// ReaderAsSource.java
package com.jdojo.script;

import java.io.IOException;
import java.io.Reader;
import java.nio.file.Files;
import java.nio.file.Path;
import java.nio.file.Paths;
import javax.script.ScriptEngine;
import javax.script.ScriptEngineManager;
import javax.script.ScriptException;

public class ReaderAsSource {
        public static void main(String[] args) {
                // Construct the script file path
                String scriptFileName = "helloscript.js";
                Path scriptPath = Paths.get(scriptFileName);

                // Make sure the script file exists. If not, print the full
                // path of the script file and terminate the program.
                if (! Files.exists(scriptPath) ) {
                        System.out.println(scriptPath.toAbsolutePath() +
                                " does not exist.");
                        return;
                }
```

```
        // Get the Nashorn script engine
        ScriptEngineManager manager = new ScriptEngineManager();
        ScriptEngine engine = manager.getEngineByName("JavaScript");

        try {
                // Get a Reader for the script file
                Reader scriptReader = Files.
                newBufferedReader(scriptPath);

                // Execute the script in the file
                engine.eval(scriptReader);
        }
        catch (IOException | ScriptException e) {
                e.printStackTrace();
        }
    }
}
```

```
Hello from JavaScript!
```

In a real-world application, you should store all scripts in files that allow modifying scripts without modifying and recompiling your Java code. You will not follow this rule in most of the examples in this chapter; you will store your scripts in String objects to keep the code short and simple.

Passing Parameters

The Java Scripting API allows you to pass parameters from the host environment (Java application) to the script engine and vice versa. In this section, you will see the technical details of parameter passing mechanisms between the host application and the script engine. There are several way to pas parameters to scripts from Java programs. In this chapter, I will explain the simplest form of parameter passing. I will discuss all other forms in Chapter 3.

Passing Parameters from Java Code to Scripts

A Java program may pass parameters to scripts. A Java program may also access global variables declared in a script after the script is executed. Let's discuss a simple example of this kind where a Java program passes a parameter to a script. Consider the program in Listing 2-3 that passes a parameter to a script.

Listing 2-3. Passing Parameters From a Java Program to Scripts

```java
// PassingParam.java
package com.jdojo.script;

import javax.script.ScriptEngine;
import javax.script.ScriptEngineManager;
import javax.script.ScriptException;

public class PassingParam {
        public static void main(String[] args) {
                // Get the Nashorn engine
                ScriptEngineManager manager = new ScriptEngineManager();
                ScriptEngine engine = manager.getEngineByName("JavaScript");

                // Store the script in a String. Here, msg is a variable
                // that we have not declared in the script
                String script = "print(msg)";

                try {
                        // Store a parameter named msg in the engine
                        engine.put("msg", "Hello from Java program");

                        // Execute the script
                        engine.eval(script);
                }
                catch (ScriptException e) {
                        e.printStackTrace();
                }
        }
}
```

```
Hello from Java program
```

The program stores a script in a String object as follows:

```
// Store a Nashorn script in a String object
String script = "print(msg)";
```

In the statement, the script is:

```
print(msg)
```

Note that msg is a variable used in the print() function call. The script does not declare the msg variable or assign it a value. If you try to execute the above script without telling the engine what the msg variable is, the engine will throw an exception stating that it does not understand the meaning of the variable msg. This is where the concept of passing parameters from a Java program to a script engine comes into play.

You can pass a parameter to a script engine in several ways. The simplest way is to use the put(String paramName, Object paramValue) method of the script engine, which accepts two arguments:

- The first argument is the name of the parameter, which needs to match the name of the variable in the script.

- The second argument is the value of the parameter.

In your case, you want to pass a parameter named msg to the script engine and its value is a String. The call to the put() method is:

```
// Store the value of the msg parameter in the engine
engine.put("msg", "Hello from Java program");
```

Note that you must call the put() method of the engine before calling the eval() method. In your case, when the engine attempts to execute print(msg), it will use the value of the msg parameter that you passed to the engine.

Most script engines let you use the parameter names that you pass to it as the variable name in the script. You saw this kind of example when you passed the value of the parameter named msg and used it as a variable name in the script in Listing 2-3. A script engine may have a requirement for declaring variables in scripts, for example, a variable name must start with a $ prefix in PHP and a global variable name contains a $ prefix in JRuby. If you want to pass a parameter named msg to a script in JRuby, your code would be as shown:

```
// Get the JRuby script engine
ScriptEngineManager manager = new ScriptEngineManager();
ScriptEngine engine = manager.getEngineByName("jruby");

// Must use the $ prefix in JRuby script
String script = "puts($msg)";

// No $ prefix used in passing the msg parameter to the JRuby engine
engine.put("msg", "Hello from Java");

// Execute the script
engine.eval(script);
```

Properties and methods of Java objects passed to scripts can be accessed in scripts, as they are accessed in Java code. Different scripting languages use different syntax to access Java objects in scripts. For example, you can use the expression msg.toString() in the example shown in Listing 2-3 and the output will be the same. In this case, you are calling the toString() method of the variable msg. Change the statement that assigns the value to the script variable in Listing 2-3 to the following and run the program, which will produce the same output:

```
String script = "println(msg.toString())";
```

Passing Parameters from Scripts to Java Code

A script engine may make variables in its global scope accessible to Java code. The get(String variableName) method of a ScriptEngine is used to access those variables in Java code. It returns a Java Object. The declaration of a global variable is scripting-language-dependent. The following snippet of code declares a global variable and assigns it a value in JavaScript:

```
// Declare a variable named year in Nashorn
var year = 1969;
```

Listing 2-4 contains a program that shows how to access a global variable in Nashorn from Java code.

Listing 2-4. Accessing Script Global Variables in Java Code

```
// AccessingScriptVariable.java
package com.jdojo.script;

import javax.script.ScriptEngine;
import javax.script.ScriptEngineManager;
import javax.script.ScriptException;

public class AccessingScriptVariable {
    public static void main(String[] args) {
        // Get the Nashorn engine
        ScriptEngineManager manager = new ScriptEngineManager();
        ScriptEngine engine = manager.getEngineByName("JavaScript");

        // Write a script that declares a global variable named year
        // and assign it a value of 1969.
        String script = "var year = 1969";

        try {
            // Execute the script
            engine.eval(script);

            // Get the year global variable from the engine
            Object year = engine.get("year");
```

```
                        // Print the class name and the value of the
                        // variable year
                        System.out.println("year's class:" + year.
                        getClass().getName());
                        System.out.println("year's value:" + year);
                }
                catch (ScriptException e) {
                        e.printStackTrace();
                }
        }
}
```

```
year's class:java.lang.Integer
year's value:1969
```

The program declares a global variable year in the script and assigns it a value of 1969 as shown:

```
String script = "var num = 1969";
```

When the script is executed, the engine adds the year variable to its state. In Java code, the get() method of the engine is used to retrieve the value of the year variable as shown:

```
Object year = engine.get("year");
```

When the year variable was declared in the script, you did not specify it data type. The conversion of a script variable value to an appropriate Java object is automatically performed. If you run the program in Java 7, your output will show java.lang.Double as the class name and 1960.0 as the value for the year variable. This is because Java 7 uses Rhino script engine that interprets 1969 as a Double whereas Java 8 uses Nashorn script engine that interprets it as an Integer.

Summary

A ScriptEngine can execute a script in a String and a Reader. The eval() method of the ScriptEngine is used execute the script. The method is overloaded and it has six versions. It lets you pass the script as the first argument and the parameters to the engine in the second.

The eval() method of the ScriptEngine is used execute the script. You can pass parameters to the script and read values from scripts back to the Java program. There are different ways to pass parameters from the Java program to scripts. You can use the put(String key, Object value) method of the ScriptEngine to pass a parameter with the name key to the script. You can use the get(String key) method to get the global variables stored in the script with the name key.

■ ■ ■

CHAPTER 3

Passing Parameters to Scripts

In this chapter, you will learn:

- Classes used in passing parameters from Java programs to scripts
- How to create and use Bindings object to hold the parameters
- How to define the scope of parameters
- How to pass parameters to scripts using different objects and scopes
- The advantages and disadvantages of different ways of passing parameters
- How to write script's output to a file

Bindings, Scope, and Context

To understand the details of the parameter passing mechanism, three terms must be understood clearly: bindings, scope, and context. These terms are confusing at first. This chapter explains the parameter passing mechanism using the following steps:

- First, it defines these terms
- Second, it defines the relationship between these terms
- Third, it explains how to use them in Java programs

Bindings

A Bindings is a set of key-value pairs where all keys must be nonempty, non-null Strings. In Java code, a Bindings is an instance of the Bindings interface. The SimpleBindings class is an implementation of the Bindings interface. A script engine may provide its own implementation of the Bindings interface.

■ **Tip** If you are familiar with the `java.util.Map` interface, it is easy to understand `Bindings`. The `Bindings` interface inherits from the `Map<String,Object>` interface. Therefore, a `Bindings` is simply a `Map` with a restriction that its keys must be nonempty, non-null Strings.

Listing 3-1 shows how to use a `Bindings`. It creates an instance of `SimpleBindings`, adds some key-value pairs to it, retrieves the values of the keys, removes a key-value pair, etc. The `get()` method of the `Bindings` interface returns `null` if the key does not exist or the key exists and its value is `null`. If you want to test if a key exists, you need to use its `contains()` method.

Listing 3-1. Using Bindings Objects

```java
// BindingsTest.java
package com.jdojo.script;

import javax.script.Bindings;
import javax.script.SimpleBindings;

public class BindingsTest {
        public static void main(String[] args) {
                // Create a Bindings instance
                Bindings params = new SimpleBindings();

                // Add some key-value pairs
                params.put("msg", "Hello");
                params.put("year", 1969);

                // Get values
                Object msg = params.get("msg");
                Object year = params.get("year");
                System.out.println("msg = " + msg);
                System.out.println("year = " + year);

                // Remove year from Bindings
                params.remove("year");
                year = params.get("year");

                boolean containsYear = params.containsKey("year");
                System.out.println("year = " + year);
                System.out.println("params contains year = " + containsYear);
        }
}
```

```
msg = Hello
year = 1969
year = null
params contains year = false
```

You will not use a Bindings by itself. Often, you will use it to pass parameters from Java code to a script engine. The ScriptEngine interface contains a createBindings() method that returns an instance of the Bindings interface. This method gives a script engine a chance to return an instance of the specialized implementation of the Bindings interface. You can use this method, as shown:

```
// Get the Nashorn engine
ScriptEngineManager manager = new ScriptEngineManager();
ScriptEngine engine = manager.getEngineByName("JavaScript");

// Do not instantiate the SimpleBindings class, use the
// createBindings() method of the engine instead
Bindings params = engine.createBindings();

// Work with params as usual
```

Scope

Let's move to the next term, which is scope. A scope is used for a Bindings. The scope of a Bindings determines the visibility of its key-value pairs. You can have multiple Bindings occurring in multiple scopes. However, one Bindings may occur only in one scope. How do you specify the scope for a Bindings? I will cover this shortly.

Using the scope for a Bindings lets you define parameter variables for script engines in a hierarchical order. If a variable name is searched in an engine state, the Bindings with a higher precedence is searched first, followed by Bindings with lower precedence. The first found value of the variable is returned.

The Java Scripting API defines two scopes. They are defined as two int constants in the ScriptContext interface. They are:

- ScriptContext.ENGINE_SCOPE

- ScriptContext.GLOBAL_SCOPE

The engine scope has higher precedence than the global scope. If you add two key-value pairs with the same key to two Bindings (one in engine scope and one in global scope), the key-value pair in the engine scope will be used whenever a variable with the same name as the key has to be resolved.

Understanding the role of the scope for a Bindings is so important that I will run through another analogy to explain it. Think about a Java class that has two sets of variables: one set contains all instance variables in the class and another contains all local variables in a method. These two sets of variables with their values are two Bindings. The type of variables in a Bindings defines the scope. Just for the sake of this discussion, I will define two scopes: instance scope and local scope. When a method is executed, a variable name is looked up in the local scope Bindings first because the local variables take precedence over instance variables. If a variable name is not found in the local scope Bindings, it is looked up in the instance scope Bindings. When a script is executed, Bindings and their scopes play a similar role.

Defining the Script Context

A script engine executes a script in a context. You can think of the context as the environment in which a script is executed. A Java host application provides two things to a script engine: a script and the context in which the script needs to be executed. An instance of the ScriptContext interface represents the context for a script. The SimpleScriptContext class is an implementation of the ScriptContext interface. A script context consists of four components:

- A set of Bindings, in which each Bindings is associated with a different scope

- A Reader that is used by the script engine to read inputs

- A Writer that is used by the script engine to write outputs

- An error Writer that is used by the script engine to write error outputs

The set of Bindings in a context is used to pass parameters to the script. A reader and writers in a context control input source and output destinations of the script, respectively. For example, by setting a file writer as a writer, you can send all outputs from a script to a file.

Each script engine maintains a default script context, which it uses to execute scripts. So far, you have executed several scripts without providing script contexts. In those cases, script engines were using their default script contexts to execute scripts. In this section, I will cover how to use an instance of the ScriptContext interface by itself. In the next section, I will cover how an instance of the ScriptContext interface is passed to a ScriptEngine during script execution.

You can create an instance of the ScriptContext interface using the SimpleScriptContext class, like so:

```
// Create a script context
ScriptContext ctx = new SimpleScriptContext();
```

An instance of the SimpleScriptContext class maintains two instances of Bindings: one for engine scope and one for global scope. The Bindings in the engine scope is created when you create the instance of the SimpleScriptContext. To work with the global scope Bindings, you will need to create an instance of the Bindings interface.

By default, the SimpleScriptContext class initializes the input reader, the output writer, and the error writer for the context to the standard input System.in, the standard output System.out, and standard error output System.err, respectively. You can use the getReader(), getWriter(), and getErrorWriter() methods of the ScriptContext interface to get the references of the reader, writer, and the error writer from the ScriptContext, respectively. Setter methods are also provided to set a reader and writers. The following snippet of code shows how to obtain the reader and writers. It also shows how to set a writer to a FileWriter to write the script output to a file:

```
// Get the reader and writers from the script context
Reader inputReader = ctx.getReader();
Writer outputWriter = ctx.getWriter();
Writer errWriter = ctx.getErrorWriter();

// Write all script outputs to an out.txt file
Writer fileWriter = new FileWriter("out.txt");
ctx.setWriter(fileWriter);
```

After you create a SimpleScriptContext, you can start storing key-value pairs in the engine scope Bindings because an empty Bindings in the engine scope is created when you create the SimpleScriptContext object. The setAttribute() method is used to add a key-value pair to a Bindings. You must provide the key name, value, and the scope for the Bindings. The following snippet of code adds three key-value pairs:

```
// Add three key-value pairs to the engine scope bindings
ctx.setAttribute("year", 1969, ScriptContext.ENGINE_SCOPE);
ctx.setAttribute("month", 9, ScriptContext.ENGINE_SCOPE);
ctx.setAttribute("day", 19, ScriptContext.ENGINE_SCOPE);
```

If you want to add key-value pairs to a Bindings in global scope, you will need to create and set the Bindings first, like so:

```
// Add a global scope Bindings to the context
Bindings globalBindings = new SimpleBindings();
ctx.setBindings(globalBindings, ScriptContext.GLOBAL_SCOPE);
```

Now you can add key-value pairs to the Bindings in global scope using the setAttribute() method, like so:

```
// Add two key-value pairs to the global scope bindings
ctx.setAttribute("year", 1982, ScriptContext.GLOBAL_SCOPE);
ctx.setAttribute("name", "Boni", ScriptContext.GLOBAL_SCOPE);
```

At this point, you can visualize the state of the `ScriptContext` instance as shown in Figure 3-1.

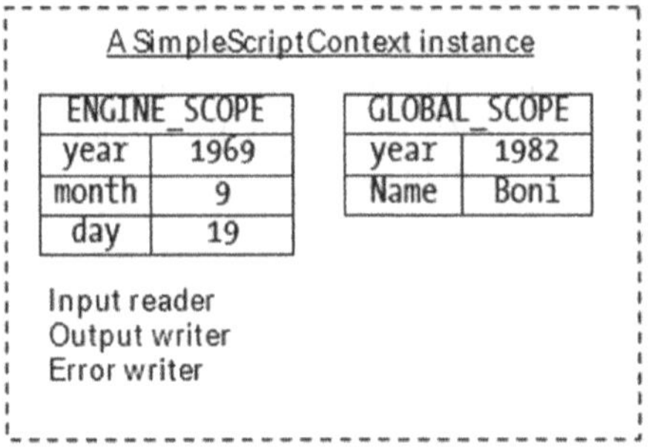

```
A SimpleScriptContext instance

ENGINE_SCOPE              GLOBAL_SCOPE
year      1969            year      1982
month      9              Name      Boni
day        19

Input reader
Output writer
Error writer
```

Figure 3-1. *A pictorial view of an instance of the SimpleScriptContext class*

You can perform several operations on a `ScriptContext`. You can set a different value for an already stored key using the `setAttribute(String name, Object value, int scope)` method. You can remove a key-value pair using the `removeAttribute(String name, int scope)` method for a specified key and a scope. You can get the value of a key in the specified scope using the `getAttribute(String name, int scope)` method.

The most interesting thing that you can do with a `ScriptContext` is to retrieve a key value without specifying its scope using its `getAttribute(String name)` method. A `ScriptContext` searches for the key in the engine scope `Bindings` first. If it is not found in the engine scope, the `Bindings` in the global scope is searched. If the key is found in these scopes, the corresponding value from the scope, in which it is found first, is returned. If neither scope contains the key, `null` is returned.

In your example, you have stored the key named year in the engine scope as well as in the global scope. The following snippet of code returns 1969 for the key year from the engine scope as the engine scope is searched first. The return type of the `getAttribute()` method is `Object`.

```
// Get the value of the key year without specifying the scope.
// It returns 1969 from the Bindings in the engine scope.
int yearValue = (Integer)ctx.getAttribute("year");
```

You have stored the key named name only in the global scope. If you attempt to retrieve its value, the engine scope is searched first, which does not return a match. Subsequently, the global scope is searched and the value `"Boni"` is returned, as shown:

```
// Get the value of the key named name without specifying the scope.
// It returns "Boni" from the Bindings in the global scope.
String nameValue = (String)ctx.getAttribute("name");
```

You can also retrieve the value of a key in a specific scope. The following snippet of code retrieves values for the key "year" from the engine scope and the global scope:

```
// Assigns 1969 to engineScopeYear and 1982 to globalScopeYear
int engineScopeYear = (Integer)ctx.getAttribute("year", ScriptContext.
ENGINE_SCOPE);
int globalScopeYear = (Integer)ctx.getAttribute("year", ScriptContext.
GLOBAL_SCOPE);
```

■ **Tip** The Java Scripting API defines only two scopes: engine and global. A subinterface of the ScriptContext interface may define additional scopes. The getScopes() method of the ScriptContext interface returns a list of supported scopes as a List<Integer>. Note that a scope is represented as an integer. The two constants, ENGINE_SCOPE and GLOBAL_SCOPE in the ScriptContext interface, are assigned values 100 and 200, respectively. When a key is searched in multiple Bindings occurring in multiple scopes, the scope with the lower integer value is searched first. Because the value 100 for the engine scope is lower than the value 200 for the global scope, the engine scope is searched for a key first when you do not specify the scope.

Listing 3-2 shows how to work with an instance of a class implementing the ScriptContext interface. Note that you do not use a ScriptContext in your application by itself. It is used by script engines during script execution. Most often, you manipulate a ScriptContext indirectly through a ScriptEngine and a ScriptEngineManager, which is discussed in detail in the next section.

Listing 3-2. Using an Instance of the ScriptContext Interface

```
// ScriptContextTest.java
package com.jdojo.script;

import java.util.List;
import javax.script.Bindings;
import javax.script.ScriptContext;
import javax.script.SimpleBindings;
import javax.script.SimpleScriptContext;
import static javax.script.ScriptContext.ENGINE_SCOPE;
import static javax.script.ScriptContext.GLOBAL_SCOPE;
```

```java
public class ScriptContextTest {
        public static void main(String[] args) {
                // Create a script context
                ScriptContext ctx = new SimpleScriptContext();

                // Get the list of scopes supported by the script context
                List<Integer> scopes = ctx.getScopes();
                System.out.println("Supported Scopes: " + scopes);

                // Add three key-value pairs to the engine scope bindings
                ctx.setAttribute("year", 1969, ENGINE_SCOPE);
                ctx.setAttribute("month", 9, ENGINE_SCOPE);
                ctx.setAttribute("day", 19, ENGINE_SCOPE);

                // Add a global scope Bindings to the context
                Bindings globalBindings = new SimpleBindings();
                ctx.setBindings(globalBindings, GLOBAL_SCOPE);

                // Add two key-value pairs to the global scope bindings
                ctx.setAttribute("year", 1982, GLOBAL_SCOPE);
                ctx.setAttribute("name", "Boni", GLOBAL_SCOPE);

                // Get the value of year without specifying the scope
                int yearValue = (Integer)ctx.getAttribute("year");
                System.out.println("yearValue = " + yearValue);

                // Get the value of name
                String nameValue = (String)ctx.getAttribute("name");
                System.out.println("nameValue = " + nameValue);

                // Get the value of year from engine  and global scopes
                int engineScopeYear = (Integer)ctx.getAttribute("year",
                ENGINE_SCOPE);
                int globalScopeYear = (Integer)ctx.getAttribute("year",
                GLOBAL_SCOPE);

                System.out.println("engineScopeYear = " + engineScopeYear);
                System.out.println("globalScopeYear = " + globalScopeYear);
        }
}
```

```
Supported Scopes: [100, 200]
yearValue = 1969
nameValue = Boni
engineScopeYear = 1969
globalScopeYear = 1982
```

Putting Them Together

In this section, I will show you how instances of Bindings and their scopes, ScriptContext, ScriptEngine, ScriptEngineManager, and the host application work together. The focus will be on how to manipulate the key-value pairs stored in Bindings in different scopes using a ScriptEngine and a ScriptEngineManager.

A ScriptEngineManager maintains a set of key-value pairs in a Bindings. It lets you manipulate those key-value pairs using the following four methods:

- void put(String key, Object value)

- Object get(String key)

- void setBindings(Bindings bindings)

- Bindings getBindings()

The put() method adds a key-value pair to the Bindings. The get() method returns the value for the specified key; it returns null if the key is not found. The Bindings for an engine manager can be replaced using the setBindings() method. The getBindings() method returns the reference of the Bindings of the ScriptEngineManager.

Every ScriptEngine, by default, has a ScriptContext known as its default context. Recall that, besides readers and writers, a ScriptContext has two Bindings: one in the engine scope and one in the global scope. When a ScriptEngine is created, its engine scope Bindings is empty and its global scope Bindings refers to the Bindings of the ScriptEngineManager that created it.

By default, all instances of the ScriptEngine created by a ScriptEngineManager share the Bindings of the ScriptEngineManager. It is possible to have multiple instances of ScriptEngineManager in the same Java application. In that case, all instances of ScriptEngine created by the same ScriptEngineManager share the Bindings of the ScriptEngineManager as their global scope Bindings for their default contexts.

The following snippet of code creates a ScriptEngineManager, which is used to create three instances of ScriptEngine:

```
// Create a ScriptEngineManager
ScriptEngineManager manager = new ScriptEngineManager();

// Create three ScriptEngines using the same ScriptEngineManager
ScriptEngine engine1 = manager.getEngineByName("JavaScript");
ScriptEngine engine2 = manager.getEngineByName("JavaScript");
ScriptEngine engine3 = manager.getEngineByName("JavaScript");
```

Now, let's add three key-value pairs to the Bindings of the ScriptEngineManager and two key-value pairs to the engine scope Bindings of each ScriptEngine:

```
// Add three key-value pairs to the Bindings of the manager
manager.put("K1", "V1");
manager.put("K2", "V2");
manager.put("K3", "V3");
```

```
// Add two key-value pairs to each engine
engine1.put("KE11", "VE11");
engine1.put("KE12", "VE12");
engine2.put("KE21", "VE21");
engine2.put("KE22", "VE22");
engine3.put("KE31", "VE31");
engine3.put("KE32", "VE32");
```

Figure 3-2 shows a pictorial view of the state of the ScriptEngineManager and three ScriptEngines after the snippet of code is executed. It is evident from the figure that the default contexts of all ScriptEngines share the Bindings of the ScriptEngineManager as their global scope Bindings.

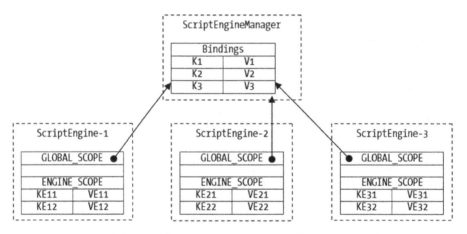

Figure 3-2. *A pictorial view of three ScriptEngines created by a ScriptEngineManager*

The Bindings in a ScriptEngineManager can be modified in the following ways:

- By using the put() method of the ScriptEngineManager

- By getting the reference of the Bindings using the getBindings() method of the ScriptEngineManager, and then using the put() and remove() method on the Bindings

- By getting the reference of the Bindings in the global scope of the default context of a ScriptEngine using its getBindings() method, and then using the put() and remove()method on the Bindings

When the Bindings in a ScriptEngineManager is modified, the global scope Bindings in the default context of all ScriptEngines created by this ScriptEngineManager are modified because they share the same Bindings.

The default context of each ScriptEngine maintains an engine scope Bindings separately. To add a key-value pair to the engine scope Bindings of a ScriptEngine, use its put() method, as shown:

```
ScriptEngine engine1 = null; // get an engine

// Add an "engineName" key with its value as "Engine-1" to the
// engine scope Bindings of the default context of engine1
engine1.put("engineName", "Engine-1");
```

The get(String key) method of the ScriptEngine returns the value of the specified key from its engine scope Bindings. The following statement returns "Engine-1", which is the value for the engineName key:

```
String eName = (String)engine1.get("engineName");
```

It is a two-step process to get to the key-value pairs of the global scope Bindings in the default context of a ScriptEngine. First, you need to get the reference of the global scope Bindings using its getBindings() method, as shown:

```
Bindings e1Global = engine1.getBindings(ScriptContext.GLOBAL_SCOPE);
```

Now you can modify the global scope Bindings of the engine using the e1Global reference. The following statement adds a key-value pair to the e1Global Bindings:

```
e1Global.put("id", 89999);
```

Because of the sharing of the global scope Bindings of a ScriptEngine by all ScriptEngines, this snippet of code will add the key "id" with its value to the global scope Bindings of the default context of all ScriptEngines created by the same ScriptEngineManager that created engine1. Modifying the Bindings in a ScriptEngineManager using code as shown here is not recommended. You should modify the Bindings using the ScriptEngineManager reference instead, which makes the logic clearer to the readers of the code.

Listing 3-3 demonstrates the concepts discussed in this section. A ScriptEngineManager adds two key-value pairs with keys n1 and n2 to its Bindings. Two ScriptEngines are created; they add a key called engineName to their engine scope Bindings. When the script is executed, the value of the engineName variable in the script is used from the engine scope of the ScriptEngine. The values for variables n1 and n2 in the script are retrieved from the global scope Bindings of the ScriptEngine. After executing the script for the first time, each ScriptEngine adds a key called n2 with a different value to their engine scope Bindings. When you execute the script for the second time, the value for the n1 variable is retrieved from the global scope Bindings of the engine, whereas the value for the variable n2 is retrieved from the engine scope Bindings as shown in the output.

Listing 3-3. Using Global and Engine Scope Bindings of Engines Created by the Same ScriptEngineManager

```java
// GlobalBindings.java
package com.jdojo.script;

import javax.script.ScriptEngine;
import javax.script.ScriptEngineManager;
import javax.script.ScriptException;

public class GlobalBindings {
        public static void main(String[] args) {
                ScriptEngineManager manager = new ScriptEngineManager();

                // Add two numbers to the Bindings of the manager that will be
                // shared by all its engines
                manager.put("n1", 100);
                manager.put("n2", 200);

                // Create two JavaScript engines and add the name of the engine
                // in the engine scope of the default context of the engines
                ScriptEngine engine1 = manager.
                getEngineByName("JavaScript");
                engine1.put("engineName", "Engine-1");

                ScriptEngine engine2 = manager.
                getEngineByName("JavaScript");
                engine2.put("engineName", "Engine-2");

                // Execute a script that adds two numbers and prints the
                // result
                String script = "var sum = n1 + n2; "
                        + "print(engineName + ' - Sum = ' + sum)";

                try {
                        // Execute the script in two engines
                        engine1.eval(script);
                        engine2.eval(script);

                        // Now add a different value for n2 for each engine
                        engine1.put("n2", 1000);
                        engine2.put("n2", 2000);

                        // Execute the script in two engines again
                        engine1.eval(script);
                        engine2.eval(script);
                }
```

```
                catch (ScriptException e) {
                        e.printStackTrace();
                }
        }
}
```

```
Engine-1 - Sum = 300
Engine-2 - Sum = 300
Engine-1 - Sum = 1100
Engine-2 - Sum = 2100
```

The story of the global scope Bindings shared by all ScriptEngines that are created by a ScriptEngineManager is not over yet. It is as complex, and confusing, as it can get! Now the focus will be on the effects of using the setBindings() method of ScriptEngineManager class and the ScriptEngine interface. Consider the following snippet of code:

```
// Create a ScriptEngineManager and two ScriptEngines
ScriptEngineManager manager = new ScriptEngineManager();
ScriptEngine engine1 = manager.getEngineByName("JavaScript");
ScriptEngine engine2 = manager.getEngineByName("JavaScript");

// Add two key-value pairs to the manager
manager.put("n1", 100);
manager.put("n2", 200);
```

Figure 3-3 shows the state of the engine manager and its engines after the above script is executed. At this point, there is only one Bindings stored in the ScriptEngineManager and two ScriptEngines are referring to it as their global scope Bindings.

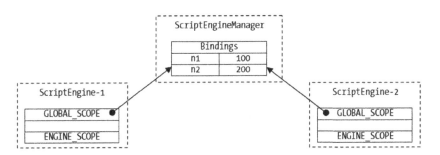

Figure 3-3. *Initial state of ScriptEngineManager and two ScriptEngines*

Let's create a new Bindings and set it as the Bindings for the ScriptEngineManager using its setBindings() method, like so:

```
// Create a Bindings, add two key-value pairs to it, and set it as the new
// Bindings for the manager
Bindings newGlobal = new SimpleBindings();
newGlobal.put("n3", 300);
newGlobal.put("n4", 400);
manager.setBindings(newGlobal);
```

Figure 3-4 shows the state of the ScriptEngineManager and two ScriptEngines after the code is executed. Notice that the ScriptEngineManager has a new Bindings and the two ScriptEngines are still referring to the old Bindings as their global scope Bindings.

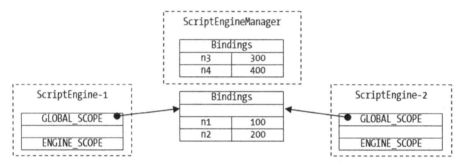

Figure 3-4. *State of ScriptEngineManager and two ScriptEngines after a new Bindings is set to the ScriptEngineManager*

At this point, any changes made to the Bindings of the ScriptEngineManager will not be reflected in the global scope Bindings of the two ScriptEngines. You can still make changes to the Bindings shared by the two ScriptEngines and both ScriptEngines will see the changes made by either of them.

Let's create a new ScriptEngine, as shown:

```
// Create a new ScriptEngine
ScriptEngine engine3 = manager.getEngineByName("JavaScript");
```

Recall that a ScriptEngine gets a global scope Bindings at the time it is created and that Bindings is the same as the Bindings of the ScriptEngineManager. The state of the ScriptEngineManager and three ScriptEngines, after this statement is executed, are shown in Figure 3-5.

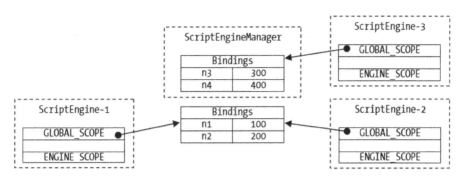

Figure 3-5. *State of ScriptEngineManager and three ScriptEngines after the third ScriptEngine is created*

Here is another twist to the so-called globalness of the global scope of ScriptEngines. This time, you will use the setBindings() method of a ScriptEngine to set its global scope Bindings. Figure 3-6 shows the state of the ScriptEngineManager and three ScriptEngines after the following snippet of code is executed:

```
// Set a new Bindings for the global scope of engine1
Bindings newGlobalEngine1 = new SimpleBindings();
newGlobalEngine1.put("n5", 500);
newGlobalEngine1.put("n6", 600);
engine1.setBindings(newGlobalEngine1, ScriptContext.GLOBAL_SCOPE);
```

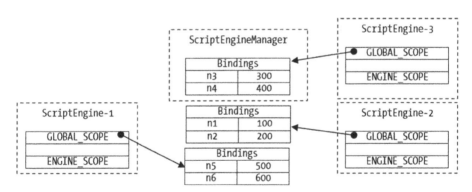

Figure 3-6. *State of ScriptEngineManager and Three ScriptEngines After a New Global Scope Bindings Is Set for engine1*

> ■ **Tip** By default, all ScriptEngines that a `ScriptEngineManager` creates share its `Bindings` as their global scope `Bindings`. If you use the `setBindings()` method of a `ScriptEngine` to set its global scope `Bindings` or if you use the `setBindings()` method of a `ScriptEngineManager` to set its `Bindings`, you break the "globalness" chain as discussed in this section. To keep the "globalness" chain intact, you should always use the `put()` method of the `ScriptEngineManager` to add key-value pairs to its `Bindings`. To remove a key-value pair from the global scope of all ScriptEngines created by a `ScriptEngineManager`, you need to get the reference of the `Bindings` using the `getBindings()` method of the `ScriptEngineManager` and use the `remove()` method on the `Bindings`.

Using a Custom ScriptContext

In the previous section, you saw that each `ScriptEngine` has a default script context. The `get()`, `put()`, `getBindings()`, and `setBindings()` methods of the `ScriptEngine` operate on its default `ScriptContext`. When no `ScriptContext` is specified to the `eval()` method of the `ScriptEngine`, the default context of the engine is used. The following two versions of the `eval()` method of the `ScriptEngine` use its default context to execute the script:

- `Object eval(String script)`
- `Object eval(Reader reader)`

You can pass a `Bindings` to the following two versions of the `eval()` method:

- `Object eval(String script, Bindings bindings)`
- `Object eval(Reader reader, Bindings bindings)`

These versions of the `eval()` method do not use the default context of the `ScriptEngine`. They use a new `ScriptContext` whose engine scope `Bindings` is the one passed to these methods and the global scope `Bindings` is the same as for the default context of the engine. Note that these two versions of the `eval()` method keep the default context of the `ScriptEngine` untouched.

You can pass a `ScriptContext` to the following two versions of the `eval()` method:

- `Object eval(String script, ScriptContext context)`
- `Object eval(Reader reader, ScriptContext context)`

These versions of the `eval()` method use the specified context to execute the script. They keep the default context of the `ScriptEngine` untouched.

The three sets of the eval() method let you execute scripts using different isolation levels:

- The first set lets you share the default context by all scripts

- The second set lets scripts use different engine scope Bindings and share the global scope Bindings

- The third set lets scripts execute in an isolated ScriptContext

Listing 3-4 shows how scripts are executed in different isolation levels using the different version of the eval() method. The program uses three variables called msg, n1, and n2. It displays the value stored in the msg variable. The values of n1 and n2 are added and the sum is displayed. The script prints what values of n1 and n2 were used in computing the sum. The value of n1 is stored in the Bindings of ScriptEngineManager that is shared by the default context of all ScriptEngines. The value of n2 is stored in the engine scope of the default context and the custom contexts. The script is executed twice using the default context of the engine, once in the beginning and once in the end, to prove that using a custom Bindings or a ScriptContext in the eval() method does not affect the Bindings in the default context of the ScriptEngine. The program declares a throws clause in its main() method to keep the code shorter.

Listing 3-4. Using Different Isolation Levels for Executing Scripts

```
// CustomContext.java
package com.jdojo.script;

import javax.script.Bindings;
import javax.script.ScriptContext;
import javax.script.ScriptEngine;
import javax.script.ScriptEngineManager;
import javax.script.ScriptException;
import javax.script.SimpleScriptContext;
import static javax.script.SimpleScriptContext.ENGINE_SCOPE;
import static javax.script.SimpleScriptContext.GLOBAL_SCOPE;

public class CustomContext {
        public static void main(String[] args) throws ScriptException {
                ScriptEngineManager manager = new ScriptEngineManager();
                ScriptEngine engine = manager.getEngineByName("JavaScript");

                // Add n1 to Bindings of the manager, which will be shared
                // by all engines as their global scope Bindings
                manager.put("n1", 100);
```

```
                   // Prepare the script
                   String script = "var sum = n1 + n2;" +
                               "print(msg + " +
                               "' n1=' + n1 + ', n2=' + n2 + " +
                               "', sum=' + sum);";

                   // Add n2 to the engine scope of the default context of the
                   // engine
                   engine.put("n2", 200);
                   engine.put("msg", "Using the default context:");
                   engine.eval(script);

                   // Use a Bindings to execute the script
                   Bindings bindings = engine.createBindings();
                   bindings.put("n2", 300);
                   bindings.put("msg", "Using a Bindings:");
                   engine.eval(script, bindings);

                   // Use a ScriptContext to execute the script
                   ScriptContext ctx = new SimpleScriptContext();
                   Bindings ctxGlobalBindings = engine.createBindings();
                   ctx.setBindings(ctxGlobalBindings, GLOBAL_SCOPE);
                   ctx.setAttribute("n1", 400, GLOBAL_SCOPE);
                   ctx.setAttribute("n2", 500, ENGINE_SCOPE);
                   ctx.setAttribute("msg", "Using a ScriptContext:",
                   ENGINE_SCOPE);
                   engine.eval(script, ctx);

                   // Execute the script again using the default context to
                   // prove that the default context is unaffected.
                   engine.eval(script);
              }
}
```

```
Using the default context: n1=100, n2=200, sum=300
Using a Bindings: n1=100, n2=300, sum=400
Using a ScriptContext: n1=400, n2=500, sum=900
Using the default context: n1=100, n2=200, sum=300
```

Return Value of the eval() Method

The eval() method of the ScriptEngine returns an Object, which is the last value in the script. It returns null if there is no last value in the script. It is error-prone, and confusing at the same time, to depend on the last value in a script. The following snippet of code shows some examples of using the return value of the eval() method for Nashorn. The comments in the code indicate the returned value from the eval() method:

```
Object result = null;

// Assigns 3 to result because the last expression 1 + 2 evaluates to 3
result = engine.eval("1 + 2;");

// Assigns 7 to result because the last expression 3 + 4 evaluates to 7
result = engine.eval("1 + 2; 3 + 4;");

// Assigns 6 to result because the last statement v = 6 evaluates to 6
result = engine.eval("1 + 2; 3 + 4; var v = 5; v = 6;");

// Assigns 7 to result. The last statement "var v = 5" is a
// declaration and it does not evaluate to a value. So, the last
// evaluated value is 3 + 4 (=7).
result = engine.eval("1 + 2; 3 + 4; var v = 5;");

// Assigns null to result because the print() function returns undefined
// that is translated to null in Java.
result = engine.eval("print(1 + 2)");
```

It is better not to depend on the returned value from the eval() method. You should pass a Java object to the script as a parameter and let the script store the returned value of the script in that object. After the eval() method is executed, you can query that Java object for the returned value. Listing 3-5 contains the code for a Result class that wraps an integer. You will pass an object of the Result class to the script that will store the returned value in it. After the script finishes, you can read the integer value stored in the Result object in your Java code. The Result needs to be declared public so it is accessible to the script engine. The program in Listing 3-6 shows how to pass a Result object to a script that populates the Result object with a value. The program contains a throws clause in the main() method's declaration to keep the code short.

Listing 3-5. A Result Class That Wraps an Integer

```java
// Result.java
package com.jdojo.script;

public class Result {
        private int val = -1;

        public void setValue(int x) {
                val = x;
        }

        public int getValue() {
                return val;
        }
}
```

Listing 3-6. Collecting the Return Value of a Script in a Result Object

```java
// ResultBearingScript.java
package com.jdojo.script;

import javax.script.ScriptEngine;
import javax.script.ScriptEngineManager;
import javax.script.ScriptException;

public class ResultBearingScript {
        public static void main(String[] args) throws ScriptException {
                // Get the Nashorn engine
                ScriptEngineManager manager = new ScriptEngineManager();
                ScriptEngine engine = manager.getEngineByName("JavaScript");

                // Pass a Result object to the script. The script will store the
                // result of the script in the result object
                Result result = new Result();
                engine.put("result", result);

                // Store the script in a String
                String script = "3 + 4; result.setValue(101);";

                // Execute the script, which uses the passed in
                // Result object to return a value
                engine.eval(script);
```

```
        // Use the result object to get the returned value from
        // the script
        int returnedValue = result.getValue(); // Will be 101

        System.out.println("Returned value is " + returnedValue);
    }
}
```

```
Returned value is 101
```

Reserved Keys for Engine Scope Bindings

Typically, a key in the engine scope `Bindings` represents a script variable. Some keys are reserved and they have special meanings. Their values may be passed to the engine by the implementation of the engine. An implementation may define additional reserved keys.

Table 3-1 contains the list of all reserved keys. Those keys are also declared as constants in the `ScriptEngine` interface. An implementation of a script engine is not required to pass all these keys to the engine in the engine scope bindings. As a developer, you are not supposed to use these keys to pass parameters from a Java application to a script engine.

Table 3-1. *The List of Reserved Keys for Engine Scope Bindings*

Key	Constant in ScriptEngine Interface	Meaning of the Value of the Key
"javax.script.argv"	ScriptEngine.ARGV	Used to pass an array of Object to pass a set of positional argument
"javax.script.engine"	ScriptEngine.ENGINE	The name of the script engine
"javax.script.engine_version"	ScriptEngine.ENGINE_VERSION	The version of the script engine
"javax.script.filename"	ScriptEngine.FILENAME	Used to pass the name of the file or the resource that the source of the script
"javax.script.language"	ScriptEngine.LANGUAGE	The name of the language supported by the script engine
"javax.script.language_version"	ScriptEngine.LANGUAGE_VERSION	The version of the scripting language supported by the engine
"javax.script.name"	ScriptEngine.NAME	The short name of the scripting language

Changing the Default ScriptContext

You can get and set the default context of a ScriptEngine using its getContext() and setContext() methods, respectively, as shown:

```
ScriptEngineManager manager = new ScriptEngineManager();
ScriptEngine engine = manager.getEngineByName("JavaScript");

// Get the default context of the ScriptEngine
ScriptContext defaultCtx = engine.getContext();

// Work with defaultCtx here

// Create a new context
ScriptContext ctx = new SimpleScriptContext();

// Configure ctx here

// Set ctx as the new default context for the engine
engine.setContext(ctx);
```

Note that setting a new default context for a ScriptEngine will not use the Bindings of the ScriptEngineManager as its global scope Bindings. If you want the new default context to use the Bindings of the ScriptEngineManager, you need set it explicitly as shown:

```
// Create a new context
ScriptContext ctx = new SimpleScriptContext();

// Set the global scope Bindings for ctx the same as the Bindings for
// the manager
ctx.setBindings(manager.getBindings(), ScriptContext.GLOBAL_SCOPE);

// Set ctx as the new default context for the engine
engine.setContext(ctx);
```

Sending Scripts Output to a File

You can customize the input source, output destination, and error output destination of a script execution. You need to set appropriate reader and writers for the `ScriptContext` that is used to execute a script. The following snippet of code will write the script output to a file named `jsoutput.txt` in the current directory:

```
// Create a FileWriter
FileWriter writer = new FileWriter("jsoutput.txt");

// Get the default context of the engine
ScriptContext defaultCtx = engine.getContext();

// Set the output writer for the default context of the engine
defaultCtx.setWriter(writer);
```

The code sets a custom output writer for the default context of the `ScriptEngine` that will be used during the execution of scripts that use the default context. If you want to use a custom output writer for a specific execution of a script, you need to use a custom `ScriptContext` and set its writer.

■ **Tip** Setting a custom output writer for a `ScriptContext` does not affect the destination of the standard output of the Java application. To redirect the standard output of the Java application, you need to use the `System.setOut()` method.

Listing 3-7 shows how to write output of a script execution to a file named `jsoutput.txt`. The program prints the full path of the output file on the standard output. You may get a different output when you run the program. You need to open the output file in a text editor to see the script's output.

Listing 3-7. Writing the Output of Scripts to a File

```
// CustomScriptOutput.java
package com.jdojo.script;

import java.io.File;
import java.io.FileWriter;
import java.io.IOException;
import javax.script.ScriptContext;
import javax.script.ScriptEngine;
import javax.script.ScriptEngineManager;
import javax.script.ScriptException;
```

```java
public class CustomScriptOutput {
        public static void main(String[] args) {
                // Get the Nashorn engine
                ScriptEngineManager manager = new ScriptEngineManager();
                ScriptEngine engine = manager.getEngineByName("JavaScript");

                // Print the absolute path of the output file
                File outputFile = new File("jsoutput.txt");
                System.out.println("Script output will be written to " +
                                outputFile.getAbsolutePath());

                FileWriter writer = null;

                try {
                        writer = new FileWriter(outputFile);

                        // Set a custom output writer for the engine
                        ScriptContext defaultCtx = engine.getContext();
                        defaultCtx.setWriter(writer);

                        // Execute a script
                        String script =
                                "print('Hello custom output writer')";
                        engine.eval(script);
                }
                catch (IOException | ScriptException e) {
                        e.printStackTrace();
                }
                finally {
                        if (writer != null) {
                                try {
                                        writer.close();
                                }
                                catch (IOException e) {
                                        e.printStackTrace();
                                }
                        }
                }
        }
}
```

Script output will be written to C:\jsoutput.txt

Summary

You can pass parameters to the script using the ScriptContext. An instance of the Bindings interface serves as the parameter holder. The Bindings interface inherits from the Map interface imposing a restriction that its keys must be nonempty, non-null Strings. The SimpleBinding class is an implementation of the Bindings interface. It is preferred to use the createBindings() method of ScriptEngine to get an instance of the Bindings interface giving ScriptEngine a chance to returned a specialized implementation of the Bindings interface. A Bindings is associated with a scope that can be an engine scope or a global scope. Parameters passed in the engine scope takes precedence over the parameters passed in the global scope. Parameters passed can be local to a script engine, local to a script execution, or global to all script engines created by a ScriptManager.

A script engine executes a script in a context that consists of four components: a set of Bindings, where each Bindings is associated with a different scope, a Reader that is used by the script engine to read inputs, a Writer that is used by the script engine to write outputs, and an error Writer that is used by the script engine to write error outputs. An instance of the ScriptContext interface represents a context for the script execution. The SimpleScriptContext class is an implementation of the ScriptContext interface.

The set of Bindings in a context is used to pass parameters to the script. A reader and writers in a context control input source and output destinations of the script, respectively. For example, by setting a file writer as a writer, you can send all outputs from a script to a file. Every ScriptEngine has a default ScriptContext that is used to execute scripts when no ScriptContext is passed to the eval() method. The getContext() method of ScriptEngine returns the default context of the engine. You can also pass a separate ScriptContext with the eval() method that will be used to execute your script, leaving the default ScriptContext of the engine untouched.

CHAPTER 4

▓ ▓ ▓

Writing Scripts in Nashorn

In this chapter, you will learn:

- How to write scripts in Nashorn

- The difference between running the script in strict mode and nonstrict mode

- How to declare variables and write comments

- Primitive and object data types, and how to convert values of one data type to another data type

- Operators, statements, and creating and invoking functions in Nashorn

- Different ways of creating and using objects

- Variable scoping and hoisting

- About built-in global objects and functions

Nashorn is a runtime implementation of the ECMAScript 5.1 specification on the JVM. ECMAScript defines its own syntax and constructs for declaring variables, writing statements, operators, creating and using objects, collections, iterating over collections of data, and so on. Nashorn is 100 percent compliant with the ECMAScript 5.1, so you have a new set of language syntax to learn when you work with Nashorn. For example, working with objects in Nashorn is entirely different from working with objects in Java.

This chapter assumes that you have at least a beginner-level understanding of the Java programming language. I will not explain details of the constructs and syntax offered by Nashorn that work the same way as they work in Java. For example, I will not explain what the assignment operator = in Nashorn does. Rather, I will simply mention that the assignment operator = works the same in Nashorn and Java. The power of Nashorn is that it lets you use Java libraries inside scripts. However, to use Java libraries inside Nashorn, you must know the Nashorn syntax and constructs. This chapter gives you a brief overview of Nashorn syntax and constructs.

Strict and Nonstrict Modes

Nashorn can operate in two modes: strict and nonstrict. Some features of ECMAScript cannot be used in strict mode. Typically, features that are error-prone are not allowed in strict mode. Some features that work in nonstrict mode will generate an error in strict mode. I will list the features that are applicable to strict mode while explaining the specific features. You can enable strict mode in your scripts in two ways:

- Using the -strict option with the jjs command
- Using the "use strict" or 'use strict' directive

The following command invokes the jjs command-line tool in strict mode and attempts to assign a value of 10 to a variable named empId without declaring the variable. You receive an error that says that the variable empId is not defined:

```
C:\> jjs -strict
jjs> empId = 10;
<shell>:1 ReferenceError: "empId" is not defined
jjs> exit()
```

The solution is to use the keyword var (discussed shortly) to declare the empId variable in strict mode.

The following command invokes the jjs command-line tool in nonstrict mode (without the -strict option) and attempts to assign a value of 10 to a variable named empId without declaring the variable. This time, you do not receive an error; rather, the value of the variable (that is, 10) is printed:

```
C:\> jjs
jjs> empId = 10;
10
jjs>exit()
```

Listing 4-1 shows a script using the use strict directive. The directive is specified in the beginning of the script or functions. The use strict directive is simply the string "use strict". You can also enclose the directive in single quotes like 'use strict'. The script assigns a value to a variable without declaring the variable, which will generate an error because strict mode is enabled.

Listing 4-1. A Script with the Strict Mode Directive

```
// strict.js

"use strict"; // This is the use strict directive.
empId = 10;   // This will generate an error.
```

Identifiers

An identifier is a name given to variables, functions, labels, and so on in scripts. An identifier in Nashorn is a sequence of Unicode characters with the following rules:

- It may contain letters, digits, underscores, and dollar signs
- It must not start with a digit
- It must not be one of the reserved words
- Characters in the identifier may be replaced with a Unicode escape sequence that would be of the form \uxxxx where xxxx is the Unicode numeric value of the character in hexadecimal format

The following are examples of valid identifiers:

- `empId`
- `emp_id`
- `_empId`
- `emp$Id`
- `num1`
- `\u0061bc` (same as abc because \u0061 is the Unicode escape sequence for the character a)

The following are examples of invalid identifiers:

- `4num` (Cannot start with a digit)
- `emp id` (Cannot contain spaces)
- `emp+id` (Cannot contains the + sign)
- `break` (break is a reserved word and cannot be used as an identifier)

Tables 4-1, 4-2, and 4-3 list the reserved words in Nashorn. Reserved words listed in Table 4-1 are already in use as keywords. You are familiar with most of these keywords in Java. In Nashorn, they have the same meaning; for example, for, do, and while are used to denote looping constructs, whereas break and continue are used to break out of loops and continue with the next iteration in the loop. I will explain the keywords specific to Nashorn in this chapter briefly. Tables 4-2 and 4-3 list keywords that are not in use yet, but they will be used in the future.

Using any reserved words as identifiers generates an error. The reserved words in Table 4-3 will generate an error only in strict mode. They can be used in nonstrict mode without any errors.

Table 4-1. *The List of Reserved Words in Nashorn Used as Keywords*

break	do	instanceof	typeof
case	else	new	var
catch	finally	return	void
continue	for	switch	while
debugger	function	this	with
default	if	throw	
delete	in	try	

Table 4-2. *The List of Future Reserved Words in Nashorn*

class	enum	extends	super
const	export	import	

Table 4-3. *The List of Future Reserved Words in Strict-Mode in Nashorn*

implements	let	private	public
yield	interface	package	protected
static			

Comments

Nashorn supports two types of comments:

- Single-line comments
- Multi-line comments

The syntax for writing comments in Nashorn is the same as that of Java. The following are examples of comments:

```
// Let us declare a variable named empId (A single-line comment)
var empId;

/* Let us declare a variable named empList
   and another variable named deptId (A multi-line comment)
*/
var empList;
var deptId;
```

Declaring Variables

Scripting languages are loosely typed. The type of a variable is not known at compile-time. The type of a variable can change during the execution of the program. The type of a variable is determined at runtime based on the value stored in the variable. For example, the same variable can store a number at one point and a string at another. This rule in Nashorn is significantly different from Java that is a strongly typed language and type of a variable is known at its declaration.

In Nashorn, the keyword var is used to declare a variable. Variable declaration is known as a variable statement in ECMAScript terminology:

```
// Declare a variable named msg
var msg;
```

Note that, unlike Java, you do not specify the data type of the declared variable in Nashorn. You can declare multiple variables in one variable statement. The variable names are separated by a comma:

```
// Declare three variables
var empId, deptId, emplList;
```

■ **Tip** In strict mode, it is an error to name a variable either eval or arguments.

A variable is initialized to undefined when declared. I will discuss data types and the undefined value in the next section. You can also initialize a variable with a value at the time of declaration:

```
/* Declare and initialize variables deptId, and emplList. deptId is
   initialized to the number 400 and emplList is initialized to an
   array of strings.
*/
var deptId = 400, emplList = ["Ken", "Lydia", "Simon"];
```

Note that you can create an array in Nashorn using an array literal that contains a comma-separated list of array elements enclosed in brackets. I will discuss arrays in detail in Chapter 7.

In nonstrict mode, you can omit the keyword var in the variable declaration:

```
// Declare a variable named greeting without using the keyword var
greeting = "Hello";
```

Data Types

Data types in can be divided into two categories: Primitive types and Object types. Primitive types include the following five data types:

- Undefined
- Null
- Number
- Boolean
- String

The Undefined Type

The Undefined type has only one value that is called undefined. A variable in Nashorn that is declared but is assigned a value has the value undefined. You can also assign the value undefined to a variable explicitly. In addition, you can compare another value with undefined. The following snippet of code shows how to use the value undefined:

```
// empId is initialized to undefined implicitly
var empId;

// deptId is initilaized to undefined explicitly
var deptId = undefined;

// Print the values of empId and deptId
print("empId is", empId)
print("deptId is", deptId);

if (empId == undefined) {
        print("empId is undefined")
}

if (deptId == undefined) {
        print("deptId is undefined")
}
```

```
empId is undefined
deptId is undefined
empId is undefined
deptId is undefined
```

The Null Type

The Null type has only one value that is called null. Even though the value null is considered to be of primitive type, it is typically used where an object is expected but there is no valid object to be specified. The following snippet of code shows how to use the value null:

```
var person = null;
print("person is", person);
```

```
person is null
```

The Number Type

Unlike Java, Nashorn does not distinguish between integers and floating-point numbers. It has only one type called Number to represent both types of numeric values. Numbers are stored in a double-precision 64-bit IEEE floating-point format. All numeric constants are called number literals. Like Java, you can represent number literals in decimal, hexadecimal, octal, and scientific notations. Nashorn defines three special values of number type: non-a-number, positive infinity, and negative infinity. In scripts, these special values are represented by NaN, +Infinity, and –Infinity, respectively. The positive infinity value can also be represented as simply Infinity, without a leading + sign. The following snippet of code shows how to use number literals and special number type values:

```
var empId = 100;              // An integer of type Number
var salary = 1500.678;        // A lfoating-point number of type Number
var hexNumber = 0x0061;       // Same as 97 is decimal
var octalNumber = 0141;       // Same 97 in decimal
var scientificNumber = 0.97E2; // Same 97 in decimal
var notANumber = NaN;
var posInfinity = Infinity;
var negInfinity = -Infinity;

// Print all values
print("empId =", empId);
print("salary =", salary);
print("hexNumber =", hexNumber);
print("octalNumber =", octalNumber);
print("scientificNumber =", scientificNumber);
print("notANumber =", notANumber);
print("posInfinity =", posInfinity);
print("negInfinity =", negInfinity);
```

```
empId = 100
salary = 1500.678
hexNumber = 97
octalNumber = 97
scientificNumber = 97
notANumber = NaN
posInfinity = Infinity
negInfinity = -Infinity
```

The Boolean Type

The Boolean type represents a logical entity that be either true or false. Like Java, Nashorn has two literals, true and false, of the Boolean type:

```
Var isProcessing = true;
var isProcessed = false;
print("isProcessing =", isProcessing);
print("isProcessed =", isProcessed);
```

```
isProcessing = true
isProcessed = false
```

The String Type

The String type includes all finite, ordered sequences of zero or more Unicode characters. A sequence of characters enclosed in double quotes or single quotes is known as a string literal. The number of characters in the sequence is known as the length of the string. The following are examples of using string literals:

```
var greetings = "Hi there";    // A string literal of length 8
var title = 'Scripting in Java'; // A string literal enclosed in single quotes
var emptyMsg = "";             // An empty string of length zero
```

A string literal can contain single quotes if it is enclosed in double quotes and vice versa. If a string literal is enclosed in double quotes, you need to escape the double quote using a backslash if you want to include a double quote inside the string. The same is true for strings enclosed in single quotes. The following snippet of code shows you some examples:

```
var msg1 = "It's here and now.";
var msg2 = 'He said, "He is happy."';
var msg3 = 'It\'s here and now.';
var msg4 = "He said, \"He is happy.\"";
```

```
print(msg1);
print(msg2);
print(msg3);
print(msg4);
```

```
It's here and now.
He said, "He is happy."
It's here and now.
He said, "He is happy."
```

Unlike Java, a string literal in Nashorn can be written in mutiple lines. You need to use a backslash at the end of the line as the continuation character. Notice that the backslash and the line terminator are not part of the string literal. Here is an example that writes the string literal, Hello World! in three lines:

```
// Assigns the string, Hello world!, to msg using a multi-line string
literal
var msg = "Hello \
world\
!";

print(msg);
```

```
Hello world!
```

If you want to insert a newline character in a multiline string literal, you will need to use the escape sequence \n as follows. Notice that I have placed the beginning and last quotes at a separate line that makes the multiline text more readable:

```
// Uses a multi-line string with embedded newlines
var lucyPoem = "\
STRANGE fits of passion have I known:\n\
And I will dare to tell,\n\
But in the lover's ear alone,\n\
What once to me befell.\
";

print(lucyPoem);
```

```
STRANGE fits of passion have I known:
And I will dare to tell,
But in the lover's ear alone,
What once to me befell.
```

A character in a string literal may appear literally or in the form of an escape sequence. You can use Unicode escape sequences to represent any character. Some of the characters such as line separator, carriage return, and so on cannot be represented literally and they must appear as escape sequences. Table 4-4 lists the escape sequences defined in Nashorn.

Table 4-4. *Single Character Escape Sequences in Nashorn*

Character Escape Sequence	Unicode Escape Sequence	Character Name
\b	\u0008	backspace
\t	\u0009	horizontal tab
\n	\u000A	line feed (new line)
\v	\u000B	vertical tab
\f	\u000C	form feed
\r	\u000D	carriage return
\"	\u0022	double quote
\'	\u0027	single quote
\\	\u005C	backslash

There is a significant difference in how Nashorn and Java interpret Unicode escape sequences. Unlike Java, Nashorn does not interpret Unicode escape sequences as the actual character before executing the code. The following single-line comment, character literal, and string literal in Java will not compile because the compiler converts the \u000A as a new line before compiling the program:

```
// This, \u000A, is a new line, making the single line comment invalid
char c = '\u000A';
String str = "Hello\u000Aworld!";
```

In Java, you must replace \u000A with \n in this code to work. The following snippet of code in Nashorn works fine:

```
// This, \u000A, is a new line that is valid in Nashorn
var str = "Hello\u000AWorld!";
print(str);
```

```
Hello
World!
```

I will defer the discussion of the Object type until I finish explaining the basic constructs in Nashorn such as operators, statements, loops, and so on.

Operators

Nashorn supports many operators. Most of them are the same as Java operators. I will list all operators in this section and discuss a few of them here. I will discuss others in subsequent sections when appropriate. Table 4-5 lists operators in Nashorn.

Table 4-5. *The List of Operators in Nashorn*

Operator	Name	Syntax	Description
++	Increment	++i i++	Increments the operand by 1.
--	Decrement	--i i--	Decrements the operand by 1.
delete		delete prop	Deletes the specified property from an object.
void		void expr	Discards the return value of the specified expression.
typeof		typeof expr	Returns a String describing the type of the specified expression.
+	Unary Plus	+op	Converts the operand to the Number type.
-	Unary Negation	-op	Converts the operand to the Number type and then negates the converted value.
~	Bitwise NOT	~op	Uses the operand as a 32-bit signed integer, flips its bits, and returns the result as a 32-bit signed integer.
!	Logical NOT	!expr	Returns true if expr evaluates to false. Returns false if expr evaluates to true.
+	Numeric addition/ string concatenation	op1 + op2	Performs a string concatenation if one of the operands is a string or they can be converted to string. Otherwise, performs numeric addition.
-	Subtraction	op1 - op2	Performs numeric subtraction on the two operands, converting them to numbers if they are not numbers.

(continued)

61

Table 4-5. (*continued*)

Operator	Name	Syntax	Description
/	Division	op1 / op2	Preforms division and returns the quotient of the two operands.
*	Multiplication	op1 * op2	Performs multiplication and returns product of the operands.
%	Remainder	op1 % op2	Uses the left operand as the dividend and the right operand as the divisor of a division operation and returns the remainder.
in		prop in obj	Returns true if the obj contains a property named prop. Otherwise, returns false. Here, prop is a string or a value convertible to string and obj is an object.
instanceof		obj instanceof cls	Returns true of obj is an instance of the class cls. Otherwise, return false.
<	Less-than	op1 < op2	Returns true of op1 is less than op2. Otherwise, returns false.
<=	Less-than-or-equal	op1 <= op2	Returns true of op1 is less than or equal to op2. Otherwise, returns false.
>	Greater-than	op1 > op2	Returns true of op1 is greater than op2. Otherwise, returns false.
>=	Greater-than-or-equal	op1 >= op2	Returns true of op1 is greater than or equal to op2. Otherwise, returns false.
==	Equality	op1 == op2	Returns true if op1 and op2 are equal. Otherwise, returns false. Type conversions are applied, if necessary. For example, "2" == 2 returns true because the string "2" s converted to the number 2 and then both operands are equal.
!=	Inequality	op1 != op2	Returns true if op1 and op2 are not equal. Otherwise, returns false. Type conversions are applied, if necessary.
===	Identity or strict equality	op1 === op2	Returns true if the types and values of the two operands are the same. Otherwise, returns false. The expression, "2" === 2 returns false "2" is a string and 2 is a number. Both expressions "2" === "2" and 2 === 2 return true.

(*continued*)

Table 4-5. (*continued*)

Operator	Name	Syntax	Description
! ==	Non-identity or strict inequality	op1 !== op2	Returns true if the operands are not equal and/or not of the same type. Both expressions "2" !== 2 and 2 !==3 return true. In the first expression, types of operands do not match (string and number) and, in the second one, the values of the operands do not match.
<<	Bitwise left shift	op1 << op2	Performs a bitwise left shift operation on op1 by the amount specified by op2. Before performing the left shift, op1 is converted to a 32-bit signed integer. The result is also a 32-bit signed integer.
>>	Bitwise signed right shift	op1 >> op2	Performs a sign-filling bitwise right shift operation on op1 by the amount specified by op2. The new bits on the left are filled with the original most significant bit that keeps the sign of the op1 and the result the same. Converts op1 to a 32-bit signed integer and the result is also a 32-bit signed integer.
>>>	Bitwise unsigned right shift	op1 >>> op2	Performs a zero-filling bitwise right shift operation on op1 by the amount specified by op2. The new bits on the left are filled with zeros that makes the result an unsigned 32-bit integer.
&	Bitwise AND	op1 & op2	Performs a bitwise AND operation on each pair of bits of op1 and op2. If both bits are 1, the resulting bit is 1. Otherwise, the resulting bit is 0.
|	Bitwise OR	op1 | op2	Performs a bitwise OR operation on each pair of bits of op1 and op2. If either bit is 1, the resulting bit is 1. If both bits are 0, the resulting bit is 0.
^	Bitwise XOR	op1 ^ op2	Performs a bitwise XOR operation on each pair of bits of op1 and op2. If bits are different, the resulting bit is 1. Otherwise, the resulting bit is 0.
&&	Logical AND	op1 && op2	Returns op1 or op2. If op1 is false or can be converted to false, op1 is returned. Otherwise, op2 is returned.

(*continued*)

Table 4-5. (*continued*)

Operator	Name	Syntax	Description
`||`	Logical OR	`op1 || op2`	Returns op1 or op2. If op1 is `true` or can be converted to `true`, op1 is returned. Otherwise, op2 is returned.
`?:`	Conditional or ternary operator	`op1 ? op2 : op3`	If op1 evaluates to true, returns the value of op2. Otherwise, returns the value of op3.
`=`	Assignment	`op1 = op2`	Assigns the value of op2 to op1 and returns op2.
`+=, -=, *=, /=, %=, <<=, >>=, >>>=, &=, ^=, |=`	Compound assignment	`op1 op= op2`	Works as if a statement like `op1 = op1 op op2` is executed. Applies the operation (+, =, *, /, %, etc.) on op1 and op2, assigns the result to op1 and returns the result.
`,`	Comma operator	`op1, op2, op3...`	Evaluates each of its operands from left to right and returns the value of the last operand. Used in locations where one expression is required, but you want to use multiple expressions, for example, in a `for` loop header.

Operators have precedence. In an expression, operators with the higher precedence are evaluated before operators with the lower precedence. Like Java, you can enclose part of an expression in parentheses that has the highest precedence. The following is the list of precedence of operators. Operators at level 1 have higher precedence than those at level 2. Operators at the same level have the same precedence:

1. ++ (Postfix increment), -- (postfix decrement)

2. !, ~, + (Unary plus), - (Unary negation), ++ (Prefix increment), -- (Prefix decrement), `typeof`, `void`, `delete`

3. `*, /, %`

4. + (Addition), - (Subtraction)

5. `<< , >>, >>>`

6. `<, <=, >, >=, in, instanceof`

7. `==, !=, ===, !==`

8. `&`

9. `^`

10. `|`

11. &&

12. ||

13. ? :

14. =, +=, -=, *=, /=, %=, <<=, >>=, >>>=, &=, ^=, |=

15. , (Comma operator)

I will discuss a few of the operators in this section. These operators in Nashorn are either not in Java or work very differently:

- The equality operator (==) and strict equality operator (===)

- The Logical AND (&&) and Logical OR (||) Operators

The == operator works almost the same way as it works in Java. It checks both operands for equality, performing the type conversions such as string to number, if possible. For example, "2" == 2 returns true because the string "2" is converted to the number 2 and then both operands are equal. The expression 2 == 2 also returns true because both operands are of type number and they are equal in values. By contrast, the === operator checks the types as well as values of both operands for equality. If either of them are not the same, it returns false. For example, "2" === 2 returns false because one operand is a string and another is a number. Their types do not match, even though their values, when converted to either string or number, match.

In Java, the && and || operators work with Boolean operands and they return true or false. In Nashorn, that is not the case; these operators return one of the operands' value that can be of any type. In Nashorn, any type of values can be converted to the Boolean value true or false. Values that can be converted to true are called *truthy* and values that can be converted to false are called *falsy*. I will provide the complete list of truthy and falsy values in the next section of this chapter.

The && and || operators work with truthy and falsy operands and return one of the operands value that may not be necessarily a Boolean value. The && and || operators also known as short circuit operators because they do not evaluate the second operand if the first operand itself can determine the result.

The && operator returns the first operand if it is falsy. Otherwise, it returns the second operand. Consider the following statement:

```
var result = true && 120; // Assigns 120 to result
```

The statement assigns 120 to result. The first operand to && is true, so it evaluates the second operand and returns it. Consider another statement:

```
var result = false && 120; // Assigns false to result
```

The statement assigns false to result. The first operand to && is false, so it does not evaluate the second operand. It simply returns the first operand.

The || operator returns the first operand if it is truthy. Otherwise, it returns the second operand. Consider the following statement:

```
var result = true || 120; // Assigns true to result
```

The statement assigns true to result. The first operand to || is true, so it returns the first operand. Consider another statement:

```
var result = false || 120; // Assigns 120 to result
```

The statement assigns 120 to result. The first operand to || is false, so it evaluates the second operand and returns its value.

Type Conversion

Things that are not allowed in Java are allowed in Nashorn, such as using a number or a string where a Boolean value is expected. Consider the following snippet of code in Nashorn, which adds a Boolean value to a number:

```
var n1 = true + 120;
var n2 = false + 120;
print("n1 = " + n1);
print("n2 = " + n2);
```

```
n1 = 121
n2 = 120
```

The expression true + 120 is not allowed in Java. However, it is allowed in Nashorn. Notice that Nashorn implicitly converts true is to the number 1 and false to the number 0. There are a lot of implicit conversions performed by Nashorn. You need to have a good understanding of them to write a bug-free code in Nashorn. The following sections explain those conversions in detail.

To Boolean Conversion

In Nashorn, you can use a truthy or falsy value whenever a Boolean value is required. For example, the condition in an if statement does not need to yield a Boolean value. It can be any truthy or falsy value. Table 4-6 lists the types of values and their corresponding converted Boolean values.

Table 4-6. *The List of Value Types and Their Corresponding Converted Boolean Values*

Value Type	Converted Boolean Value
Undefined	false
Null	false
Boolean	Identity conversion
Number	Evaluates to false if the argument is +0, -0, or NaN; otherwise, evaluates to true
String	The empty string evaluates to false. All other strings evaluate to true
Object	true

You can also use the Boolean() global function to explicitly convert a value to the Boolean type. The function takes the value to be converted as an argument. The following snippet of code contains some examples of implicit and explicit conversions to the Boolean type:

```
var result;
result = undefined ? "undefined is truthy" : "undefined is falsy";
print(result);

result = null ? "null is truthy" : "null is falsy";
print(result);

result = 100 ? "100 is truthy" : "100 is falsy";
print(result);

result = 0 ? "0 is truthy" : "0 is falsy";
print(result);

result = Boolean("") ? "The empty string is truthy"
                     : "The empty string is falsy";
print(result);

result = 'Hello' ? "'Hello' is truthy" : "'Hello' is falsy";
print(result);
```

```
undefined is falsy
null is falsy
100 is truthy
0 is falsy
The empty string is falsy
'Hello' is truthy
```

To Number Conversion

Values of all types in Nashorn can be implicitly or explicitly converted to the Number type. Table 4-7 lists the types of values and their corresponding converted numeric values.

Table 4-7. *The List of Value Types and Their Corresponding Converted Numeric Values*

Value Type	Converted Number Value
Undefined	NaN
Null	+0
Boolean	The Boolean value true is converted to 1 and false to 0
Number	Identity conversion
String	The empty string and a string containing only whitespaces are converted to zero. A string whose contents after trimming the leading and trailing whitespaces can be interpreted as a number is converted to the corresponding numeric value. If the numeric content of the string is too large or too small, it is converted to +Infinity or −Infinity, respectively. All other strings are converted to NaN
Object	If the contents of the object can be interpreted as a number, the object is converted to the corresponding numeric value; otherwise, the object is converted to NaN

You can use the Number() global function to explicitly convert a value to the Number type. The function takes the value to be converted as an argument and returns a number. The following snippet of code contains some examples of implicit and explicit conversions to the Number type:

```
var result;
result = Number(undefined);
print("undefined is converted to", result);

// Any number + NaN is NaN
result = 10 + undefined;
print("10 + undefined is", result);
```

```
result = Number("");
print("The empty string is converted to", result);

result = Number('Hello');
print("'Hello' is converted to", result);

// Convertes to the number 1982, ignoring leading and trailing whitespaces
result = Number(' 1982 ');
print("' 1982 ' is converted to", result);

result = Number(new Object(88));
print("new Object(88) is converted to", result);

result = Number(new Object());
print("new Object() is converted to", result);

// A very big number in a string
result = Number("10E2000");
print("10E2000 is converted to", result);
```

```
undefined is converted to NaN
10 + undefined is NaN
The empty string is converted to 0
'Hello' is converted to NaN
' 1982 ' is converted to 1982
new Object(88) is converted to 88
new Object() is converted to NaN
10E2000 is converted to Infinity
```

To String Conversion

Values of all types in Nashorn can be implicitly or explicitly converted to the String type.
Table 4-8 lists the types of values and their corresponding converted String values.

Table 4-8. *The List of Value Types and Their Corresponding Converted String Values*

Value Type	Converted String Value
Undefined	"undefined"
Null	"null"
Boolean	The Boolean value true is converted to "true" and false to "false"
Number	+0, 0, and -0 are converted to "0"; NaN is converted to "NaN"; Infinity (or +Infinity) is converted to "Infinity"; -Infinity is converted to "-Infinity". All other numbers are converted to their corresponding string representation in either decimal or scientific notation. Bigger numbers may not be converted exactly
String	Identity conversion
Object	If the object is a wrapper for a primitive value, it returns the primitive value as a String; otherwise, the String representation of the object by calling the toString() method is returned. If toString() method does not exist in the object, the string representation of the returned value of the valueOf() method is returned

You can use the String() global function to explicitly convert a value to the String type. The function takes the value to be converted as an argument and returns a String. The following snippet of code contains some examples of implicit and explicit conversions to the String type:

```
var result;
result = String(undefined);
print("undefined is converted to", result);

result = String(true);
print("true is converted to", result);

result = String(9088);
print("9088 is converted to", result);

result = String(0x786A);
print("0x786A is converted to", result);

result = String(900000000000000000000);
print("900000000000000000000 is converted to", result);

result = String(9000000000000000000000);
print("9000000000000000000000 is converted to", result);

result = String(new Object(1982));
print("new Object(1982) is converted to", result);
```

```
result = String(new Object());
print("new Object() is converted to", result);
```

```
undefined is converted to undefined
true is converted to true
9088 is converted to 9088
0x786A is converted to 30826
900000000000000000000 is converted to 900000000000000000000
900000000000000000000 is converted to 9e+21
new Object(1982) is converted to 1982
new Object() is converted to [object Object]
```

Statements

Nashorn contains most of the statements that you have in Java. Most of the statement types work in a very similar way to Java. The following is the list of statement types in Nashorn:

- Block Statement
- Variable Statement
- Empty Statement
- Expression Statement
- The if Statement
- Iteration (or loop) Statements
- The continue Statement
- The break Statement
- The return Statement
- The with Statement
- The switch Statement
- Labelled Statements
- The throw Statement
- The try Statement
- The debugger Statement

As in Java, you can use a semicolon to terminate a statement. Unlike Java, however, a statement terminator is optional. Nashorn will insert semicolons in many cases. Most of the time, you can omit the semicolon as the statement terminator without any problem.

Nashorn will insert them automatically as it feels necessary. In some cases, the automatic insertion of a semicolon may cause a misinterpretation of the program. The following rules are used to insert a semicolon automatically:

- A semicolon in automatically inserted if the parser encounters source text that is not allowed in the statement currently being parsed and the text is preceded by at least one line terminator

- A semicolon is inserted after a statement if the statement is followed by a closing brace (})

- A semicolon is inserted at the end of the program

- A semicolon is not inserted automatically if it will be parsed as an empty statement (I will explain empty statements later in this chapter). A semicolon is also not inserted in the header of a for statement

Consider the following code:

```
var x = 1, y = 3, z = 5
x = y
z++
printf("x = %d, y = %d, z = %d", x, y, z)
```

The parser will automatically insert semicolons as statement terminators as if you have written the code as follows:

```
var x = 1, y = 3, z = 5;
x = y;
z++;
printf("x = %d, y = %d, z = %d", x, y, z);
```

Consider the following code:

```
var x = 10, y = 20
if (x > y)
else x = y
```

The parser will insert a semicolon after the variable statement and the assignment statement x = y, but not after the if statement. The transformed code will be as follows:

```
var x = 10, y = 20;
if (x > y)
else x = y;
```

A semicolon is not automatically inserted after the if statement because the inserted semicolon will be interpreted as an empty statement. This code will not compile because the if statement has a condition but a statement is missing.

The parser keeps parsing the source code until it finds an offending token. It does not always insert a semicolon before a line terminator. Consider the following code:

```
var x
x
=
200
printf("x = %d", x)
```

The parser will treat the three lines of source code (second to fourth) as one assignment statement (x = 200) and insert a semicolon after 200. The transformed code will be as follows:

```
var x;
x
=
200;
printf("x = %d", x);
```

Consider the following code that prints 20:

```
var x = 200, y = 200, z
z = Math.sqrt
(x + y).toString()
print(z)
```

The parser does not insert a semicolon at the end of the third line (z = Math.sqrt). It thinks that the (in the following line is the start of the argument list for a function Math.sqrt. The transformed code looks as follows:

```
var x = 200, y = 200, z;
z = Math.sqrt
(x + y).toString();
print(z);
```

However, the writer of the code might have meant to assign the function reference Math.sqrt to the variable named z. In that case, the automatic insertion of semicolons changes the intended meaning of the code. If you insert the semicolon yourself after the assignment statement, the code output is different:

```
var x = 200, y = 200, z;
z = Math.sqrt;       // Assigns Math.sqrt function reference to z
(x + y).toString(); // Converts x + y to a string and ignores the result
print(z);
```

```
function sqrt() { [native code] }
```

If you had written the same code using the keyword void to ignore the result of the expression (x + y).toString(), the parser would have added a semicolon after the text z = Math.sqrt. The following code works as if you intended to assign the function reference Math.sqrt to the variable named z:

```
var x = 200, y = 200, z    // A semicolon is inserted here
z = Math.sqrt              // A semicolon is inserted here
void (x + y).toString()    // A semicolon is inserted here
print(z)                   // A semicolon is inserted here
```

```
function sqrt() { [native code] }
```

The reason that a semicolon was inserted at the end of the second line is that the keyword void is an offending token in the third line. The keyword void cannot be part of the assignment statement that started in the second line.

■ **Tip** I advise using a semicolon as the statement terminator everywhere it is required. Depending on the automatic insertion of semicolons may sometimes lead to subtle bugs.

I will discuss these statement types briefly in the following sections.

Block Statement

A block statement works similar to that of in Java. It is a group of zero or more statements enclosed in braces ({ }). Unlike Java, variables declared inside a block statement does not have a local scope to that block. They can be accessed before and after the block statement in which they are declared. The following snippet of code demonstrates this:

```
var empId = 100;

// Print empId and deptId. Note that deptId has not been
// declared yet, but you can access it.
print("empId = " + empId + ", deptId = " + deptId);

// A block statement
{
        var deptId = 200;
        print("empId = " + empId + ", deptId = " + deptId);

        // Compute the area of a circle
        var radius = 2.3;
        var area = Math.PI * radius * radius;
        printf("Radius = %.2f, Area = %.2f", radius, area);
}
```

```
print("empId = " + empId + ", deptId = " + deptId);
```

```
empId = 100, deptId = undefined
empId = 100, deptId = 200
Radius = 2.30, Area = 16.62
empId = 100, deptId = 200
```

In the code, the variable deptId is declared local to the block. However, you were able to access it outside (before as well as after) the block. This is not a bug in Nashorn. This works as designed, based on the variable scoping rules. Variable scoping in Nashorn works quite differently from that of in Java. I will discuss variable's scoping in the section *Variable Scoping and Hoisting*.

Variable Statement

A variable statement is used to declare and, optionally, initialize variables. I have already discussed the variable statement in the section *Declaring Variables*. Examples of variable statements are as follows:

```
// Declare a variable named empId
var empId;

// Declare a variable named deptId and initialize it to 200
var deptId = 200;
```

Empty Statement

A semicolon is used as an empty statement. The empty statement in Nashorn works the same way as that of in Java. It has no effect. It can be used anywhere a statement is required. Like Java, a for statement in Nashorn is used for iteration purpose. The following code uses a for statement to print integers 1 through 10. An empty statement is used as the body of the statement:

```
// The semicolon at the end is the empty statement
for(var i = 1; i <= 10; print(i++));
```

Expression Statement

An expression statement is a statement that consists of an expression with/without side effects. The following are some examples of expression statements:

```
var i = 100; // A variable statement
i++;         // An expression statement
print(i);    // An expression statement
```

The if Statement

The if statement in Nashorn works the same way it works in Java. Its general syntax is:

```
if(condition)
        statement;
```

You can also have an else part for an if statement:

```
if(condition)
        statement-1;
else
        statement-2;
```

If the condition evaluates to true, statement-1 is executed; otherwise, statement-2 is executed. Notice that the condition can be any type of expression, not necessarily a Boolean expression. The condition expression is evaluated and converted to a Boolean type value. The following snippet of code shows how to use an if and an if-else statements:

```
var x = 100, y = 200;

if (x <= y)
        printf("%d <= %d", x, y);

// The print() function returns undefined that evaluates to a Boolean false.
if (print(x)) {
        print("Inside if");
}
else {
        print("Inside else")
}
```

```
100 <= 200
100
Inside else
```

Notice that the expression print(x) is used as the condition for the second if statement. The print() function prints the value of the variable x and returns undefined. The value undefined is converted to the Boolean false (please refer to the section *To Boolean Conversion*) that will execute the statement associated with the else part.

Iteration Statements

Nashorn supports five types of iteration statements:

- The while Statement
- The do-while Statement
- The for Statement
- The for..in Statement
- The for..each..in Statement

The while, do-while, and for statements in Nashorn works the same as in Java. I will not discuss them in detail because as a Java developer you know how to use them. The following code demonstrates their use:

```
// Print first 3 natural numbers using the while,
// do-while, and for statements
var count;

print("Using the while statement...");
count = 1;
while (count <= 3) {
        print(count);
        count++;
}

print("Using the do-while statement...");
count = 1;
do {
        print(count);
        count++;
} while (count <= 3);

print("Using the for statement...");
for(var i = 1; i <= 3; i++) {
        print(i);
}
```

```
Using the while statement...
1
2
3
Using the do-while statement...
1
2
3
Using the for statement...
1
2
3
```

The for..in statement is used to iterate over indices of arrays or property names of objects. It can be used with collections such as arrays, lists, maps, any Nashorn objects, and so on. Its syntax is:

```
for(var index in object)
        Statement;
```

First, the object is evaluated. If it evaluates to null or undefined, the entire for.. in statement is skipped. If it evaluates to an object, the statement assigns the enumerable property to the index and executes the body. The index is of the string type. In case of an array, the index is the index of the array element as a string. In case of any other collections such as a list or a map (a Nashorn object is also a map), the property of the object is assigned to index. You can use the bracket notation (object[index]) to access the value of the property. The following code demonstrates how to use the for..in statement to iterate over the indices of an array:

```
// Create an array of three strings
var empNames = ["Ken", "Fred", "Li"];

// Use the for..in statement to iterate over indices of the array
for(var index in empNames) {
        var empName = empNames[index];
        printf("empNames[%s]=%s", index, empName);
}
```

```
empNames[0]=Ken
empNames[1]=Fred
empNames[2]=Li
```

■ **Tip** The index in the for...in statement is of String type, not Number type.

The for..each..in statement is not in the ECMAScript 5.1 specification. The Mozilla JavaScript 1.6 extension that is supported by Nashorn. As the for..in statement iterates over the indices/property names of a collection, the for..each..in statement iterates over the values in the collection. It works in the same way as the for-each statement in Java. Notice that a set is a collection of unique values without giving names to the values. You cannot iterate over a set using the for..in statement, but you can do so using a for..each..in statement. Its syntax is:

```
for(var value in object)
        Statement;
```

The following code shows how to use a for..each..in statement to iterate over the elements (not indices) of an array:

```
// Create an array of three strings
var empNames = ["Ken", "Fred", "Li"];

// Use the for..each..in statement to iterate over elements of the array
for each(var empName in empNames) {
        printf(empName);
}
```

```
Ken
Fred
Li
```

I will discuss more about the for..in and for..each..in statements in Chapter 7.

The continue, break, and return Statements

The continue, break, and return statements in Nashorn works the same as in Java. The continue and break statements can be labelled. The continue statement skips the rest of the body of the iteration statement and jumps to the beginning of the iteration statement to continue with the next iteration. The break statement jumps to the end of the iteration and switch statement in which it appears. The return statement in a function returns the control to the caller of the function. Optionally, the return statement can also return a value to the caller.

The with Statement

Nashorn executes a script in a context called execution context. It looks up an unqualified name in the script using the scope chain associated with the execution context. The name is searched in the closest scope first. If it is not found, the search continues up the scope chain until the name is found or the search is performed at the top of the scope chain. Its syntax is:

```
with(expression)
        statement
```

The with statement adds the specified expression that evaluates to an object to the head of the scope chain while executing the statement.

▪ Tip The use of the with statement is deprecated because it leads to the confusion as to where the unqualified name exists—in the object specified in the with statement or somewhere up the scope chain. It is not allowed in strict mode.

The following code demonstrates the use of the with statement:

```
var greetings = new String("Hello");

// Must use greetings.length to access the length property
// of the String object named greetings
printf("greetings = %s, length = %d", greetings, greetings.length);

with(greetings) {
        // You can use the length property of the greetings object
        // as an unqualified identifier within this with statement.
        printf("greetings = %s, length = %d", greetings, length);
}

with(new String("Hi")) {
        // The toString() and length will be resolved using the
        // new String("Hi") object
        printf("greetings = %s, length = %d", toString(), length);
}

with(Math) {
        // Compute the area of a circle
        var radius = 2.3;

        // PI and pow are resolved as properties of the Math object
        var area = PI * pow(radius, 2);
        printf("Radius = %.2f, Area = %.2f", radius, area);
}
```

```
greetings = Hello, length = 5
greetings = Hello, length = 5
greetings = Hi, length = 2
Radius = 2.30, Area = 16.62
```

The switch Statement

The switch statement in Nashorn works pretty much the same as the switch statement in Java works. Its syntax is:

```
switch(expression) {
        case expression-1:
                statement-1;
        case expression-2:
                statement-2;
        default:
                statement-3;
}
```

The expression is matched against the expressions in case clauses using the ===
operator. The statements in the first matched case clause are executed. If the case clause
contains a break statement, the control is transferred to the end of the switch statement;
otherwise, the statements following the matched case clause are executed. If no match is
found, the statements in the default clause are executed. If there are multiple matches,
only the statements in the first matched case clause are executed. In Java, the expression
must be of type int, String, or enum, whereas in Nashorn the expression can be of any
type including the Object, Null, and Undefined types. The following snippet of code
demonstrates how to use a switch statement:

```
// Define a match function that matches the passed in argument
// using a switch statement
function match(value) {
        switch (value) {
                case undefined:
                        print("Matched undefined:", value);
                        break;
                case null:
                        print("Matched null:", value);
                        break;
                case '2':
                        print("Matched string '2':", value);
                        break;
```

```
                case 2:
                        print("Matched number 2: ", value);
                        break;
                default:
                        print("No match:", value);
                        break;
        }
}

// Call the match function with different arguments
match(undefined);
match(null);
match(2);
match('2');
match("Hello");
```

```
Matched undefined: undefined
Matched null: null
Matched number 2: 2
Matched string '2': 2
No match: Hello
```

Labelled Statements

A label is simply an identifier followed with a colon. Any statement in Nashorn can be labelled by putting a label before the statement. In fact, Nashorn lets you have multiple labels for a statement. Once you have labelled a statement, you can use the same label with break and continue statements to break and continue to the label. Typically, you label outer iteration statements so that you can continue or break out of nested loops. Labelled statements work the same way as they do in Java. The following is an example of using a labeled statement and a continue statement with a label to print the lower-left half of a 3x3 matrix:

```
// Create a 3x3 matrix using an array of arrays
var matrix = [[11, 12, 13],
              [21, 22, 23],
              [31, 32, 33]];

 outerLoop:
 for(var i = 0; i < matrix.length; i++) {
        for(var j = 0; j < matrix[i].length; j++) {
                java.lang.System.out.printf("%d ", matrix[i][j]);
                if (i === j) {
                        print();
                        continue outerLoop;
                }
        }
 }
```

```
11
21 22
31 32 33
```

The throw Statement

A throw statement is used to throw a user-defined exception. It works similar to the throw statement in Java. Its syntax is:

```
throw expression;
```

In Java, a throw statement throws an object of the Throwable class or one of its subclasses; the expression must evaluate to a Throwable instance. In Nashorn, a throw statement can throw a value of any type that may include a number or a string. Nashorn has few built-in objects that can be used as error objects to be thrown in the throw statement. Such objects are Error, TypeError, RangeError, SyntaxError, etc. The following snippet of code shows how to throw a RangeError when empId is not between 1 and 10000:

```
var empId = -900;
if (empId <= 0 || empId >= 10000) {
        throw new RangeError(
        "empId must be between 1 and 10000. Found: " + empId);
}
```

When you run the code, it will print the stack trace of the error on the standard error. Like Java, Nashorn lets you handle the errors that are thrown. You will need to use a try-catch-finally statement to handle the thrown errors, which I will discuss in the next section.

The try Statement

The try-catch-finally statement in Nashorn works the same way as it works in Java. The try block contains one or more statements to execute that may throw errors. If the statements throw an error, the control is transferred to the catch block. Finally, the statements in the finally block are executed. Like in Java, you can have three combination of try, catch, and finally blocks: try-catch, try-finally, and try-catch-finally. Unlike Java, ECMAScript supports only one catch block per try block. Nashorn supports Mozilla JavaScript 1.4 extension that allows multiple catch block per try block. The syntax for using the try block is:

```
/* A try-catch block */
try {
        // Statements that may throw errors
}
```

```
catch(identifier) {
        // Handle the error here
}

/* A try-finally block */
try {
        // Statements that may throw errors
}
finally {
        // Perform cleanup work here
}

/* A try-catch-finally block */
try {
        // Statements that may throw errors
}
catch(identifier) {
        // Handle the error here
}
finally {
        // Perform cleanup work here
}
```

■ **Tip** In strict mode, it is a SyntaxError to use eval or arguments as the identifier in a catch block.

The following is a try block with multiple catch blocks supported as a Nashorn extension where e is an identifier. You can use any other identifier in place of e:

```
/* A try block with multiple catch blocks */
try {
        // Statements that may throw errors
}
catch (e if e instanceof RangeError) {
        // Handle RangeError here
}
catch (e if e instanceof TypeError) {
        // Handle TypeError here
}
catch (e) {
        // Handle other errors here
}
```

Consider the code in Listing 4-2. It defines two functions: isInteger() and factorial(). The isInteger() function returns true if its argument is an integer; otherwise, it returns false. The factorial() function computes and returns the factorial of a natural number. It throws a TypeError is its argument is not a number and a RangeError if its argument is not a number greater than or equal to 1.

Listing 4-2. The Contents of the factorial.js file

```
// factorial.js

// Returns true if n is an integer. Otherwise, returns false.
function isInteger(n) {
        return typeof n === "number" && isFinite(n) && n%1 === 0;
}

// Define a function that computes and returns the factorial of an integer
function factorial(n) {
        if (!isInteger(n)) {
                throw new TypeError(
                        "The number must be an integer. Found:" + n);
        }

        if(n < 0) {
                throw new RangeError(
                        "The number must be greater than 0. Found: " + n);
        }

        var fact = 1;
        for(var counter = n; counter > 1; fact *= counter--);

        return fact;
}
```

The program in Listing 4-3 uses the factorial() function to compute factorial for a number and a String. The load() function is used to load the program from the factorial.js file. The message property of the Error object (or its subtype) contains the error message. The program uses the message property to display the error message. The factorial() function throws a TypeError when "Hello" is passed to it as an argument. The program handles the error and displays the error message.

Listing 4-3. The Contents of the File factorial_test.js

```
// factorial_test.js

// Load the factorial.js file that contains the factorial() function
load("factorial.js");
```

```
try {
        var fact3 = factorial(3);
        print("Factorial of 3 is", fact3);

        var factHello = factorial("Hello");
        print("Factorial of 3 is", factHello);
}
catch (e if e instanceof RangeError) {
        print("A RangeError has occurred.", e.message);
        print("Error:", e.message);
}
catch (e if e instanceof TypeError) {
        print("A TypeError has occurred.", e.message);
}
catch (e) {
        print(e.message);
}
```

```
Factorial of 3 is 6
A TypeError has occurred. The number must be an integer. Found:Hello
```

Nashorn extends the Error object provided by ECMAScript. It add several useful properties to get the details of the error thrown. Table 4-9 lists such properties with their descriptions.

Table 4-9. *The List of the Proeprties of Error Object in Nashorn*

Property	Type	Description
lineNumber	Number	The line number in the source code from where the error object was thrown
columnNumber	Number	The column number in the source code from where the error object was thrown
fileName	String	The file name of the source script
stack	String	The script stack trace as a string
printStackTrace()	function	Prints full stack trace, including all Java frames, from where error was thrown from
getStackTrace()	function	Returns an array of java.lang.StackTraceElement instance for ECMAScript frames only
dumpStack()	function	Prints stack trace of the current thread as the java.lang.Thread.dumpStack() method does in Java. The dumpStack() is a function property of the Error object and you will need to call it as Error.dumpStack()

Listing 4-4 shows another version of the program in Listing 4-3. This time, you use only catch block and print the error's details using the Nashorn extensions for the Error object.

Listing 4-4. The Contents of the File factorial_test2.js

```
// factorial_test2.js

load("factorial.js");

try {
        // throw new TypeError("A type error occurred.");
        var fact3 = factorial(3);
        print("Factorial of 3 is", fact3);

        var factHello = factorial("Hello");
        print("Factorial of 3 is", factHello);
}
catch (e) {
        printf("Line %d, column %d, file %s. %s",
                e.lineNumber, e.columnNumber, e.fileName, e.message);

}
```

```
Factorial of 3 is 6
Line 10, column 8, file factorial.js. The number must be an integer.
Found:Hello
```

The debugger Statement

The debugger statement is for debugging purpose. It does not take any action by itself. If a debugger is active, the implementation may cause a breakpoint but it is not required to do so when it encounters a debugger statement. The syntax is:

debugger;

The NetBeans 8.0 IDE supports the debugger statement in debug mode. I will show how to debug Nashorn scripts using a debugger statement in Chapter 13.

Defining Functions

In Nashorn, a function is a block of executable, parameterized code that is declared once and can be executed multiple times. Executing a function is called *calling* or *invoking* the function. A function is an object; it can have properties, and it can be passed around as an argument to another function; it can be assigned to a variable. A function can have the following parts:

- A name
- Formal parameters
- A body

A function may optionally be given a name. When a function is called, you can pass some values that are called arguments of that function. The arguments are copied to the function's formal parameters. The body of the function consists of a series of statements. A function may optionally return a value using a `return` statement. If no `return` statement is used to return from the function, by default, the value `undefined` is returned. A function in Nashorn can be defined in many ways, as described in subsequent sections.

■ **Tip** You may think of a `function` in Nashorn as a method in Java. However, be aware that a function in Nashorn is an object and it is used in many different ways that a method in Java cannot be used.

Function Declaration

You can declare a function using the `function` statement as follows:

```
function functionName(param1, param2...) {
      function-body
}
```

The keyword `function` is used to declare a function. The `functionName` is the name of the function that can be any identifier. The `param1`, `param2`, and so on are formal parameter names. A function may have zero formal parameters and, in that case, the function name is followed with an opening and a closing parentheses. The body of the function that consists of zero or more statements is enclosed in braces.

■ **Tip** In strict mode, you cannot use eval and arguments as the function name or the name of formal parameters of the function.

So far, everything in a function declaration seems like a method declaration in Java. However, there are two significant differences:

- A function declaration does not have a return type

- A function specifies only the names of the formal parameters, not their types

The following is an example of a function named adder that takes two parameters and returns a value by applying the + operator on them:

```
// Applies the + operator on parameters named x and y,
// and returns the result
function adder(x, y) {
        return x + y;
}
```

Calling a function is the same as calling a method in Java. You need to use the function name followed with the comma-separated list of arguments enclosed in parentheses. The following snippet of code calls the adder function with two arguments with values 5 and 10, and assigns the returned value from the function to a variable named sum:

```
var sum = adder(5, 10); // Assigns 15 to sum
```

Consider the following snippet of code and the output:

```
var sum1 = adder(5, true); // Assigns 6 to sum1
var sum2 = adder(5, "10"); // Assigns "510" to sum2
print(sum1, typeof sum1);
print(sum2, typeof sum2);
```

```
6 number
510 string
```

This will be a surprise for you. You might have written the adder() function keeping in mind to add two numbers. However, you were able to pass arguments of type Number, Boolean, and String. In fact, you can pass any type of arguments to this function. This is because Nashorn is a loosely typed language and type-checking is performed at runtime. All values are converted to the expected types in a given context. In the first call, adder(5, true), the Boolean value true was converted automatically to the number 1; in the second call, adder(5, "10"), the number 5 was converted to the String "5" and the + operator worked as the string concatenation operator. If you want type-safety for the parameters in functions, you will need to validate them yourself as you did inside the factorial() function in Listing 4-2.

> ■ **Tip** Every function has a read-only property, named length, which contains the number of formal parameters of the function. In our case, adder.length will return 2 because the adder() function declares two formal parameters named x and y.

A function is an object. The function name is the reference to the function object. You can assign the function name to another variable and pass it to other functions. The following snippet of code assigns the reference of the adder() function to a variable named myAdder and calls the function using the myAdder variable:

```
// Assigns the reference of the adder function to the variable myAdder
var myAdder = adder;

// Call the function (adder()) referenced by myAdder
var sum = myAdder(5, 10);
print(sum);
```

```
15
```

Working with Function Arguments

Before I discuss how argument passing in functions works, consider the following snippet of code that calls the adder() function with zero to three arguments:

```
var sum1 = adder();          // Passes no arguments
var sum2 = adder(10);        // Passes only one arguments
var sum3 = adder(10, 5);     // Passes two arguments
var sum4 = adder(10, 5, 9);  // Passes three arguments - one extra
print("sum1 = " + sum1)
print("sum2 = " + sum2)
print("sum3 = " + sum3)
print("sum4 = " + sum4)
```

```
sum1 = NaN
sum2 = NaN
sum3 = 15
sum4 = 15
```

First thing to notice is that the code executes without any errors, that is, Nashorn lets you pass arguments to a function that are fewer or greater than the number of formal parameters of the function. This feature can be good or bad depending on how you think about it. In a good sense, you can think that all functions in Nashorn are varargs where some of the formal parameters can be named. In a bad sense, you can argue that you need to validate the number of arguments passed to the function if you want the callers to pass the same number of arguments as the number of declared formal parameters.

Inside every function body, an object reference named arguments is available. It acts like an array, but it is an object, not an array. Its length property is the number of actual arguments passed to the function. The actual arguments are stored in the arguments object using indexes 0, 1, 2, 3, and so on. The first argument is arguments[0], the second argument is arguments[1], and so on. The following rules are applied for arguments for a function call:

- The passed arguments to the function are stored in the arguments object

- If the number of passed arguments is less than the declared formal parameters, the unfilled formal parameters are initialized to undefined

- If the number of passed arguments is greater than the number of formal parameters, you can access the additional arguments using the arguments object. In fact, you can access all arguments all the time using the arguments object

- If an argument is passed for a formal parameter, the formal parameter name and the arguments object indexed property for that formal parameter are bound to the same value. Changing the parameter value or the corresponding value in the arguments object changes both

Listing 4-5 shows the code for an avg() function that compute average of passed arguments. The function does not declare any formal parameters. It checks that at least two arguments are passed and all arguments must be numbers (primitive numbers or Number objects).

Listing 4-5. A Function Using the arguments Object to Access All Passed Arguments

```
// avg.js

function avg() {
        // Make sure at least two arguments are passed
        If (arguments.length < 2) {
                throw new Error(
                "Minimum 2 arguments are required to compute average.");
        }

        // Compute the sum of all arguments
        var sum = 0;
        for each (var arg in arguments) {
                if (!(typeof arg === "number" ||
                    arg instanceof Number)) {
                        throw new Error("Not a number: " + arg);
                }
```

```
                sum += arg;
        }

        // Compute and return the average
        return sum / arguments.length;
}
```

The following snippet of code calls the avg() function:

```
// Load avg.js file, so the avg() function is available
load("avg.js");

printf("avg(1, 2, 3) = %.2f", avg(1, 2, 3));
printf("avg(12, 15, 300, 8) = %.2f", avg(12, 15, 300, 8));
```

```
avg(1, 2, 3) = 2.00
avg(12, 15, 300, 8) = 83.75
```

Function Expression

A function expression is a function that can be defined anywhere an expression can be defined. The function expression looks very similar to a function declaration except that the function name is optional. The following is an example of a function expression that defines a function as part of an assignment expression:

```
var fact = function factorial(n) {
                    if (n <= 1) {
                            return 1;
                    }

                    var f = 1;
                    for(var i = n; i > 1; f *= i--);

                    return f;
            };
```

```
/* Here, you can use the variable name fact to call the function,
   not the function name factorial.
*/
```

```
var f1 = fact(3);
var f2 = fact(7);
printf("fact(3) = %d", f1);
printf("fact(10) = %d", f2);
```

```
fact(3) = 6
fact(10) = 5040
```

Notice the semicolon at the end of the closing brace in the function expression that is the assignment statement terminator. You have given the function expression a name called `factorial`. However, the name `factorial` is not available to be used as a function name, except inside the function body itself. If you want to call the function, you must use the variable in which you have stored the function reference. The following code shows the use of the function name of the function expression inside the function body. This code uses a recursive function call to compute the factorial:

```
var fact = function factorial (n) {
                    if (n <= 1) {
                            return 1;
                    }

                    // Uses the function name factorial to call itself
                    return n * factorial(n - 1);
            };

var f1 = fact(3);
var f2 = fact(7);
printf("fact(3) = %d", f1);
printf("fact(10) = %d", f2);
```

```
fact(3) = 6
fact(10) = 5040
```

The function name in a function expression is optional. The code may be written as follows:

```
// There is no function name in the function expression. It is an
// anonymous function.
var fact = function (n) {
                    if (n <= 1) {
                            return 1;
                    }

                    var f = 1;
                    for(var i = n; i > 1; f *= i--);

                    return f;
            };

var f1 = fact(3);
var f2 = fact(7);
printf("fact(3) = %d", f1);
printf("fact(10) = %d", f2);
```

```
fact(3) = 6
fact(10) = 5040
```

You can also define a function expression and call it in the same expression. The following code shows how to define and call a function expression in two different ways:

```
// Load the avg.js file, so the avg() function will be available
load("avg.js");

// Encloses the entire expression in (). Defines a function expression and calls
// it at the same time.
(function printAvg(n1, n2, n3){
        // Call the avg() function
        var average = avg(n1, n2, n3);
        printf("Avarage of %.2f, %.2f and %.2f is %.2f.", n1, n2, n3,
        average);
}(10, 20, 40));

// Uses the void operator to create an expression. Defines a function
// expression and calls it at the same time.
void function printAvg(n1, n2, n3) {
        var average = avg(n1, n2, n3);
        printf("Avarage of %.2f, %.2f and %.2f is %.2f.", n1, n2, n3, average);
}(10, 20, 40);
```

```
Avarage of 10.00, 20.00 and 40.00 is 23.33.
Avarage of 10.00, 20.00 and 40.00 is 23.33.
```

First, the avg.js file is loaded that defines the avg() function. A function expression needs to be enclosed in parentheses or preceded by the void operator to help the parser not to confuse it as a function declaration. The function arguments list follows the function expression closing brace. In the second case, you have used the void operator instead of parentheses. The parser will be able to parse the function argument properly as it expects an expression after the void operator, not a function declaration. You could have dropped the function name in the code in both function expressions.

Nashorn supports a Mozilla JavaScript 1.8 extension that is a shorthand for defining a function expression whose body consists of only one expression. In that case, you can drop the braces and the return statement from the function's body. The following code defines the adder function expression using the shorthand syntax:

```
// The function expressions' body does not use {} and a return statement
var adder = function(x, y) x + y;

// Call the function using the adder variable
printf("adder(10, 5) = %d", adder(10, 5));
```

```
adder(10, 5) = 15
```

As a Java developer, you can compare function expressions with lambda expressions and anonymous classes. Typically, function expressions are used as callbacks and to encapsulate business logic that should not be exposed to the global scope.

The Function( ) Constructor

You can also create a function object using the Function constructor or the Function function. It lets you creates a function object from a string. A constructor in Nashorn is a function that is used to create a new object using the new operator. Nashorn has a built-in function, named Function, which can be used as a constructor function. The syntax to create a function using the Function constructor is:

```
var func = new Function("param1", "param2"..., "function-body");
```

You can also simply use Function as a function, as shown:

```
var func = Function("param1", "param2"..., "function-body");
```

param1, param2, and so on are names of the formal parameters of the new function being defined. The function body is the body of the function. All parameters to Function are passed as strings. If you pass only one parameter, it is considered the body of the function. You can also specify all parameter names in one string by separating the names with a comma, as shown:

```
var func = Function("param1, param2,...", "function-body");
```

The following code creates the adder() function that we had created earlier. This time, we use the Function object:

```
// Create a function that takes two arguments and returns
// the value after applying the + operator
var adder = new Function("x", "y", "return x + y;")
```

```
printf("adder(10, 15) = %d", adder(10, 15));
printf("adder('Hello', ' world') = %s", adder('Hello', ' world'));
```

```
adder(10, 15) = 25
adder('Hello', ' world') = Hello world
```

Sometimes, you may need an empty function that takes no parameters and performs no logic. An empty function always return undefined when called. You can create such an empty function by not specifying any parameters to the Function, as shown:

```
// Define an empty function
var emptyFunction = Function();

// Print the string form of the new function
print(emptyFunction);

// Call the function that will return undefined
var nothing = emptyFunction();
print(nothing);
```

```
function () {
}
undefined
```

You are advised not to use the Function object to define functions because the runtime cannot apply optimization to the function body contained in the string and the function is created every time the expression using Function is encountered.

The Object Type

An Object in Nashorn is a collection of properties. There are two types of properties:

- Named Data Property
- Named Accessor Property

A named data property associates a name with a value. The value can be a primitive value, an object, or a function. You can think of a named data property of an Object in Nashorn as an instance variable or a method of a Java object.

A named accessor property associates a name with one or two accessor functions. Those functions are also known as getter and setter. Accessor function are used to get or set a value. When the named accessor property is used (assigned a value or read) the corresponding accessor function is called. You can think of a named accessor property as getter/setter methods of a Java object.

You can also specify some Boolean attributes to the properties of an Object. For example, you can set the `writable` attribute of an Object to `false` to make the property read-only. There are several ways to create objects in Nashorn:

- Using an Object Literal

- Using a Constructor Function

- Using `Object.create()` Method

The following section will explain how to create objects using these methods.

Using an Object Literal

An object literal is an expression that creates and initializes an object. The syntax to use an object literal is:

```
{propName1:value1, propName2:value2, propName3:value3,...}
```

The object literal is enclosed in braces. Each property consists of a name-value pair. The name and value of the property are separated by a colon. Two properties are separated by a comma. A trailing comma after the last property value is allowed. In the object literal, propName1, propName2, and so on are the names of the properties and value1, value2, and so on are their values. The name of a property can be an identifier, a string enclosed in single or double quotes, or simply a number. If the property name contains whitespaces, it must be enclosed in single or double quotes. You can also use the empty string as the property name of an object.

The properties that you define this way are called *own* properties of the object. Notice that an object may inherit properties from its prototype and those properties are called *inherited* properties. The following statement creates few objects using object literals:

```
// An object with no own properties
var emptyObject = {};

// An object with two own properties named x and y
var origin2D = {x:0, y:0};

// An object with three own properties named x, y, and z
var origin3D = {x:0, y:0, z:0};

// An object with whitespaces in property names
var redColor = {"red value": 1.0,
                green: 0.0,
                "black value": 0.0,
                alpha: 1.0};
```

Accessing Object's Properties

You can access properties of an object using property accessor expressions using one of the two syntax:

- Using the Dot Notation
- Using the Bracket Notation

The dot notation uses the following syntax:

```
objectExpression.property
```

The objectExpression is an expression that evaluates to the reference to the object and the property is the property name.

The bracket notation uses an array-like syntax:

```
objectExpression[propertyExpression]
```

The objectExpression is an expression that evaluates to the reference to the object. It is followed with an opening bracket and a closing bracket. The propertyExpression is an expression that is convertible to a string and that is the property name being accessed.

■ **Tip** If the property name contains whitespaces or stored in a variable, you must use the bracket notation, not the dot notation, to access the property.

Consider the following object from the previous section:

```
// An object with whitespaces in the property names
var redColor = {"red value": 1.0,
                green: 0.0,
                "black Value": 0.0,
                alpha: 1.0};
```

The following statement reads the value of the alpha property of the object into a variable named alphaValue:

```
// Assigns 1.0 to alphaValue
var alphaValue = redColor.alpha;
```

If the property accessor expression appears on the right side of the assignment operator, you are setting a new value for the property. The following statement sets the alpha property of the redColor object to 0.5:

```
// Make the color semi-transparent
redColor.alpha = 0.5;
```

The following snippet of code performs the same actions using the bracket notation:

```
// Assigns 1.0 to alphaValue
var alphaValue = redColor["alpha"];

// Make the color semi-transparent
redColor["alpha"] = 0.5;
```

The "red value" and "black value" properties contain a space, so you can use only the bracket notation to access them:

```
// Assigns 1.0 to redValue
var redValue = redColor["red value"];

// Assigns 0.8 to the "red value" property
redColor["red value"] = 0.8
```

When you use the bracket notation, you can use any expression that can be converted to the property name as a string. The following snippet of code assigns the value 0.8 to the "red Value" property in two ways:

```
var prop = "red value";
redColor[prop] = 0.8;                        // Using a variable
redColor["red" + " " + "value"] = 0.8;  // Using an expression
```

Consider the following code that defines a point2D object with two properties named x and y, and attempts to read a nonexisting property named z:

```
// Define a point2D object
var point2D = {x:10, y:-20};

// Try accessing x, y, and z properties
var x = point2D.x;
var y = point2D.y;
var z = point2D.z;
print("x = " + x + ", y =" + y + ", z = " + z);
```

```
x = 10, y =-20, z = undefined
```

Are you surprised by the output? Accessing a nonexisting property of an object in Nashorn does not generate an error. If you read a nonexisting property, undefined is returned; if you set a nonexisting property, a new property with the same name is created with the new value. The following code shows this behavior:

```
// Create an object with one property x
var point3D = {x:10};

// Create a new property named y and assign -20 to it
point3D.y = -20;

// Create a new property named z and assign 35 to it
point3D.z = 35;

// Print all properties of point3D
print("x = " + point3D.x + ", y =" + point3D.y + ", z = " + point3D.z);
```

```
x = 10, y =-20, z = 35
```

How do you know the difference between a nonexisting property and an existing property with the value undefined? You can use the in operator to know whether a property exists in an object. The syntax is:

```
propertyNameExpression in objectExpression
```

The propertyNameExpression evaluates to a string that is the name of the property. The objectExpression evaluates to an object. The in operator returns true if the object has a property with the specified name; otherwise, it returns false. The in operator searches own as well as inherited properties of the object. The following code shows how to use the in operator:

```
// Create an object with x and y properties
var colorPoint2D = {x:10, y:20};

// Check if the object has a property named x
var xExists = "x" in colorPoint2D;
print("Property x exists: " + xExists + ", x = " + colorPoint2D.x);

// Check if the object has a property named color
var colorExists = "color" in colorPoint2D;
print("Property color exists: " + colorExists + ", color = " +
colorPoint2D.color);
```

```
// Add a color property and set it to undefined, and then, perform the check
colorPoint2D.color = undefined;
colorExists = "color" in colorPoint2D;
print("Property color exists: " + colorExists + ", color = " +
colorPoint2D.color);
```

```
Property x exists: true, x = 10
Property color exists: false, color = undefined
Property color exists: true, color = undefined
```

The following statement creates an object with three properties; two of them contain data values and another a function. It shows you how to use the property that is a function. You need to call the function passing the arguments, if any:

```
// A person object with fName, lName, and getFullName properties
var john = {fName: "John",
            lName: "Jacobs",
            getFullName: function () {
                            return this.fName + " " + this.lName;
                        }
        };

var fullName = john.getFullName();
print("Full name is " + fullName);
```

```
Full name is John Jacobs
```

Notice the use of the keyword this inside the function. The keyword this refers to the object on which the function is called.

■ **Tip** If the data property of an object has a function as its value, such a function is known as a method of the object. In other words, a method is a function defined as a property of an object.

You can also access the property that is a function using the bracket notation. The syntax looks a bit awkward. This function call that uses the dot notation can be replaced with the bracket notation, as shown:

```
var fullName = john["getFullName"]();
print("Full name is " + fullName);
```

```
Full name is John Jacobs
```

Defining Accessor Properties

An accessor property is also called getter and setter methods. You can think of an accessor property as a set of getXxx() and setXxx() methods in a Java class. When the xxx property is read, the getter method with the xxx name is called; when the xxx property is set, the setter method with the xxx name is called. The getter method declares no formal parameters. The setter method declares one formal parameter. A property can have only a getter method, only a setter method, or both. The following is the syntax for defining the accessor property:

```
{ prop1: value1, /* A data property */
  prop2: value2, /* A data property */

  /* The getter for the property propName */
  get propName() {
      // Getter method's body goes here
  },

  /* The setter for the property propName */
  set propName(propValue) {
      // Setter method's body goes here
  }
}
```

Defining an accessor property is the same as declaring functions with the keyword function replaced with the keywords get and set. The keywords get and set are used to define the getter and setter methods, respectively. Notice that you do not use a colon to define the accessor property, but you still need to use a comma to separate two properties of the object. The following code defines an object with two data properties named fName and lName, and an accessor property named fullName:

```
// A person object with fName and lName as data proeprties
// and fullName as an accessor property
var john = {fName: "John",
            lName: "Jacobs",
            get fullName() {
```

```
            return this.fName + " " + this.lName;
        },
        set fullName(name) {
            names = name.split(" ");
            if(names.length === 2) {
                this.fName = names[0];
                this.lName = names[1];
            }
            else {
                    throw new Error("Full name must be in the form
                    'fName lName'.");
            }
        }
    };

// Get the full name using the fullName accessor property and print it
print("Full name is " + john.fullName);

// Set a new full name
john.fullName = "Ken McEwen";

// Get the new full name and print it
print("New full name is " + john.fullName);
```

```
Full name is John Jacobs
New full name is Ken McEwen
```

Notice that you set the first and the last names of the person by setting the fullName property. When you set the value of the fullName property, the value is passed to the setter method of the property that sets the first and last names, provided the value follows the "fName lName" format.

Setting Property Attributes

You can set attributes for data and accessor properties of an object. Table 4-10 lists the attributes of properties. Note that not all attributes are applicable to all types of properties.

Table 4-10. The List of Property Attributes and Their Descriptions

Attribute	Type	Applicable To	Description
value	Any type	Data Property Only	The value of the property
writable	Boolean	Data Property Only	Specifies whether the value of the property can be changed. If false, the property is read-only. Otherwise, the property is read-write. The default is true
get	function	Accessor Property Only	The getter method for the property or undefined. The default is undefined
set	function	Accessor Property Only	The setter method of the property of undefined. The default is undefined
enumerable	Boolean	Both	If set to false, the property of the object cannot be enumerated using the for..in and for..each..in loops. The default is true
configurable	Boolean	Both	It set to false, the property cannot be deleted and attributes for the property cannot be changed. The default is true

You can read and set the property attributes using an object called the property descriptor. The following statement create a property descriptor that has the value property to 10 and writable property to false:

```
var descriptor = {value:10, writable:false};
```

Creating a property descriptor does not do anything. It just creates an object. You need to use one of the following three methods of Object to define a new property with attributes, to change the attributes of an already defined property, and to read the property descriptor of an existing property:

- Object.defineProperty(object, "propertyName", propertyDescriptor)

- Object.defineProperty(object, "propertyName", attributeObject)

- Object.getOwnPropertyDescriptor(object, "propertyName")

The defineProperty() function lets you define a new property with attributes or change attributes of an existing property. Using the defineProperties() function, you can do the same but with multiple properties. The getOwnPropertyDescriptor() function returns the descriptor for the specified property of the object. All three functions work with the own properties of an object.

The following code defines an origin2D object to define the origin in a 2D coordinate system and makes both x and y properties nonwritable:

```
// Define an object
var origin2D = {x:0, y:0};

// Read the property descriptors for x and y
var xDesc = Object.getOwnPropertyDescriptor(origin2D, "x");
var yDesc = Object.getOwnPropertyDescriptor(origin2D, "y");
printf("x.value = %d, x.writable = %b", xDesc.value, xDesc.writable);
printf("y.value = %d, y.writable = %b", yDesc.value, yDesc.writable);

// Make x and y non-writable
Object.defineProperty(origin2D, "x", {writable:false});
Object.defineProperty(origin2D, "y", {writable:false});

print("After setting x and y non-writable... ")

// Read the property descriptors for x and y again
var xDesc = Object.getOwnPropertyDescriptor(origin2D, "x");
var yDesc = Object.getOwnPropertyDescriptor(origin2D, "y");
printf("x.value = %d, x.writable = %b", xDesc.value, xDesc.writable);
printf("y.value = %d, y.writable = %b", yDesc.value, yDesc.writable);
```

```
x.value = 0, x.writable = true
y.value = 0, y.writable = true
After setting x and y non-writable...
x.value = 0, x.writable = false
y.value = 0, y.writable = false
```

The following code shows you how to add a new property using the Object.defineProperty() function:

```
// Define an object with no properties
var origin2D = {};

// Add two non-writable x and y properties to origina2D with their
value set to 0.
Object.defineProperty(origin2D, "x", {value:0, writable:false});
Object.defineProperty(origin2D, "y", {value:0, writable:false});
```

In this code, you could have used the `defineProperties()` function to define both x and y properties in one shot. Both functions `defineProperty()` and `defineProperties()` return the object on which the property or properties are being set so that you can chain their calls. The following code rewrites the previous example:

```
// Create an empty object
var origin2D = {};

// Add two non-writable x and y properties to origina2D
// with their value set to 0.
Object.defineProperties(origin2D, {x: {value:0, writable: false},
                                    y: {value:0, writable: false}});
```

■ **Tip** When you add a property to an object in the object literal or by assigning a value to the property, the default values for `writable`, `enumerable`, and `configurable` properties are set to `true`. When you use a property descriptor to define a property or alter the property's attributes, the default values for these attributes in the property descriptor is `false`. Make sure you specify values for all attributes that needs to be set to `true` when using a property descriptor.

Once you set the `writable` attribute of a property to `false`, changing its value has no effect. In strict mode, changing the value of a nonwritable property generates an error:

```
var point = {x:0, y:10};
printf("x = %d", point.x);

// Make x non-writable
Object.defineProperty(point, "x", {writable: false});

// Try changing the value of x
point.x = 100; // Has no effect, because x is non-writable

printf("x = %d", point.x);
```

```
x = 0
x = 0
```

Defining a constant in Nashorn is not straightforward. You will need to use the Object.defineProperty() function to define a constant. The following code defines a constant named MAX_SIZE in the global scope. The keyword this refers to the global object in the following code:

```
// Define a constant named MAX_SIZE with a value 100
Object.defineProperty(this, "MAX_SIZE", {value:100, writable:false,
configurable:false});

printf("MAX_SIZE = %d", MAX_SIZE);
```

```
MAX_SIZE = 100
```

You can iterate over enumerable properties of an object using the for..in and for.. each..in iterator statements. The following code creates an object with two properties that are enumerable by default, uses the for..in and for..each..in statements to iterate over the properties, changes one of the properties to nonenumerable, and iterates over the properties again:

```
// Create an object with two properties x and y
var point = {x:10, y:20};

// Using for..in reports x and y as properties
for(var prop in point) {
        printf("point[%s] = %d", prop, point[prop]);
}

// Make x non-enumerable
Object.defineProperty(point, "x", {enumerable: false});

print("After making x non-enumerable");

// Using for..in reports only y as property
// because x is now non-enumerable
for(var prop in point) {
        printf("point[%s] = %d", prop, point[prop]);
}
```

```
point[x] = 10
point[y] = 20
After making x non-enumerable
point[y] = 20
```

Deleting Properties of an Object

You can delete a configurable property of an object using the delete operator. Its syntax is:

```
delete property;
```

The following snippet of code creates an object with two properties x and y, iterator over the properties, delete the property named x, and iterates over the properties again. The second time, the property x and its value are not printed because it has been deleted:

```
// Create an object with two properties x and y
var point = {x:10, y:20};

for(var prop in point) {
        printf("point[%s] = %d", prop, point[prop]);
}

// Delete property x from the point object
delete point.x;
print("After deleting x");

for(var prop in point) {
        printf("point[%s] = %d", prop, point[prop]);
}
```

```
point[x] = 10
point[y] = 20
After deleting x
point[y] = 20
```

In strict mode, it is an error to delete to a property whose configurable attribute is set to false. Deleting a nonconfigurable property in nonstrict mode has no effect.

Using a Constructor Function

A constructor function (or simply a constructor) is a function that is used with the new operator to create an object. It is customary to start a constructor with an uppercase letter. The following code creates a function named Person that is intended to be used as a constructor:

```
// Declare a constructor named Person
function Person(fName, lName) {
        this.fName = fName;
        this.lName = lName;
        this.fullName = function () {
                        return this.fName + " " + this.lName;
                }
}
```

Notice that a constructor is simply a function like any other function, and it can also be called as a function without using the new keyword. The outcome may be very different, depending on how the function is written. I will discuss such scenarios shortly.

The keyword this inside a constructor refers to the object being constructed when the function is called with the new operator. In this case, this.fName inside the Person function refers to the fName property of the new object being constructed. So are lName and toString. The Person constructor simply adds three properties to the object being created. The following snippet of code creates two objects using the Person constructor and prints their string representations:

```
// Create few Person objects
var john = new Person("John", "Jacobs");
var ken = new Person("Ken", "McEwen");

// The print() function calls the toString() method when
// it needs to convertan object to a string
print(john);
print(ken);
```

```
John Jacobs
Ken McEwen
```

Let's try using Person simply as a function, not as a constructor:

```
// Print details
printf("fName = %s, lName = %s", this.fName, this.lName);

// Call the Person function
var john = Person("John", "Jacobs");

// Print details
printf("fName = %s, lName = %s, full name = %s", this.fName, this.lName,
this.fullName());

// Call the Person function
var ken = Person("Ken", "McEwen");

// The print two person references
print("john = " + john);
print("ken = " + ken);

printf("fName = %s, lName = %s, full name = %s", this.fName, this.lName,
this.fullName());
```

```
fName = undefined, lName = undefined
fName = John, lName = Jacobs, full name = John Jacobs
john = undefined
ken = undefined
fName = Ken, lName = McEwen, full name = Ken McEwen
```

You can observe the following points in the code:

- The code prints the value of this.fName and this.lName. The printf() function is called in the global context and the keyword this refers to the global object. Because you have not defined any fName and lName properties for the global object, values for both properties are returned as undefined.

- The Person() function is called and its return value is stored in the john variable. The Person() function is called in the global context, so the keyword this inside the function refers to the global object. The function adds three properties to the global object.

- The printf() function is used to print the details of the global object (referred to by this) to confirm that the previous call to the Person() function added those properties to the global object.

- The Person() function is called again with different arguments. The first call had already added three properties to the global object. This call simply updates them with new values. This is confirmed by reading these properties from the global object again.

- Because the Person() function does not return a value explicitly, it returns undefined by default that is confirmed by the last two lines in the output.

If you do not pass any arguments a constructor, you can omit the parentheses in the new object creation expression. The following code calls Person as a constructor function without passing any arguments that will default the actual parameters inside the function to undefined. Notice that the new operator is simply followed with the constructor name:

```
// Create a person with both names as undefined
var person = new Person;  // No arguments list
print(person.fullName());

// Set the names for the person
person.fName = "Ken";
person.lName = "Smith";
print(person.fullName());
```

```
undefined undefined
Ken Smith
```

Typically, a constructor does not use a return statement in its body. If it returns no value or a primitive value, the new object is used, ignoring the primitive value. If it returns an object, the returned object is used as the value of the invocation of the new operator. It may sound odd that the return value of the constructor may change the returned object of the new operator; however, it is a powerful feature of the language. You can use this to implement a function that can be used as a function as well as a constructor and both return an object. You can use it for caching an object and returning the cached object when a new object already exists in the cache. Listing 4-6 shows such a technique.

Listing 4-6. The Contents of the Logger.js File

```
// Logger.js

// Declare a function object named Logger
function Logger() {
        // A private method
        function getLogger() {
                if (!Logger.logger) {
                        // Create a new logger and store its reference in
                        // the looger pproperty of the Logger function
                        Logger.logger = {log: function(msg) {
                                                print(msg);
                                        }
                        };
                }

                return Logger.logger;
        }

        return getLogger();
}

// Create two logger objects
var logger1 = new Logger(); // A constructor call
var logger2 = new Logger(); // A constructor call
var logger3 = Logger();     // A function call

// Check if the logger is cached
print("logger1 === logger2 is " + (logger1 === logger2));
print("logger1 === logger3 is " + (logger1 === logger3));
logger1.log("Hello 1");
logger2.log("Hello 2");
logger3.log("Hello 3");
```

```
logger1 === logger2 is true
logger1 === logger3 is true
Hello 1
Hello 2
Hello 3
```

When Logger is called for the first time, as a function or a constructor, it creates an object with a log() method, caches the object in the logger property of the Logger function, and returns the object. When Logger is called again, it simply returns the cached object.

Using a constructor, you can maintain private state for objects. This is done using closure. If you define a variable with the keyword var inside a function, that variable has local scope. It is only accessible inside the function. A nested function captures its enclosing scope including the local variables declared in its outer function. Listing 4-7 demonstrates the concept of maintaining the private state for an object using a constructor. It creates a Sequence object that maintains the current value that is accessible only through the methods curValue() and nextValue(). Notice that when the object is created, the local variable currentValue is captured by both function. When the functions are called, they work on the same captured variables, as shown in the output.

Listing 4-7. The Contents of the Sequence.js File

```
// Sequence.js

// This object generates strictly increasing sequence numbers
function Sequence() {
        var currentValue = 0;

        // Using Nashorn extension syntax to define one-liner functions
        this.nextValue = function () ++currentValue;
        this.curValue = function () currentValue;
}

// Create a Sequence object
var empId = new Sequence();

print("empId sequence...");
printf("Current Value = %d, next Value = %d", empId.curValue(),
empId.nextValue());
printf("Current Value = %d, next Value = %d", empId.curValue(),
empId.nextValue());
printf("Current Value = %d, next Value = %d", empId.curValue(),
empId.nextValue());
```

```
// Create a Sequence object
var deptId = new Sequence();

print("deptId sequence...");
printf("Current Value = %d, next Value = %d", deptId.curValue(),
deptId.nextValue());
printf("Current Value = %d, next Value = %d", deptId.curValue(),
deptId.nextValue());
printf("Current Value = %d, next Value = %d", deptId.curValue(),
deptId.nextValue());
```

```
empId sequence...
Current Value = 0, next Value = 1
Current Value = 1, next Value = 2
Current Value = 2, next Value = 3
deptId sequence...
Current Value = 0, next Value = 1
Current Value = 1, next Value = 2
Current Value = 2, next Value = 3
```

Object Inheritance

Unlike Java, Nashorn does not have classes. Nashorn works with objects only. It supports prototype-based object inheritance. Apart from the collection of properties, every object in Nashorn has a prototype that is an object or the null value. You can access the reference of the prototype of an object using the __proto__ property. Notice that there are two underscores before and after the word proto in the property name __proto__. This property is deprecated and you can use the following two functions to get and set the prototype of an object:

- Object.getPrototypeOf(object)
- Object.setPrototypeOf(object, newPrototype)

If a property in an object is accessed, first its own properties are searched. If the property is found, it is returned. If the property is not found, the prototype of the object is search. If the property is not found, the prototype of the prototype of the object is searched, and so on. The search continues until the property is found in the prototype chain or the entire prototype chain is searched. This search is the same as in class-based inheritance in Java, where properties are searched up the class inheritance chain until the java.lang.Object class is searched.

■ **Tip** In Java, the class inheritance always extends up to the java.lang.Object class. In Nashorn, Object.prototype is the default prototype of an object. However, you can set the prototype to any object, including the null value.

Consider the code in Listing 4-8.

Listing 4-8. The Contents of the file prototype.js

```
// prototype.js

var point = {x: 10,
             y: 20,
             print: function() {
                        printf("(%d, %d)", this.x, this.y);
                     }
            };

var coloredPoint = {color: "red",
                    print: function() {
                             printf("(%d, %d, %s)", this.x, this.y,
                                       this.color);
                          }
                   };

// Set the point object as the prototype of the coloredPoint object
// That is, the coloredPoint object inherits from the point object.
Object.setPrototypeOf(coloredPoint, point);

print("After setting the prototype for coloredPoint...");

// Call the print() methods of both objects
point.print();
coloredPoint.print();

// Change the x and y values in the point object.
point.x = 100;
point.y = 200;

print("After setting the x and y properties for point...");

// Print the two points details again
point.print();
coloredPoint.print();

/* Call the toString() method that is defined in Object.prototype object and are
   available in point and coloredPoint object through prototype chain.
*/
print(point.toString());
print(coloredPoint.toString());

// Print prototypes of objects
```

```
print("Object.getPrototypeOf(point) === Object.prototype is " +
      (Object.getPrototypeOf(point) === Object.prototype));
print("Object.getPrototypeOf(colorPoint) === point is " +
      (Object.getPrototypeOf(coloredPoint) === point));
print("Object.getPrototypeOf(colorPoint) === Object.prototype is " +
      (Object.getPrototypeOf(coloredPoint) === Object.prototype));
```

```
 After setting the prototype for coloredPoint...
(10, 20)
(10, 20, red)
After setting the x and y properties for point...
(100, 200)
(100, 200, red)
[object Object]
[object Object]
Object.getPrototypeOf(point) === Object.prototype is true
Object.getPrototypeOf(colorPoint) === point is true
Object.getPrototypeOf(colorPoint) === Object.prototype is false
```

You can observe the following points in the code:

- It defines a point object with three properties named x, y, and print

- It defines another object, called coloredPoint, with two properties named color and print. At this point, the two objects are unrelated.

- It sets the point object as the prototype of the coloredPoint object using the Object.setPrototypeOf() function, so now the coloredPoint object inherits from the point object. At this point, the coloredPoint object inherits all properties of the point object, including the properties x and y. Notice that only one copy of x and y exists and they are shared by both point and coloredPoint objects.

- It calls the print() method on both objects. The output confirms that both objects called their versions of the print() method. This is a case of property overriding. The coloredPoint object overrides the print() method of the point object. This works the same as in Java.

- It changes the values for the x and y properties on the point object and calls the print() method of both objects again. The output confirms that the values of x and y were changed for both point and coloredPoint objects.

- It calls the `toString()` method on both objects and they print the same string. This is another case of inheritance. The `point` object does not set its prototype, so its prototype is, by default, set to `Object.prototype` object, where `Object` is a built-in object in Nashorn. The `toString()` method is defined in `Object.prototype` and it is inherited by default by all objects. The `coloredPoint` object inherited it from the `point` object and the `point` object inherited it from the `Object.prototype` object.

- Finally, it compares the prototypes of objects and prints the results. The output confirms the prototype chain as discussed.

Figure 4-1 depicts the prototype chain for the `point` and `coloredPoint` objects. Notice that the `Object.prototype` has its prototype set to `null`, indicating the end of the prototype chain. You could have set the prototype for the `point` object to `null`, thus eliminating the `Object.prototype` from the prototype chain.

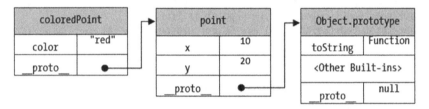

Figure 4-1. *The Prototype Chain for the point and coloredPoint Objects*

In the previous example, you saw that the two objects shared the same properties named x and y. You do not really want to share object's states. Typically, you want each object to have its own state. You could have solved this problem by redeclaring the x and y properties in the `coloredPoint` object. If you set the x and y properties on `coloredObject`, `coloredObject` will get new x and y properties of its own. The following demonstrates this:

```
var point = {x: 10,
            y: 20,
            print: function() {
                    printf("(%d, %d)", this.x, this.y);
            }
        };

var coloredPoint = {color: "red",
                print: function() {
                        printf("(%d, %d, %s)", this.x,
                        this.y, this.color);
                }
            };
```

```
Object.setPrototypeOf(coloredPoint, point);

// Call the print() methods of both objects
point.print();
coloredPoint.print();

// Change the x and y values in the point object
point.x = 100;
point.y = 200;

// Add own x and y properties to the coloredPoint object
coloredPoint.x = 300;
coloredPoint.y = 400;

// Call the print() methods of both objects
point.print();
coloredPoint.print();
```

```
(10, 20)
(10, 20, red)
(100, 200)
(300, 400, red)
```

■ **Tip**   The prototype chain is searched when reading the object's property, not when updating them. Recall that updating a property that does not exists adds a new property to the object on which the property is set.

In the previous example, you saw how the prototype inheritance chain works in Nashorn. You created objects using the object literals and set up object's prototype using the Object.setPrototypeOf() function. You can also do the same, though a bit differently, using function constructors. A function in Nashorn is also an object and, by default, the prototype of a function is set to Function.prototype object. The Function. prototype has Object.prototype as its prototype. Function.prototype contains several useful methods and properties that can be used with all functions. For example, it overrides the toString() method of the Object.prototype and the method prints the source code for the function. The following code demonstrates this:

```
// Create a function object called log
function log(str) {
        print(new Date() + ": " + str);
}
```

```
// Call toString() method on the log object
print(log.toString());
```

```
function log(str) {
    print(new Date() + ": " + str);
}
```

Every function in Nashorn has a property named prototype, which is another object. Do not confuse the prototype property of a function with the prototype object (or simply prototype) of the function. The prototype property of a function is set automatically as the prototype for all objects created using that function as a constructor. The prototype property has a property named constructor that refers back to the function itself.

Listing 4-9 creates a constructor function called Point and adds two methods named toString() and distance() to its prototype property.

Listing 4-9. The Contents of the Point.js File

```
// Point.js

// Define the Point constructor
function Point(x, y) {
        this.x = x;
        this.y = y;
}

// Override the toString() method in Object.prototype
Point.prototype.toString = function() {
        return "Point(" + this.x + ", " + this.y + ")";
};

// Define a new method called distance()
Point.prototype.distance = function(otherPoint) {
        var dx = this.x - otherPoint.x;
        var dy = this.y - otherPoint.y;
        var dist = Math.sqrt(dx * dx + dy * dy);
        return dist;
};
```

The code in Listing 4-10 uses the `Point` constructor to create two objects and calculates the distance between them.

Listing 4-10. The Contents of the PointTest.js File

```
// PointTest.js

load("Point.js");

// Create two Point object, compute the distnce
// between them, and print the results
var p1 = new Point(100, 200);
var p2 = new Point(-100, -200);
var dist = p1.distance(p2);
printf("Distance between %s and %s is %.2f.", p1.toString(), p2.toString(),
dist);
```

```
Distance between Point(100, 200) and Point(-100, -200) is 447.21.
```

If you create a `Point` object, its prototype will automatically be set as `Point.prototype` object, so the new object will inherit the `toString` and `distance` methods. The following snippet of code demonstrates this:

```
// Create two Point objects, compute and print the distnce between them
var p1 = new Point(100, 200);
var p2 = new Point(-100, -200);
var dist = p1.distance(p2);
printf("Distance between %s and %s is %.2f.", p1.toString(), p2.toString(),
dist);
```

```
Distance between Point(100, 200) and Point(-100, -200) is 447.21
```

Listing 4-11 contains the code for the `ColoredPoint` constructor. I will explain more about this after the listing.

Listing 4-11. The Contents of the ColoredPoint.js File

```
// ColoredPoint.js

load("Point.js");

function ColoredPoint(x, y, color) {
        // Call the Point constructor function binding this,
        // which is the current ColoredPoint object context
```

```
        // as this for the Point invocation, so the x and y
        // properties will be added to the current ColoredPoint object
        Point.call(this, x, y);

        // Add a color property to the new object
        this.color = color;
};

// Set a new object whose prototype is Point.prototype as
// the prototype for the ColoredPoint function
ColoredPoint.prototype = Object.create(Point.prototype);

// Set the constructor property of the prototype
ColoredPoint.prototype.constructor = ColoredPoint;

// Override the toString() method of the Point.prototype object
ColoredPoint.prototype.toString = function() {
        return "ColoredPoint(" + this.x + ", " + this.y + ", " + this.color + ")";
};
```

First, the code loads the Point.js file that contains the definition of the Point constructor function.

The first statement in the ColoredPoint constructor calls the Point() function passing the x and y arguments. It is important to understand the intention of this statement. It is the same as calling the superclass constructor in Java from the subclass constructor. You are in the process of creating a ColoredPoint object and you want to call the Point function as the constructor, so the ColoredPoint object being created is initialized as a Point first. You may be tempted to use Point(x, y) instead of Point. call(this, x, y). However, that will not work. The confusion comes from the meaning of the keyword this. When you call the Point() function from the ColoredPoint function, you need to point the keyword this in the Point() function to the new ColoredPoint object being created. When you call Point(x, y), the keyword this inside the Point() function points to the global object, not the ColoredPoint object being created. The call() method of a function lets you pass the this reference as the first argument. In this case, you passed the this reference that is available in the ColorPoint() function, so the Point() function executes in the same context as the ColoredPoint function. The statements this.x = x and this.y = y inside the Point() function will add x and y properties to the new ColoredPoint object.

Now, you need to set up the prototype chain for objects that will be created using the ColoredPoint function. This is done by setting the prototype property of the ColoredPoint function to an object whose prototype is Point.prototype. The Object. create() function does this, like so:

```
// Set a new object whose prototype is Point.prototype as the prototype for the
// ColoredPoint function
ColoredPoint.prototype = Object.create(Point.prototype);
```

The statement replaced the prototype property of the ColoredPoint function that will also reset the constructor property of the prototype property. The following statement restores the constructor property:

```
// Set the constructor property of the prototype
ColoredPoint.prototype.constructor = ColoredPoint;
```

ColoredPoint objects will inherit the toString() method from Point.prototype. To make sure that a ColoredPoint returns its color component when the toString() method is called on it. To achieve this, you override the toString() method, as shown:

```
// Override the toString() method of the Point.prototype object
ColoredPoint.prototype.toString = function() {
        return "ColoredPoint(" + this.x + ", " + this.y + ", " + this.color + ")";
};
```

Listing 4-12 shows the code that tests the Point and ColoredPoint functions. It creates an object of each type and computes the distance between them. Finally, the results are printed.

Listing 4-12. The Contents of the ColoredPointTest.js File

```
// ColoredPointTest.js

load("Point.js");
load("ColoredPoint.js")

// Create a Point and a ColoredPoint objects
var p1 = new Point(100, 200);
var p2 = new ColoredPoint(25, 50, "blue");

// Compute the distance between two points
var p1Top2 = p1.distance(p2);
var p2Top1 = p2.distance(p1);
printf("Distance of %s from %s = %.2f", p1.toString(), p2.toString(), p1Top2);
printf("Distance of %s from %s = %.2f", p2.toString(), p1.toString(), p2Top1);
```

```
Distance of Point(100, 200) from ColoredPoint(25, 50, red) = 167.71
Distance of ColoredPoint(25, 50, red) from Point(100, 200) = 167.71
```

Figure 4-2 depicts the prototype chain of the Point and ColoredPoint functions and their objects. The figure may seem intimidating at first. Once you understand the linking of an object with its prototype using the __proto__ property and the prototype property of a function, the rest is linking of the objects by their references.

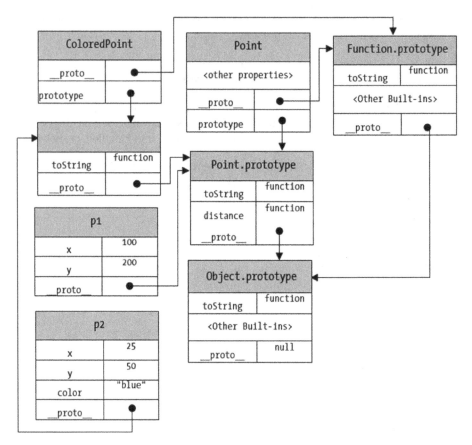

Figure 4-2. *The Prototype Chain for the Point and ColoredPoint Functions and Their Objects*

Using Object.create( ) Method

The Object.create() method is another way to create an object by specifying the object's prototype and initial properties. Its syntax is:

```
Object.create(prototypeObject, propertiesObject)
```

The function returns the reference of the new object. The prototypeObject is an object or null that is set as the prototype of the new object. The propertiesObject is optional; it is a property descriptor that contains the initial list of properties for the new object. The following two statements are equivalent. Both create empty object whose prototype is Object.prototype:

```
var obj1 = {};
var obj2 = Object.create(Object.prototype);
```

The following statement creates an empty object with null as its prototype:

```
var obj = Object.create(null);
```

Listing 4-13 creates an object to represent the origin in a 2D plane. It uses Point.prototype as the prototype of the new object. It specifies x and y properties for the object. Note that the writable, enumerable and configurable properties are set to false by default in a property descriptor. So, the origin2D object is nonmutable. The code also prints the properties of the new object that proves that x and y properties are nonenumerable. Note that the new object inherits the toString and distance properties from the Point. prototype object.

Listing 4-13. Using Object.create() to Create an Object

```
// ObjectCreate.js

load("Point.js");

// Create a non-writable, non-enumerable, non-configurable
// Point to represent the origin
var origin2D = Object.create(Point.prototype, {x:{value:0}, y:{value:0}});

print("After creating:", origin2D);

// Cannot change x and y properties of origin2D.
// They are non-writable by default.
origin2D.x = 100; // No effect
origin2D.y = 100; // No effect

print("After changing x and y:", origin2D);

print("origin2D instanceof Point = " + (origin2D instanceof Point));
```

```
print("origin2D properties:");
for(var x in origin2D) {
        print(x);
}
```

```
After creating: Point(0, 0)
After changing x and y: Point(0, 0)
origin2D instanceof Point = true
origin2D properties:
toString
distance
```

Binding Object Properties

Nashorn lets you bind properties of one object to another object using the
Object.bindProperties(target, source) method where target is the object whose
properties will be bound to the properties of source. Listing 4-14 shows how to bind
properties of one object to another object.

Listing 4-14. Binding Properties of One Object to Another Object

```
// bindproperties.js

var trg = {};
var src = {x:100, y:200, z:300};

// Bind properties of sourceObject to targetObject
Object.bindProperties(trg, src);

// Print properties using trg
printf("trg-1: x=%d, y=%d,z=%d", trg.x, trg.y, trg.z);

// Now change z using trg
trg.z = 30;   // Using src.z = 30 will have the same efect

// Print the properties using both objects and both
// should have the new value of z as 30
printf("trg-2: x=%d, y=%d,z=%d", trg.x, trg.y, trg.z);
printf("src-2: x=%d, y=%d,z=%d", src.x, src.y, src.z);

// Now add a new property to trg
trg.u = 30;
```

```
// At this point, trg has the property named u, but src does not.
printf("trg-3: x=%d, y=%d,z=%d, u=%d", trg.x, trg.y, trg.z, trg.u);
printf("src-3: x=%d, y=%d,z=%d, u=%s", src.x, src.y, src.z, src.u);

// Now add a new property to src
src.v = 30;

// Contrary to our expectation, trg.v does not exist. It may indicate a bug.
printf("trg-4: x=%d, y=%d,z=%d, u=%d, v=%s", trg.x, trg.y, trg.z, trg.u,
trg.v);
printf("src-4: x=%d, y=%d,z=%d, u=%s, v=%d", src.x, src.y, src.z, src.u,
src.v);
```

```
trg-1: x=100, y=200,z=300
trg-2: x=100, y=200,z=30
src-2: x=100, y=200,z=30
trg-3: x=100, y=200,z=30, u=30
src-3: x=100, y=200,z=30, u=undefined
trg-4: x=100, y=200,z=30, u=30, v=undefined
src-4: x=100, y=200,z=30, u=undefined, v=30
```

There are two practical uses of the Object.bindProperties() method:

- To enumerate the properties of Java objects inside Nashorn scripts

- You can import an object's properties into global scope as if those properties are declared globally

You cannot enumerate the properties of Java objects using the for..in or for.. each..in statements in Nashorn. Notice that we are talking about Java objects, not Nashorn objects. The solution is to bind the properties of Java objects to a Nashorn object and use one of these iteration statements on the Nashorn object. Listing 4-15 shows how to iterate over the properties of java.util.HashSet object.

Listing 4-15. Iterating Over Properties of Java Objects

```
// bindjavaobject.js

var trg = {};
var src = new java.util.HashSet();

// Try iterating src properties
print("Iterating over src properties:");
for (var propName in src) {
        print(propName); // Will not get here
}
```

```
// Bind properties of the java.util.HashSet object referenced by src to trg
Object.bindProperties(trg, src);

// Try iterating src properties
print("Iterating over trg properties:");
for (var propName in trg) {
        print(propName);
}
```

```
Iterating over src properties:
Iterating over trg properties:
getClass
wait
notifyAll
notify
remove
removeAll
iterator
stream
hashCode
toArray
parallelStream
add
spliterator
forEach
containsAll
clear
isEmpty
removeIf
contains
size
addAll
equals
clone
toString
retainAll
class
empty
```

Listing 4-16 show code that creates a logger object that has only one property called log that is a function. It uses the Object.bindProperties() method to bind the property of the object to the global object referenced by this. Once, the bind takes place, you can use the function log() as if it is a global function. When the code is loaded, it prints the location of the log file.

Listing 4-16. Binding an Object's Properties to the Global Object

```
// loadglobals.js

// Create a function obejct using a function expression
var Logger = function () {
        var LOG_FILE = new java.io.File("nashorn_app.log");
        var printer = new java.io.PrintWriter(
                new java.io.FileWriter(LOG_FILE, true /*append*/), true
                /*autoflush*/);

        this.log = function (msg) {
                printer["println(String)"](java.time.LocalDateTime.now() +
                ": " + msg);
        };

        // Print the path for the log file
        print("Logs using the log(msg) global function will be written to " +
                        LOG_FILE.absolutePath);
};

// Bind a Logger object to the global object.
// Here, this refers to the global object
Object.bindProperties(this, new Logger());
```

The following code loads the loadglobals.js file and uses the log() function as if it is a global function. You may get a different output. The logged messages will be stored in the file located printed in the output. You can use this technique to import as many global objects int the global scope you need. All that you need to do is to add all such properties to an object and bind that object to the global object this:

```
// Load the globals
load("loadglobals.js");

// Now you can use the log() method as a global function
log("Hello logger!");
```

```
Logs using the log(msg)  global function will be written to
C:\nashorn_app.log
```

Locking Objects

Object provides several methods that let you lock down objects. These methods give you finer control as to what parts or features of the object are locked down:

- You can prevent extensions of the object (or make it nonextensible) so new properties cannot be added to it

- You can seal the object so that the existing properties cannot be deleted and new properties cannot be added

- You can freeze the object so that the existing properties cannot be deleted, new properties cannot be added, and properties are read-only

The Object.preventExtensions(obj) method lets you make the specified object nonextensible. The Object.seal(obj) method seals the specified object. The Object.freeze(obj) method freezes the specified object. Notice that once you make an object nonextensible, sealed, or frozen, there is no way to reverse these properties. You can use the Object.isExtensible(obj), Object.isSealed(obj), and Object.isFrozen(obj) methods to check if the specified object is extensible, sealed, and frozen, respectively. In strict mode, an error is thrown if you try to make changes to the object that are not allowed; for example, adding a new property to a nonextensible object throws an error.

■ **Tip** Preventing extensions, sealing, and freezing an object affects only that object, not its prototype. It is still possible to make changes to its prototype and the object will inherit those changes. If you want to freeze the object completely, you will need to freeze all objects along the object's prototype chain.

Listing 4-17 shows how to prevent extensions of an object. It also shows that you can add a property to the prototype of an otherwise nonextensible object and the object will inherit that property. The code makes the point object nonextensible and adding a property named z does not add the property to the object. However, you are able to add the same property to Object.prototype and the point object inherits it.

Listing 4-17. Preventing Extensions of Objects

```
// preventextensions.js

var point = {x:1, y:1};
print("isExtensible() = " + Object.isExtensible(point));

// Make point non-extensible
Object.preventExtensions(point);
print("isExtensible() = " + Object.isExtensible(point));
```

```
// Try adding a new property to point
point.z = 1; // Will throw an error in strict mode

// Check if the property z was added to point
print("point has property z = " + ("z" in point));

// point inherits from Object.prototype. Let us add a property
// named z in Object.prototype
Object.prototype.z = 1;

// Check if the property z was added to point. Now point inherits
// the proeprty named z from Object.prototype.
print("point has property z = " + ("z" in point));

// The following statement has no effect as the point object
// is still non-extensible.
point.z = 100;

print("z = " + point.z); // Reads the Object.prototype.z
```

```
isExtensible() = true
isExtensible() = false
point has property z = false
point has property z = true
z = 1
```

Accessing Missing Properties

Nashorn provides an extension to allow you to add a method to an object that is called when a nonexistent property of an object is accessed. You can also provide such a method for nonexistent methods. The property names are __noSuchProperty__ and __noSuchMethod__. Notice the two underscores before and after the property names. Both properties are functions. If you are working on a project and need this behavior everywhere, you should add these hooks to the Object.prototype, so they are available in all objects by default. Listing 4-18 shows how to add these properties to the Object. prototype. The function for the __noSuchProperty__ is passed the property name being accessed. The function for the __noSuchMethod__ is passed the method name and all arguments used in the method call. You can access all arguments using the arguments object inside the function.

Listing 4-18. Adding Missing Property and Method Hooks

```
// missingprops.js

var point = {x:10, y:20};

// Add no such property and no such method hooks
Object.prototype.__noSuchProperty__ = function (prop) {
        throw Error("No such property: " + prop);
};

Object.prototype.__noSuchMethod__ = function () {
        var desc = arguments[0] + "(";
        if (arguments.length > 1) {
                desc += arguments[1];
        }

        for (var i = 2; i < arguments.length; i++) {
                desc += ", " + arguments[i];
        }

        desc += ")";
        throw Error("No matching method found: " + desc);
};

// Try accessing point.z. Will throw an Error.
try {
        var z = point.z;
}
catch(e) {
        print(e.message);
}

// try calling a ono-existent method named dustance
try {
        point.distance(10, 20);
}
catch(e) {
        print(e.message);
}
```

```
No such property: z
No matching method found: distance(10, 20)
```

Serializing Objects

Nashorn supports serializing and desterilizing of object using a built-in object called JSON. JSON is also an acronym that stands for **J**ava**S**cript **O**bject **N**otation that specifies how a JavaScript object is converted to a string and vice versa. JSON is a Data Interchange Format described in RFC 4627 at http://www.ietf.org/rfc/rfc4627.txt. The JSON object contains two methods:

- JSON.stringify(value, replacer, indentation)
- JSON.parse(text, reviver)

The JSON.stringify() method converts a Nashorn value into a string. The JSON.parse() method converts a string in JSON format into a Nashorn value.

The value parameter in the stringify() method can be an object or a primitive value. Not all types of values can be stringified. For example, undefined cannot be stringified. NaN and Infinity are stringified as null.

The replacer argument is a function or an array. If replacer is a function, it is takes two parameter. The first parameter is the name of the property being stringified and the second one is the value of the property. The returned value of the function is used as the final value to be stringified. If the function returns undefined or no value, the property is not stringified. The first time replacer is called with the empty string as the property name and the object being stringified as the value. Subsequent calls pass the property name and the property value of the property being stringified. If replacer is an array, it contains the names of the properties to be stringified. Any properties not appearing in the array will not be stringified.

The indentation is a number or a string used for indentation in the output. If it is a number, it is the number of spaces to be used for indentation. Its value is capped at 10. If it is a string such as "\t", it is used for indentation at each level. The replacer and indentation parameters are optional in the stringify() method.

The reviver is a function that is called when the JSON text is being parsed into an object. It takes two parameters. The first parameter is the name of the property being parsed and the second one is the value of the property. If the function returns null or undefined, the corresponding property is deleted.

Listing 4-19 demonstrates the use of the JSON object. It stringifies an object. During stringification, it multiplies the values of the properties by 2. During parsing, it applies the reverse logic to restore the object.

Listing 4-19. Using the JSON Object to Stringify and Parse Objects

```
// json.js
var point = {x: 10, y: 20};

function replacer (key, value) {
        if (key === "x" || key === "y") {
                // Multiply the value by 2
                return value * 2;
        }
}
```

```
        else {
                // Simply return the value
                return value;
        }
}

function reviver (key, value) {
        if (key === "x" || key === "y") {
                // Divide the value by 2
                return value / 2;
        }
        else {
                return value;
        }
}

var pointString = JSON.stringify(point, replacer, "  ");
print("Stringified object is");
print(pointString);

var obj = JSON.parse(pointString, reviver);

print("Parsed object proeprties are");
for(var prop in obj) {
        print("obj[" + prop + "] =  " + obj[prop]);
}
```

```
Stringified object is
{
  "x": 20,
  "y": 40
}
Parsed object proeprties are
obj[x] =  10
obj[y] =  20
```

Dynamically Evaluating Scripts

Nashorn contains a global function called eval(string). It takes a string containing
Nashorn code as an argument, executes the code, and returns the last evaluated value in
the code. The following snippet of code shows a trivial example of adding two numbers
using the eval() function:

```
// Assigns 300 to sum
var sum = eval("100 + 200");
```

You will not use the eval() function for such a trivial computation. Nashorn can execute an arithmetic expression like 100 + 200 without using the eval() function. You will use it when you get Nashorn code as a string at runtime.

The eval() function is executed in the context of the caller. If it is called from the global context, it executes in the global context. If it is called from a function, it executes in the context of the function.

Listing 4-20 demonstrates the context of the eval() function execution. The first time, it is called in the global context, so it defined a new variable z and sets it to 300 in the global context. It reads the value of x from the global context, multiplies it with 2, and returns 200 that is set to y. The second time, it is called from the function and it works on local variables x, y, and x of the function.

Listing 4-20. The Contents of the EvalTest.js File

```javascript
// EvalTest.js

var x = 100;
var y = eval("var z = 300; x * 2;"); // Called from the global context
print(x, y, z);

function testEval() {
        var x = 300;

        // Called from the function context
        var y = eval("var z = 900; x * 2;");
        print(x, y, z);
}

testEval();
```

```
100 200 300
300 600 900
```

Variable Scoping and Hoisting

Java supports block-level scoping. A variable declared in a block is local to that block and it is not accessible before and after the block. Nashorn (and all JavaScript implementations) support two scopes:

- Global Scope

- Function Scope

Variable and function declarations in the global code are available everywhere in the global scope. Similarly, variable and function declarations in a function are available everywhere inside the function.

Consider the code and its output in Listing 4-21. The output will surprise you if you have not worked with JavaScript before.

Listing 4-21. Declaration Hoisting in Nashorn

```
// beforehoisting.js

// Try accessing empId variable before declaring it
print("1. empId = " + empId);

// Declare and initialize empId now
var empId = 100;

function test() {
        if (empId === undefined) {
                var empId = 200;
        }
        print("2. empId = " + empId);
}

// Call the test function
test();

print("3. empId = " + empId);
```

```
1. empId = undefined
2. empId = 200
3. empId = 100
```

The first output shows that you can access a variable before declaring it. The variable value is undefined. Inside the test() function, you would expect that expression empId === undefined will read the value of empId from the global scope and it will evaluate to false. However, the output shows otherwise. The second output shows that the if condition inside the test() function evaluated to true and the empId local variable was set to 200. The third output shows that the function call did not affect the global variable empId and its value remained 100.

You can understand this variable's scoping behavior in two ways:

- As a *two-phase process*: First, all declarations are processed. Second, the code is executed. Because all declarations are processed before executing the code, all variable and function declarations are available when the code is executed, irrespective of the place where they were declared. Of course, you need to take into account the global and function scopes of those declarations.

- As *declaration hoisting*: This simply means that all variable and function declarations are moved to the top in their respective scope. This is the same as saying that you have declared all variables and functions at the top in the global and function scopes.

Listing 4-22 shows the same code as in Listing 4-21 but after the declarations are hoisted. This time, you will not have any problem in understanding the output.

Listing 4-22. Reorganized Code after Declaration Hoisting

```
// afterhoisting.js

var empId; // Hoisted

function test() {
        var empId; // Hoisted
        if (empId === undefined) {
                empId = 200; // Left after hoisting
        }
        print("2. empId = " + empId);
}

// Try accessing empId variable before declaring it
print("1. empId = " + empId);

// Declare and initialize empId now
empId = 100; // Left after hoisting

// Call the test function
test();

print("3. empId = " + empId);
```

```
1. empId = undefined
2. empId = 200
3. empId = 100
```

Notice that hoisting occurs for function declarations, not for function expressions, which enables you to call functions before they are declared. One more thing to remember: only variable declarations are hoisted, not the assignment part in the variable declarations, as shown in Listing 4-22.

Using Strict Mode

You can use the strict mode in Nashorn script by using the "use strict" directive. It is used in the beginning of the global code or the beginning of the function code. If it is used in the beginning of the global code, all code is considered executing in string mode. If it occurs in the beginning of the function code, only that function code executes in the strict mode. You can also use the "use strict" directive in the script executed by the eval() function.

The following snippet of code uses the "use strict" directive for the global scope:

```
"use strict";

// An error. Using a variable without declaring it with var
x = 10;

// other code goes here
```

The following code will throw an error when the test() function is called because the function uses the "use strict" directive and it uses a variable named y without declaring it with the keyword var:

```
x = 10; // OK. The global code is not in strict mode

function test() {
        "use strict";
        y = 100; // Will cause an error when executed
}

test();
```

Built-in Global Objects

Nashorn defines many built-in objects. I will discuss some of them in the subsequent sections.

The Object Object

Nashorn provides a built-in object called Object. You can think of it similar to the java.lang.Object class in Java. Object in Nashorn serves as the base object for other objects. It has several useful properties that are used to work with all types of objects. I have already discussed many of them in previous sections.

Object is a function that can also be used as a constructor. It accepts an optional parameter. If you call the Object function, it has the same effect of calling the Object constructor with the new operator. If you pass an object to the function, it returns the reference of the same object. If you pass a primitive value, it returns a wrapper object that wraps the primitive value. You can get the primitive value using the valueOf() method on the returned object. Calling the function without an argument creates an empty object. The following code illustrates how to use Object:

```
var str = "Hello";

// Assigns a wrapper for str to p1 because str is a primitive type
var p1 = new Object(str);

print("p1.valueOf() is", p1.valueOf());
print("typeof p1 is", typeof p1);
print("p1.valueOf() === str is", p1.valueOf() === str);

var msg = new String("Hello");

// Assigns the reference of msg to p2. new Object(msg) returns
// the reference of msg because msg is an object.
var p2 = new Object(msg);

print("p2 === msg is", p2 === msg);
print("p2.valueOf() is", p2.valueOf());
print("typeof p2 is", typeof p2);
print("p2.valueOf() === msg is", p2.valueOf() === msg);
```

```
p1.valueOf() is Hello
typeof p1 is object
p1.valueOf() === str is true
p2 === msg is true
p2.valueOf() is Hello
typeof p2 is object
p2.valueOf() === msg is false
```

Table 4-11 contains the list of properties and methods of Object with their descriptions.

Table 4-11. *The List of Properties and Methods of Object with Their Descriptions*

Property/Method	Description
Object.prototype	It is the prototype object for Object. Its writable, enumerable, and configurable properties are set to false
Object.prototype.constructor	Contains reference to the constructor function that creates the object
Object.create(p, descriptor)	Creates a new object setting the specified p as the prototype and adding all properties in the descriptor to the new object. The descriptor parameter is optional
Object.defineProperties(obj, descriptors)	Creates or updates properties of the specified object
Object.defineProperty(obj, prop, descriptor)	Creates or updates the specified property with of the specified object
Object.freeze(obj)	Freezes the specified object by making it nonextensible, nonconfigurable, and making all its properties read-only
Object.getOwnPropertyDescriptor(obj, prop)	Returns a property descriptor for the specified property of the specified object
Object.getOwnPropertyNames(obj)	Returns an array containing names of all own properties of the specified object. The array also includes the nonenumerable properties
Object.getPrototypeOf(obj)	Returns the prototype of the specified object
Object.isExtensible(obj)	Returns true of the specified object is extensible, false otherwise
Object.isFrozen(obj)	Returns true of the specified object is frozen, false otherwise
Object.isSealed(obj)	Returns true of the specified object is sealed, false otherwise
Object.keys(obj)	Returns an array containing the names of all enumerable, noninherited properties of the specified object
Object.preventExtensions(object)	Makes the specified object nonextensible so that no new properties can be added to the object

(continued)

Table 4-11. (*continued*)

Property/Method	Description
Object.prototype.hasOwnProperty(prop)	Returns true if the object has the specified property as its own property; returns false otherwise
Object.prototype.isPrototypeOf(obj)	Returned true if the specified object is the prototype of the object on which the isPrototypeOf() method is called
Object.prototype.propertyIsEnumerable(prop)	Returns true if the specified property is enumerable; returns false otherwise
Object.prototype.toLocaleString()	Returned a localized string representation of the object. It is intended to be overridden by objects. By default, it returns a string returned by the toString() method
Object.prototype.toString()	Returns a string representation of the object. It is intended to be overridden by objects. By default, it returns a string [object class] where class is the class name of the object such as String, Date, Object, and so on
Object.prototype.valueOf()	If the object wraps a primitive value, it returns that primitive value. Otherwise, it returns the object itself
Object.seal(obj)	Seals the specified object
Object.setPrototypeOf(obj, proto)	Sets the specified proto as the prototype of the specified obj

The Function Object

The Function object is a function that can be called as a function or a constructor. Calling it as a function works the same way as calling it as a constructor. It creates a new function object from a string. It takes variable number of arguments and it has the following signature:

```
Function(p1, p2, p3,..., body);
```

Here, p1, p2, p3, and so on are the names of the formal parameters of the new function and body is the body of the function. The last argument is always the body of the function. If it is called without any arguments, it creates an empty function with no formal parameters and an empty body. The following snippet of code creates a function that takes two parameters and returns the result of applying the + operator on both arguments. Calling adder(10, 20) will return 30:

```
var adder = new Function("p1", "p2", "return p1 + p2");
```

Function.prototype is an object that itself is a Function object. Function. prototype is set as the prototype object for all functions you create. So, all properties available in Function.prototype are available in all functions. The following properties are defined in Function.prototype:

- Function.prototype.constructor
- Function.prototype.toString()
- Function.prototype.apply(thisArg, argArray)
- Function.prototype.call(thisArg, arg1, arg2,...)
- Function.prototype.bind(thisArg, arg1, arg2,...)

The Function.prototype.constructor property is set to the built-in Function constructor.

The Function.prototype.toString() method returns an implementation-dependent representation of the function object. The following code shows how to use this method and the values it returns for different types of object. Note that for the user-defined functions, it returns the function declaration as a string and for built-in function the body of the function is returned as [native code]:

```
function adder(n1, n2) {
        return n1 + n2;
}

// Call the toString() method of the user-defined adder function
var adderStr = adder.toString();

// Call the toString() method of the built-in print function
var printStr = print.toString;

print("adderStr: \n" + adderStr);
print("printstr:\n" + printStr);
```

```
adderStr:
function adder(n1, n2) {
    return n1 + n2;
}
printstr:
function toString() { [native code] }
```

The apply() and call() methods are used for the same purpose. Both are used to call a method for an object. They differ only in argument types. The first argument to both methods are an object in whose context the method is called. The apply() method lets you specify the arguments to the method in an array whereas the call() method lets you specify each argument separately. These methods let you call a method of an object on any other objects. You can use these methods to call the overridden methods of an object.

The following code shows how to call the toString() method of the Object. prototype on a String object:

```
// Create a String object
var str = new String("Hello");

// Call the toString() method of the String object
var stringToString = str.toString();

// Call the toString() method of the Object.prototype object on str
var objectToString = Object.prototype.toString.call(str);

print("String.toString(): " + stringToString);
print("Object.prototype.toString(): " + objectToString);
```

```
String.toString(): Hello
Object.prototype.toString(): [object String]
```

The bind() method binds a function to an object and returns a new function object. When the new function is called, it executes in the context of the bound object. It takes variable-length arguments. The first argument is the object that you want to bind with the function. The rest of the arguments are the arguments you want to bind with the function. If you bind any arguments to the function, those arguments will be used when you call the bound function.

Suppose that you want to create a function for the Point objects that will compute the distance of a Point from the origin. You can create a Point to represent the origin and bind the Point.prototype.distance function to this object to get a new function. Listing 4-23 demonstrates this technique.

Listing 4-23. Binding a Function to an Object

```
// functionbind.js

load("Point.js");

// Create a 2D origin
var origin = new Point(0, 0);

// Create a new method called distanceFromOrigin() by binding
// the distance() method of the Point to the origin object
var distanceFromOrigin = Point.prototype.distance.bind(origin);
```

```
var dist = distanceFromOrigin(new Point(0, 10));
print(dist);

// The above distanceFromOrigin() is the same as follows
var dist2 = origin.distance(new Point(0, 10));
print(dist2);
```

```
10
10
```

An important point about the Function() constructor is that the functions it creates do not use lexical scoping; instead, they are always compiled as if they were top-level functions. Listing 4-24 demonstrates this subtle point.

Listing 4-24. Testing the Captured Scoping of Functions Created by the Function Object

```
// functioncapture.js

var empId = 100; // Global

function createFunction1() {
        var empId = 200;   // Local

        // Does not capture local empId
        var test = new Function("print(empId)");
        return test;
}

function createFunction2() {
        var empId = 200; // Local

        function test () {
                print(empId); // Captures local empId
        }

        return test;
}

createFunction1()(); // Prints 100 (the global empId)
createFunction2()(); // Prints 200 (the local empId)
```

```
100
200
```

When the `createFunction1()` creates a new function using the `Function` object, the new function doesn't capture the local `empId`, rather it captures the global `empId`. However, when a nested function is declared inside the `createFunction2()` function, the new function captures the local `empId`. The output verifies this rule.

The String Object

The String object is a function. It can be used simply as a function or a constructor. When it is used as a function, it converts the argument to a primitive type string value. The following is an example of using `String` as a function:

```
var str1 = String(100); // Returns "100"
var str2 = String();    // Returns ""
```

When `String` is used as a constructor, it creates a new `String` object with its contents as the passed argument:

```
// Create a String object
var str = new String("Hello");
```

Each character in the String object is assigned an index. The first character is assigned an index of 0, the second 1, and so on. Every String object has a read-only property named `length` that contains the number of characters in the string.

`String.prototype` contains many useful methods to manipulate String objects and get its contents in different ways. Table 4-12 lists those methods. Notice that you can use all String object methods on a primitive string value; the primitive string will be automatically converted to a String object before applying the method.

Table 4-12. *The List of Methods of in String.prototype with Their Descriptions*

Method	Description
`charAt(index)`	Returns the character at the specified `index` as a primitive string value
`charCodeAt(index)`	Returns the Unicode value of the character at the specified `index`
`concat(arg1, arg2, ...)`	Returns a primitive string concatenating the contents of the object and the specified arguments
`indexOf(substring, start)`	Returns the index of the first occurrence of the substring in the object. The search starts at `start`. If `start` is not passed, the search starts at index 0
`lastIndexOf(substring, start)`	It works the same way as the `indexOf()` method, except that it searches for the `substring` from the end of the string

(continued)

Table 4-12. *(continued)*

Method	Description
localeCompare(target)	Returns a number. If the string is less than target, it returns a negative number; if string is greater than target, it returns a positive number; otherwise, it returns zero
match(regexp)	Searches the string for the specified regular expression regexp and returns the results in an array
replace(regexp, replacement)	Searches the string using the regular expression regexp, replaces the matched substrings with the replacement, and returns the result as a primitive string value
search(regexp)	Searches the string for the specified regular expression and returns the index of the first occurrence. Returns -1 if no match is found
slice(start, end)	Returns a substring contains characters from start and end indexes in the string where start is inclusive and end is exclusive. If end is not specified, it returns all characters from start. If end is negative, the index is counted from the end. "Hello".slice(1, 2) returns "e" and "Hello".slice(1, -2) returns "el"
split(delimiter, limit)	Returns an array by splitting the string around the specified delimiter. The limit is optional and it specifies the maximum number of elements returned in the array
substring(start, end)	Returns a substring of the string starting at the start and up to, but not including, the end. If either argument is NaN or negative, it is replaced with zero. If they are larger than the length of the string, they are replaced with the length of the string. If start is greater than end, they are swapped. "Hello".slice(1, 2) returns "e" and "Hello".slice(1, -2) returns "H"
toLowerCase()	Returns the lowercase equivalent of the string by replacing uppercase characters with the corresponding lowercase characters
toLocaleLowerCase()	Works the same as the toLowerCase(), except that it uses locale specific uppercase to lowercase character mapping
toUpperCase()	Returns the uppercase equivalent of the string by replacing lowercase characters with the corresponding uppercase characters

(continued)

Table 4-12. (*continued*)

Method	Description
toLocaleUpperCase()	Works the same as the toUpperCase(), except that it uses locale specific lowercase to uppercase character mapping
toString()	Returns the contents of the String object as a primitive string value
trim()	Returns a primitive string value by removing the whitespaces from the string
valueOf()	Same as toString()

The Number Object

The Number object is a function. It can be called as a function or a constructor. When it is called as a function, it converts the supplied argument to a primitive number value. If it is called with no argument, it returns the primitive number zero. When it is called as a constructor, it returns a Number object that wraps the specified argument. You can think of the Number object as the wrapper objects Integer, Long, Float, Double, Short, and Byte types in Java. The valueOf() method of the Number object returns the primitive number value stored in the object. The following code shows how to use the Number object as a function and a constructor:

```
// Converts the string "24" to a number 24 and assigns 24 to n1
var n1 = Number("24");

// Asigns zero to n2
var n2 = Number();

// Create a Number object for the nuembr 100.43
var n3 = new Number(100.43);

printf("n1 = %d, n2 = %d, n3 = %f", n1, n2, n3.valueOf());
```

```
n1 = 24, n2 = 0, n3 = 100.430000
```

The Number object contains several useful properties to work with numbers. They are listed in Table 4-13. All listed methods are defined in Number.prototype object.

Table 4-13. *The List of Properties and Method of the Number Object with Their Descriptions*

Property/Method	Description
Number.MAX_VALUE	It is the largest positive, finite value of the Number type. It is approximately 1.7976931348623157e+308
Number.MIN_VALUE	It is the smallest positive, finite value of the Number type. It is approximately 4.9e-324
Number.NaN	It is same as the global variable NaN that represents non-a-number
Number.NEGATIVE_INFINITY	Represents a negative infinity. It is the same as the global variable -Infinity
Number.POSITIVE_INFINITY	Represents a positive infinity. It is the same as the global variable Infinity
toString(radix)	Converts the Number into the specified radix. If radix is not specified, 10 is used. The radix must be a number between 2 and 36, both inclusive
toLocaleString()	Formats the number into a local specific format and returns it as a primitive string value. Currently, it returns the same value as the toString() method
valueOf()	Returns the primitive value stored in the Number object
toFixed(digits)	Returns a string representation of the number that contains exactly the specified digits after the decimal point. The number is rounded if necessary. The number is zero-padded if the digits after the decimal is less than the specified digits. If the number is greater than 1e+21, it will return a string representing the number in exponential notation. If digits is not specified, zero is assumed. The digits can be between 0 and 20
toExponential(digits)	Returns a string representation of the number in exponential notation. Contains one digit before the decimal and digits number of digits after the decimal. The digits can be between 0 and 20
toPrecision(precision)	Returns a string representation of the number with precision significant digits. It may return the number in decimal or exponential notation. If precision is not specified, it converts the number to a string and returns the result

You can call all methods of the Number object on all primitive numbers. However, you have to be careful when calling methods on primitive number values. A number can have decimal as well. The parser gets confused in the following statement:

```
var x = 1969.toString(16); // A SyntaxError
```

The parser does not know if the decimal after 1969 is part of the number or the dot to call the toString() method. You have two ways to fix it:

- You need to use two decimals in the number. The last decimal will be considered as the dot to call the following method such as 1969..toString(16).

- Enclose the number inside a pair of parenthesis such as (1969). toString(16).

The following code shows how to use methods of the Number object with primitive numbers:

```
var n1 = 1969..toString(16);
print("1969..toString(16) is " + n1);

var n2 = (1969).toString(16);
print("(1969).toString(16) is " + n2);

var n3 = (1969.79).toFixed(1);
print("(1969.79).toFixed(1) is " + n3);
```

```
1969..toString(16) is 7b1
(1969).toString(16) is 7b1
(1969.79).toFixed(1) is 1969.8
```

The Boolean Object

The Boolean object is a function. It can be called as a function or a constructor. It takes an optional argument. If it is called as a function, it converts the specified argument to a Boolean primitive value (true or false). If the argument is not specified, the function returns false. As a constructor, it wraps the specified argument into a Boolean object. Notice that if the argument is not of the Boolean type, first the argument is converted to a Boolean primitive value. For example, an argument of 100 will be converted to a Boolean true and stored as true, not as 100. Its toString() method returns a string "true" or "false", depending on the value wrapped in the Boolean object. The valueOf() method returns the primitive Boolean value wrapped in the object. The Boolean object does not have any other interesting properties or methods. The following code shows how to use the Boolean object:

```
var b1 = Boolean(100);      // Assins true to b1
var b2 = Boolean(0);        // Assins false to b1
var b3 = Boolean();         // Assigns false to b3
var b4 = new Boolean(true); // Assign a Boolean object to b4

print("Boolean(100) returns " + b1);
print("Boolean(0) returns " + b2);
print("Boolean() returns " + b3);
print("b4.valueOf() returns " + b4.valueOf());
```

```
Boolean(100) returns true
Boolean(0) returns false
Boolean() returns false
b4.valueOf() returns true
```

The Date Object

The Date object is a function. It can be called as a function or constructor. Its signature is:

```
Date(year, month, date, hours, minutes, seconds, milliseconds)
```

All parameters in the Date object are optional. When it is called as a function, it returns the current date and time as a string. You can pass arguments to it when calling it as a function; however, all arguments are always ignored. When it is called as a constructor, arguments represent the date components and are used to initialize the Date object. The following code shows how to use the Date object as a function to get the current date and time. You may get a different output when you run the code:

```
// Call Date as a function
print(Date());
print(Date(2014, 10, 4, 19, 2)); // Arguments to Date are ignored
```

```
Sat Oct 04 2014 19:07:20 GMT-0500 (CDT)
Sat Oct 04 2014 19:07:20 GMT-0500 (CDT)
```

The Date object can be called as a constructor passing arguments in the following forms:

- `new Date()`

- `new Date(milliseconds)`

- `new Date(dateString)`

- `new Date(year, month, day, hours, minutes, seconds, milliseconds)`

If the number of arguments is less than two, one of the first three forms is used. If the number of arguments is two or more, the fourth form is used. If no argument is passed, it creates a Date object with the current date and time. If only one number argument is passed, it is considered the number of milliseconds passed since midnight January 1, 1970 UTC. If only one string argument is passed, the date and time in the string is parsed and used as the date and time value for the new Date object. If two or more arguments are passed, a Date object is constructed; remaining values are set to 1 for day and 0 for hours, minutes, seconds, and milliseconds. The Date object has a static method Date.now() that returns the number of milliseconds elapsed between the midnight January 1, 1970 UTC and the current time.

The following code shows how to create Date objects passing different number of arguments to the constructor:

```
// Current date and time
print("new Date() =", new Date());

// Pass 2000 milliisesonds
print("new Date(2000) =", new Date(2000));

// Pass 2000 milliisesonds and convert to UTC date time string
print("new Date(2000).toUTCString() =", new Date(2000).toUTCString());

// Pass a date as a string. Date is considered in UTC
print('new Date("2014-14-04") =', new Date("2014-14-04"));

// Pass year and month. day will default to 1
print("new Date(2014, 10) = ", new Date(2014, 10));

// Pass year, month. day, and hour. Other parts will default to 0
print("new Date(2014, 10, 4, 10) = ", new Date(2014, 10, 4, 10));

// Milliseconds elapsed from midnight Januray 1070 and now
print("Date.now() = ", Date.now());
```

```
new Date() = Sat Oct 04 2014 19:38:46 GMT-0500 (CDT)
new Date(2000) = Wed Dec 31 1969 18:00:02 GMT-0600 (CST)
new Date(2000).toUTCString() = Thu, 01 Jan 1970 00:00:02 GMT
new Date("2014-14-04") = Fri Oct 03 2014 19:00:00 GMT-0500 (CDT)
new Date(2014, 10) =  Sat Nov 01 2014 00:00:00 GMT-0500 (CDT)
new Date(2014, 10, 4, 10) =  Tue Nov 04 2014 10:00:00 GMT-0600 (CST)
Date.now() =  1412469527013
```

There are over forty methods in the Date objects. I will briefly explain them. These methods work the same way, although on different components of the date and time. It contains getYear(), getFullYear(), getDate(), getMonth(), getHours(), getMinutes(), getSeconds(), and getMilliseconds() method that returns the 2-digit year, full year, date, month, hours, minutes, seconds, and milliseconds components of the Date object, respectively. It contains a getDay() method that returns the day of the week (0 for Sunday and 6 for Saturday). There are corresponding setter methods such as setHours(), setDate(), and so on to set the date and time components. There are another set of getters and setters that work with UTC date and time; their names are based on the pattern getUTCXxx and setUTCXxx such as getUTCYear(), getUTCHours(), setUTCYears(), setUTCHours(), and so on. The getTime() and setTime() methods work with milliseconds elapsed since midnight January 1970. The Date object contains several methods named such as toXxxString() to convert the date in a specific string format. For example, the toDateString() returns a human-readable string format of the date portion whereas toTimeString() works the same way but on the time portion.

The Date.parse(str) static method parses the specified str considering it as a date and time in the YYYY-MM-DDTHH:mm:ss.sssZ format and returns the number of milliseconds elapsed since midnight January 1, 1970 UTC and the parsed date and time.

The Math Object

The Math object contains properties that are mathematical constants and functions. Table 4-14 lists the properties of the Math object with their descriptions. The properties of the Math object are self-explanatory; I will not discuss any examples of using them.

Table 4-14. *The List of Properties and Methods of the Math Object*

Property/Method	Description
Math.E	The Number value for e, the base of the natural logarithms, which is approximately 2.7182818284590452354
Math.LN10	The Number value for the natural logarithm of 10, which is approximately 2.302585092994046
Math.LN2	The Number value for the natural logarithm of 2, which is approximately 0.6931471805599453
Math.LOG2E	The Number value for the base-2 logarithm of e, which is approximately 1.4426950408889634
Math.LOG10E	The Number value for the base-10 logarithm of e which is approximately 0.4342944819032518
Math.PI	The Number value for π, the ratio of the circumference of a circle to its diameter, which is approximately 3.1415926535897932
Math.SQRT1_2	The Number value for the square root of 0.50 which is approximately 0.7071067811865476
Math.SQRT2	The Number value for the square root of 2, which is approximately 1.4142135623730951
Math.abs(x)	Returns the absolute value of x. For example, both Math.abs(2) and Math.abs(-2) return 2

(continued)

Table 4-14. (*continued*)

Property/Method	Description
Math.acos(x), Math.asin(x), Math.atan(x)	Returns arc cosine, arc sine, and arc tangent of x
Math.atan(y, x)	Returns the arc tangent of the quotient y/x of the arguments y and x, where the signs of y and x are used to determine the quadrant of the result
Math.ceil(x)	Returns the closest integer that is greater than or equal to x
Math.cos(x), Math.sin(x), Math.tan(x)	Returns cosine, sine, and tangent of x
Math.exp(x)	Returns e raised to the power of x, where e is Math.E
Math.floor(x)	Returns the closest integer that is less than or equal to x
Math.log(x)	Returns the natural logarithm of x. That is, computes the logarithm of x base-e
Math.max(v1, v2,...)	Returns the maximum of all arguments v1, v2, and so on, converting the arguments to Number type if necessary. If no arguments are passed, -Infinity is returned
Math.min(v1, v2,...)	Returns the minimum of all arguments v1, v2, and so on, converting the arguments to Number type if necessary. If no arguments are passed, Infinity is returned
Math.pow(x, y)	Returns the result of raising x to the power y
Math.random()	Returns a random number between 0 (inclusive) and 1 (exclusive)
Math.round(x)	Returns an integer closed to x. If two integers are equally close, returns the integer that is closer to +Infinity. For example, Math.round(2.3) returns 2, Math.round(2.9) returns 3, and Math.round(2.5) returns 3
Math.sqrt(x)	Returns the square root of x

The RegExp Object

A regular expression represents a pattern in input text. The RegExp object is a function. It represents a regular expression and contains several methods and properties to match the pattern in input text. RegExp can be used as a function or a constructor. Its signature is:

```
RegExp(pattern, flags)
```

Here, `pattern` is the pattern to be matched in the input text. It can be another RegExp object or a string representing the pattern. `flags` is a string that defines the text-matching rules. It may be an empty string, `undefined`, or a string containing one or all of the characters: g, i, and m. It is a `SyntaxError` to repeat the flags in a RegExp object. Table 4-15 contains the list of flags and their descriptions.

Table 4-15. *The List of Flags Used in Regular Expressions*

Flag	Description
g	Performs a global match. The default is to stop the match after the first match
i	Performs a case-insensitive match. The default is to perform a case-sensitive match
m	Enables multiline mode. The default is single-line mode. In single-line mode, the ^ and $ characters in the pattern match the beginning and end of the input text, respectively. In multiline mode, they match the beginning and end of the input text as well as the beginning and end of lines

The RegExp object can be used as a function or a constructor with the following rules:

- If `pattern` is a `RegExp` object and `flags` is `undefined`, `pattern` is returned

- If `pattern` is a `RegExp` object and `flags` is not `undefined`, a `SyntaxError` is generated

- Otherwise, a `RegExp` object is returned that represents a pattern specified by `pattern` and `flags`

The following are examples of creating `RegExp` objects:

```
// Creates a RegExp object with a pattern to match the word
// "Java" in the input text. The g flag will perform the match
// globally and the m flag will use multiline mode.
var pattern1 = new RegExp("Java", "gm");

// Assigns pattern1 to pattern2. The constructor returns
// pattern1 because its first argument, pattern1, is a RegExp object.
var pattern2 = new RegExp(pattern1);

// Prints true
print(pattern1 === pattern2);
```

You can also create regular expressions using regular expression literals. The syntax to use a regular expression literal is:

```
/pattern/flags
```

The following are examples of creating regular expressions using the regular expression literals:

```
var pattern1 = /Java/gm;  // The same as new RegExp("Java", "gm")
var pattern2 = /Nashorn/; // The same as new RegExp("Nashorn")
```

A regular expression literal is converted to a RegExp object every time is it evaluated. According to this rule, if two regular expression literals with the same contents appear in the same program, they will evaluate to two different RegExp objects, as shown:

```
// pattern1 and pattern2 have the same contents, but they evaluate to
// different RegExp objects
var pattern1 = /Java/gm;
var pattern2 = /Java/gm;

// Prints false in both cases
print(pattern1 === pattern2);
print(/Nashoern/ === /Nashorn/);
```

The RegExp.prototype object contains three methods as listed in Table 4-16. The test() method is a specialized case of the exec() method. The toString() method returns the string form of the regular expression. You only need to learn the exec() method in detail.

Table 4-16. *The List of Methods in the RegExp.prototype Object*

Method	Description
exec(string)	Performs a match on string against the regular expression. Returns an Array object containing the results of the match or null if there was no match
test(string)	Calls the exec(string) method. Returns true if the exec() method returns not null, false otherwise. Use this method instead of the exec() method if you care about only to know whether there is a match
toString()	Returns a string of the form /pattern/gim, where gim is the flags that were specified when the RegExp object was created

Regular expressions are very powerful features of any programming language. Java supports regular expressions. If you are familiar with regular expression in Java or Perl, the following discussion will be easy to follow. The pattern in a regular expression may be very complex. Typically, the letters and digits in the pattern match the input text literally. For example, the regular expression /Java/ will try to match the word Java at any position in the input text. The following code uses the test() method to check if a regular expression matches the input text:

```
var pattern = new RegExp("Java"); // Same as var pattern = /Java/;
var match = pattern.test("JavaScript");
print(pattern + " matches \"JavaScript\": " + match);

// Perfoms a case-sensitive match that is the default
var match2 = /java/.test("JavaScript");
print("/java/ matches \"JavaScript\": " + match2);

// Performs a case-insensitive match using the i flag
var match3 = /java/i.test("JavaScript");
print("/java/i matches \"JavaScript\": " + match3);
```

```
/Java/ matches "JavaScript": true
/java/ matches "JavaScript": false
/java/i matches "JavaScript": true
```

The RegExp object has four properties, as listed in Table 4-17. The source, global, ignoreCase, and multiline properties are read-only, nonenumerable, and nonconfigurable, and they are set at the time you create the regular expression. The lastIndex property is writable, nonenumerable, and nonconfigurable.

Table 4-17. *The List of Methods in the RegExp.prototype Object*

Property	Description
source	A string that is the pattern part of the RegExp object. If you create a regular expression using new RegExp("Java", "gm"), the source property of the object is set to "Java"
global	It is a Boolean value that is set to true if the flag g is used, false otherwise
ignoreCase	It is a Boolean value that is set to true if the flag i is used, false otherwise
multiline	It is a Boolean value that is set to true if the flag m is used, false otherwise
lastIndex	It is an integer value that specifies the position in the input text where the next match will start. It is set to zero when the RegExp object is created. It may change automatically when you perform a match or you can change it in code

The exec() method searches the input text against the pattern and returns null or an Array object. When a match is not found, it returns null. When a match is found, the returned Array object has the following pieces of information:

- The first element of the array is the matched text of the input text. Subsequent elements in the array, if any, are the matched text by the capturing parentheses in the pattern. (I will discuss capturing parentheses later in this chapter.)

- The array has an index property that is set to position where the match started.

- The array has an input property that is set to the input text.

- If the search is global (using the flag g), the lastIndex property of the RegExp object is set to position in the input text immediately following the matched text. If, for a global search, a match is not found, the lastIndex property of the RegExp object is set to zero. For a nonglobal match, the lastIndex property is untouched.

Notice that the exec() method starts the search from the position defined by the lastIndex property of the RegExp object. If you are performing a global search, you can use a loop to find all matches in the input text. Listing 4-25 demonstrates how to use the exec() method.

Listing 4-25. Using the exec() Method of the RegExp Object for a Global Match

```
// regexexec.js

var pattern = /Java/g;
var text = "Java and JavaScript are not the same";

var result;
while((result = pattern.exec(text)) !== null) {
        var msg = "Matched '" + result[0] + "'" + " at " + result.index +
                    ". Next match will begin at " + pattern.lastIndex;
        print(msg);
}

print("After the search finishes, lastIndex = " + pattern.lastIndex);
```

```
Matched 'Java' at 0. Next match will begin at 4
Matched 'Java' at 9. Next match will begin at 13
After the search finishes, lastIndex = 0
```

Be careful not to use the exec() method in a loop when the search is not global, because for the nonglobal match, it does not change the lastIndex property that will make the loop an infinite loop. You should call the method only once for the nonglobal match. The following code will run forever:

```
var pattern = /Java/; // A non-global pattern
var text = "Java and JavaScript are not the same";

var result;

/* Do not use this loop. It will run forever because
   pattern is non-global.
*/
while((result = pattern.exec(text)) !== null) {
        // Code goes here
}
```

Some characters when used in certain contexts have special meaning. These characters are known as metacharacters and they are (,), [,], {, }, \, ^, $, |, ?, *, +, and the dot. I will discuss the special meanings of these characters at appropriate places in this section.

In a regular expression, a set of characters enclosed within a pair of brackets is known as a character class. The regular expression will match any of the characters in the set. For example, /[abc]/ will match a, b, or c in the input text. You can also specify a range of characters using a character class. The range is expressed using a hyphen. For example, [a-z] represents any lowercase English letters; [0-9] represents any digit between 0 and 9. If you use the character ^ in the beginning of a character class, it means complement (meaning not). For example, [^abc] means any character except a, b, and c. The character class [^a-z] represents any character except lowercase English letters. If you use the character ^ anywhere in a character class, except in the beginning, it loses the special meaning and it matches just a ^ character. For example, [abc^] will match a, b, c, or ^. Character classes also support multiple ranges and operations such as union, intersection, subtraction on those ranges. Table 4-18 shows a few examples of using ranges in character classes. Nashorn has some predefined character classes as listed in Table 4-19.

Table 4-18. *A Few Examples of Character Classes*

Character Classes	Meaning	Category
[abc]	Character a, b, or c	Simple character class
[^xyz]	A character except x, y, and z	Complement or negation
[a-p]	Characters a through p	Range
[a-cx-z]	Characters a through c, or x through z, which would include a, b, c, x, y, or z.	Union
[0-9&&[4-8]]	Intersection of two ranges (4, 5, 6, 7, or 8)	Intersection
[a-z&&[^aeiou]]	All lowercase letters minus vowels. In other words, a lowercase letter that is not a vowel. That is, all lowercase consonants.	Subtraction

Table 4-19. *The List of the Predefined Character Classes*

Predefined Character Classes	Meaning
. (a dot)	Any character (may or may not match line terminators)
\d	A digit. Same as [0-9]
\D	A non-digit. Same as [^0-9]
\s	A whitespace character. Same as [\t\n\x0B\f\r]. The list includes a space, a tab, a new line, a vertical tab, a form feed, and a carriage return characters
\S	A non-whitespace character. Same as [^\s]
\w	A word character. Same as [a-zA-Z_0-9]. The list includes lowercase letters, uppercase letter, underscore, and decimal digits
\W	A nonword character. Same as [^\w]

You can also specify the number of times a character in a regular expression may match the sequence of characters. If you want to match all two digit integers, the regular expression would be /\d\d/, which is the same as /[0-9][0-9]/. What would be the regular expression to match an integer? You cannot write the regular expression to match an integer with the knowledge you have gained so far. You need to be able to express a pattern "one digit or more" using a regular expression. Quantifiers and their meanings have been listed in Table 4-20.

Table 4-20. *Quantifiers and Their Meanings*

Quantifiers	Meaning
*	Zero or more times
+	One or more times
?	Once or not at all
{m}	Exactly m times
{m, }	At least m times
{m, n}	At least m, but not more than n times

It is important to notice that quantifiers must follow a character or character class for which it specifies the quantity. The regular expression to match any integer would be /\d+/, which specifies: "match one or more number of digits". Is this solution for matching integer correct? No, it is not. Suppose that the text is "This is text123 which contains 10 and 120". If we match the pattern /\d+/ against the text, it will match against 123, 10, and 120. The following code demonstrates this:

```
var pattern = /\d+/g;
var text = "This is text123 which contains 10 and 120";

var result;
while((result = pattern.exec(text)) !== null) {
        print("Matched '" + result[0] + "' at " + result.index +
                ". Next match will begin at " + pattern.lastIndex);
}
```

```
Matched '123' at 12. Next match will begin at 15
Matched '10' at 31. Next match will begin at 33
Matched '120' at 38. Next match will begin at 41
```

Notice that 123 is not used as an integer rather it is part of the word text123. If you are looking for integers inside the text, certainly 123 in text123 does not qualify to be an integer. You want to match all integers, which form a word in the text. You need to specify that the match should be performed only on word boundaries, not inside text having embedded integers. This is necessary to exclude integer 123 from the result. Table 4-21 lists metacharacters that match boundaries in a regular expression.

Table 4-21. *List of Boundary Matchers Inside Regular Expressions*

Boundary Matchers	Meaning
^	The beginning of a line
$	The end of a line
\b	A word boundary
\B	A nonword boundary
\A	The beginning of the input
\G	The end of previous match
\Z	The end of the input but for the final terminator, if any
\z	The end of the input

With the knowledge of boundary matchers, you can rewrite the previous example to match only integers in the input text:

```
var pattern = /\b\d+\b/g;
var text = "This is text123 which contains 10 and 120";

var result;
while((result = pattern.exec(text)) !== null) {
        print("Matched '" + result[0] + "' at " + result.index +
            ". Next match will begin at " + pattern.lastIndex);
}
```

```
Matched '10' at 31. Next match will begin at 33
Matched '120' at 38. Next match will begin at 41
```

The String object has a replace(regExp, replacement) method that you can use to perform find-and-replace operation in text. The following code finds all occurrences of the word apple in text and replaces it with the word orange:

```
var pattern = /\bapple\b/g;
var text = "I have an apple and five pineapples.";
var replacement = "orange";
var newText = text.replace(pattern, replacement);
print("Regular Expression: " + pattern + ", Input Text: " + text);
print("Replacement Text: " + replacement + ", New Text: " + newText);
```

```
Regular Expression: /\bapple\b/g, Input Text: I have an apple and five
pineapples.
Replacement Text: orange, New Text: I have an orange and five pineapples.
```

You can treat multiple characters as a unit by using them as a group. A group is created inside a regular expression by enclosing one or more characters inside parentheses. (ab), ab(z), ab(ab)(xyz), and (the((is)(are))) are examples of groups. Each group in a regular expression has a group number. The group number starts at 1. A left parenthesis starts a new group. You can back-reference group numbers in a regular expression. Suppose that you want to match text, which starts with ab followed by xy, which is followed by ab. You can write the regular expression as /abxyab/. You can also achieve the same result by forming a group that contains ab and back-reference it as /(ab)xy\1/, where \1 refers to group 1, which is (ab) in this case. Notice that the returned Array object from the exec() method of the RegExp object contains the matched text in the first element and all matched groups in subsequent elements. If you want to have a group but do not want to capture its result or back reference it, you can add the character sequence ?: to the beginning of the group; for example, (?:ab)xy contains a group with the pattern ab, but you cannot reference it as \1 and its matched text will not be populated in the Array object returned by the exec() method. A group starting with ?: is called a noncapturing group and a group not starting with ?: is called capturing group. You can also reference the captured text in the replacement text in the replace() method of the String object as $1, $2, $3, and so on, where 1, 2, 3 are the group numbers. Table 4-22 lists all character combinations that can be used in the replacement text to refer back to the matched text.

Table 4-22. *List of Boundary Matchers Inside Regular Expressions*

Characters	Replacement Text
$$	$
$&	The matched substring
$`	The portion of string that precedes the matched substring. It is a $ followed by a back quote
$'	The portion of string that follows the matched substring. It is a $ followed by a single quote
$n	Refers to the matched text for group n, where n an integer in the range 1 to 99. If group n is undefined, uses the empty String. If n is greater that the number of groups, the result is $n

Using groups and back referencing in the replacement text, you can format 10-digit phone numbers nnnnnnnnnn as (nnn) nnn-nnnn, as shown Listing 4-26.

Listing 4-26. Formatting 10-Digit Phone Numbers

```
// tendigitsphonesformatter.js

var pattern = /\b(\d{3})(\d{3})(\d{4})\b/g;
var text = "3342449999, 2229822, and 6152534734";
var replacement = "($1) $2-$3";
var formattedPhones = text.replace(pattern, replacement);
print("Phones: " + text);
print("Formatted Phones: " + formattedPhones);
```

```
Phones: 3342449999, 2229822, and 6152534734
Formatted Phones: (334) 244-9999, 2229822, and (615) 253-4734
```

In the example, the 7-digit phone number was left unformatted. Suppose that you want to format a 7-digit phone as nnn-nnnn. You can achieve this using a replacement function as the second argument to the replace() method of the String object. The replacement function is called with the following arguments for each match:

- The number of arguments is the number of groups in the regular expression plus 3

- The first argument is the matched text

- The second and subsequent arguments are the matched text for the groups, if any, starting at group 1

- The matched text for the last group is followed by the position in the input text where the match was found

- The last argument is the input text itself

The returned value from the replacement function replaces the matched text in the result returned by the replace() method. Listing 4-27 shows how to use a replacement function to format 7-digit and 10-digit phone numbers. Notice that the first group of three digits is optional in the pattern. If a group does not match in the matched text, back-referencing the group returns undefined. This logic is used in the phoneFormatter() function. If the argument named group1 is undefined, it means that a 7-digit phone number was matched; otherwise, a 10-digit phone number was matched.

Listing 4-27. Formatting 7-Digit and 10-Digit Phone Numbers Using a Replacement Function

```
// phoneformatter.js

// Formats 10-digit and 7-digit phone numbers
function phoneFormatter(macthedText, group1, group2, group3, startIndex,
inputText) {
        if (group1 === undefined) {
                // Matched a 7-digit phone number
                return group2 + "-" + group3;
        }
        else {
                // Matched a 10-digit phone number
                return "(" + group1 + ") " + group2 + "-" + group3;
        }
}

// Make the first group of 3-digits optional using the ? metacharacter
var pattern = /\b(\d{3})?(\d{3})(\d{4})\b/g;

var text = "3342449999, 2229822, and 6152534734";
```

```
// Use the phoneFormatter() function as the replacement in the replace()
// method
var formattedPhones = text.replace(pattern, phoneFormatter);
print("Phones: " + text);
print("Formatted Phones: " + formattedPhones);
```

```
Phones: 3342449999, 2229822, and 6152534734
Formatted Phones: (334) 244-9999, 222-9822, and (615) 253-4734
```

Knowing Script Location

Nashorn provides three global objects:

- __FILE__
- __DIR__
- __LINE__

Notice the two underscores before and after the names of these properties. They contain the script file name, script file's directory name, and the line number of the script that reads the __LINE__ property. The properties __FILE__, and __DIR__ may be reported as null if they are not available such as when reading scripts from standard input. Sometimes, you will get a file name that is not the real file name of your script. You may run your script in a file from a Java program using a Reader, and in that case, the file name will be reported as <eval>. Listing 4-28 contains code that prints these properties. The code is stored in a file named scriptdetails.js.

Listing 4-28. The Contents of the scriptdetails.js File

```
// scriptdetails.js

// Print the location details of the following statement
print("File Name =", __FILE__, ", Directory =",__DIR__, ", Line # =" ,__LINE__);
```

The following command runs the scriptdetails.js file on the command-line using the jjs command that prints the script details:

```
c:\>jjs c:\kishori\scriptdetails.js
File Name = c:\kishori\scriptdetails.js, Directory = c:\kishori\, Line # = 4
```

> ■ **Tip** Typically, the __FILE__, __DIR__, and __LINE__ global properties are used for debugging purposes. You can also use __DIR__ property to load scripts from locations relative to the currently running script file.

Built-in Global Functions

Nashorn defines built-in global functions. I have discussed one of such functions, named eval() that is used to evaluate a script stored in a string. In this section, I will discuss some more built-in global functions.

The parseInt( ) Function

The parseInt() function is used parse an integer from a string. It has the following signature:

```
parseInt(string, radix)
```

The function returns an integer by parsing the specified string. If radix is specified, it is considered the base of the integer in string. The leading spaces in string are ignored. If radix is not specified, undefined, or 0, radix is assumed to be 10, except when string starts with 0x or 0X (ignoring the leading spaces) in which case radix is assumed to be 16. If radix is less than 2 or greater than 36, the function returns NaN.

The parseInt() function parses only the leading portion of string that can be a valid digit in an integer represented in the specified radix. When it encounters an invalid character, it stops parsing and returns the so far parsed integer value. It returns NaN, if no leading characters can be parsed into an integer. Notice that you do not get any error when string contains invalid characters. The function always returns a value.

> ■ **Tip** The parseInt() function in Nashorn works similar to the Integer.parseInt() method in Java, except that the former is very lenient and does not throw an exception.

The following snippet of code shows the output of calling the parseInt() function with different arguments:

```
printf("parseInt('%s') = %d", "1969", parseInt('1969'));
printf("parseInt('%s') = %d", "  1969", parseInt('  1969'));
printf("parseInt('%s') = %d", "  1969 Hello", parseInt('  1969 Hello'));
printf("parseInt('%s') = %s", "Hello1969", parseInt('Hello1969'));
printf("parseInt('%s') = %d", "0x1969", parseInt('0x1969'));
printf("parseInt('%s', 16) = %d", "0x1969", parseInt('0x1969', 16));
printf("parseInt('%s', 2) = %d", "1001001", parseInt('1001001', 2));
```

```
printf("parseInt('%s') = %d", "-1969", parseInt('-1969'));
printf("parseInt('%s') = %s", "-  1969", parseInt('-  1969'));
printf("parseInt('%s') = %s", "xyz", parseInt('xyz'));
```

```
parseInt('1969') = 1969
parseInt('   1969') = 1969
parseInt('   1969 Hello') = 1969
parseInt('Hello1969') = NaN
parseInt('0x1969') = 6505
parseInt('0x1969', 16) = 6505
parseInt('1001001', 2) = 73
parseInt('-1969') = -1969
parseInt('-  1969') = NaN
parseInt('xyz') = NaN
```

The parseFloat() Function

The parseFloat() function is used parse a floating-point number from a string. It has the following signature:

```
parseFloat(string)
```

The parseFloat() function works the same way as the parseInt() function, except that the former parses string for a floating-point number. It returns NaN if string does not contain a number. The following code show the output of calling the parseFloat() function with different arguments:

```
printf("parseFloat('%s') = %f", "1969.0919", parseFloat('1969.0919'));
printf("parseFloat('%s') = %f", "  1969.0919", parseFloat('  1969.0919'));
printf("parseFloat('%s') = %f", "-1969.0919", parseFloat('-1969.0919'));
printf("parseFloat('%s') = %f", "-1.9690919e3", parseFloat('1.9690919e3'));
printf("parseFloat('%s') = %f", "1969Hello", parseFloat('1969Hello'));
printf("parseFloat('%s') = %f", "Hello", parseFloat('Hello'));
```

```
parseFloat('1969.0919') = 1969.091900
parseFloat('   1969.0919') = 1969.091900
parseFloat('-1969.0919') = -1969.091900
parseFloat('-1.9690919e3') = 1969.091900
parseFloat('1969Hello') = 1969.000000
parseFloat('Hello') = NaN
```

The isNaN() Function

The isNaN() function has the following signature:

```
isNaN(value)
```

It returns true if value results in NaN when converted to a Number; that is, it returns true if Number(value) return NaN. If the value represents a number, isNaN() returns false. Notice that isNaN() does not only check if value is NaN; it checks if value is a number or not. NaN is not considered a number, so isNaN(NaN) returns true. If you are interested in checking where value is NaN, use the expression value !== value. NaN is the only value that is not equal to itself. So, value !== value will return true if and only if value is NaN. The following code shows how to use the isNaN() function:

```
printf("isNaN(%s) = %b", NaN, isNaN(NaN));
printf("isNaN('%s') = %b", "123", isNaN('123'));
printf("isNaN('%s') = %b", "Hello", isNaN('Hello'));
printf("isNaN('%s') = %b", "97Hello", isNaN('97Hello'));
printf("isNaN('%s') = %b", "Infinity", isNaN('Infinity'));
printf("isNaN(%s) = %b", "1.89e23", isNaN(1.89e23));

var value = NaN;
if (value !== value) {
        print("value is NaN")
}
else {
        print("value is not NaN")
}
```

```
isNaN(NaN) = true
isNaN('123') = false
isNaN('Hello') = true
isNaN('97Hello') = true
isNaN('Infinity') = false
isNaN(1.89e23) = false
value is NaN
```

The isFinite( ) Function

The isFinite() function has the following signature:

isFinite(value)

It returns true if value is a finite number or it can be converted to a finite Number value. Otherwise, it returns false. In other words, if Number(value) returns NaN, +Infinity, or –Infinity, the isFinite(value) function returns false; otherwise it returns true. The following code shows how to use the isFinite() function:

```
printf("isFinite(%s) = %b", NaN, isFinite(NaN));
printf("isFinite(%s) = %b", Infinity, isFinite(Infinity));
printf("isFinite(%s) = %b", -Infinity, isFinite(-Infinity));
printf("isFinite(%s) = %b", 1089, isFinite(1089));
printf("isFinite('%s') = %b", "1089", isFinite('1089'));
printf("isFinite('%s') = %b", "Hello", isFinite('Hello'));
printf("isFinite(%s) = %b", "true", isFinite(true));
printf("isFinite(%s) = %b", "new Object()", isFinite(new Object()));
printf("isFinite(%s) = %b", "new Object(7889)", isFinite(new Object(7889)));
```

```
isFinite(NaN) = false
isFinite(Infinity) = false
isFinite(-Infinity) = false
isFinite(1089) = true
isFinite('1089') = true
isFinite('Hello') = false
isFinite(true) = true
isFinite(new Object()) = false
isFinite(new Object(7889)) = true
```

The decodeURI( ) Function

The decodeURI() function has the following signature:

decodeURI(encodedURI)

The decodeURI() function returns encodedURI after replacing the escape sequences by the characters they represent. The following code decodes a URI that contains %20 as an escape sequence that is converted to a space:

```
var encodedUri = "http://www.jdojo.com/hi%20there";
var decodedUri = decodeURI(encodedUri);
print("Encoded URI:", encodedUri);
print("Decoded URI:", decodedUri);
```

```
Encoded URI: http://www.jdojo.com/hi%20there
Decoded URI: http://www.jdojo.com/hi there
```

The decodeURIComponent( ) Function

The decodeURIComponent() function has the following signature:

```
decodeURIComponent(encodedURIComponent)
```

The decodeURIComponent() function is used to replaces the escape sequences in the URI components (values in the URI's query part) with the corresponding characters. For example, %26 needed to be used as an escape sequence in the value for an ampersand. This function will convert %26 to an ampersand. The following code shows how to use this function:

```
var encodedUriComponent = "Ken%26Donna";
var decodedUriComponent = decodeURIComponent(encodedUriComponent);
print("Encoded URI Component:", encodedUriComponent);
print("Decoded URI Component:", decodedUriComponent);
```

```
Encoded URI Component: Ken%26Donna
Decoded URI Component: Ken&Donna
```

The encodeURI( ) Function

The encodeURI() function has the following signature:

```
encodeURI(uri)
```

It returns uri after replacing certain characters with escape sequences. The following code encodes a URI that contains a space. The space character is encoded as %20.

```
var uri = "http://www.jdojo.com/hi there";
var encodedUri = encodeURI(uri);
print("URI:", uri);
print("Encoded URI:", encodedUri);
```

```
URI: http://www.jdojo.com/hi there
Encoded URI: http://www.jdojo.com/hi%20there
```

The encodeURIComponent() Function

The encodeURIComponent() function has the following signature:

```
encodeURIComponent(uriComponent)
```

It is used to replace certain characters in the URI components (values in the URI's query parts) with escape sequences. For example, an ampersand in the URI component is escaped as %26. The following code shows how to use this function:

```
var uriComponent = "Ken&Donna";
var encodedUriComponent = encodeURIComponent(uriComponent);
print("URI Component:", uriComponent);
print("Encoded URI Component:", encodedUriComponent);
```

```
URI Component: Ken&Donna
Encoded URI Component: Ken%26Donna
```

The load( ) and loadWithNewGlobal Functions

The load() and loadWIthNewGlobal() function are used to load and evaluate scripts stored in a file (locally or remotely) and a script object. Their signatures are:

- load(scriptPath)

- load(scriptObject)

- loadWIthNewGlobal(scriptPath, args1, arg2, ...)

- loadWIthNewGlobal(scriptObject, arg1, arg2,...)

Both functions load and evaluate a script. The load() function loads the script in the same global scope. Existing names in the global scope and the names in the loaded script may collide and the loaded script may overwrite the existing global values.

The loadWithNewGlobal() function loads the script in a new global scope and the names in the loaded script will not collide with the already existing names in the global scope that loads the script. The function lets you pass arguments to the new global scope. You can specify the arguments after the script path or script object. This way, the existing global scope can pass information to the new global scope. The passed arguments can be accessed in the loaded script using the arguments global object. When the loaded script in the new global scope modifies the built-in global objects, such as String, Object, and so on, those modification are not available in the caller's global scope.

■ **Tip** The loadWithNewGlobal() function is useful in executing script in a new thread using a new global scope, thus eliminating the possibility of the thread overwriting the existing global variables. Both functions return a value that is the value of the last evaluated expression in the loaded script.

You have used the load() function to load the scripts in this chapter. You can specify the local path (absolute or relative) or a URL of a script:

```
// Load a script from a local path from the current directory
load("Point.js");

// Load a script from a local path using an absolute path on Windows
load("C:\\scripts\\Point.js");

// Load a script from Internet
load("http://jdojo.com/scripts/Point.js");
```

The load() and loadWithNewGlobal() functions also support pseudo URL schemes such as nashorn and fx. The nashorn scheme is used to load Nashorn scripts; for example, load("nashorn:mozilla_compat.js") loads the built-in Mozilla compatibility script so that you can use Mozilla functionalities in Nashorn. The fx scheme is used to load JavaFX related scripts; for example, load("fx:controls.js") loads the built-in JavaFX script that imports all JavaFX control class names into the Nashorn code, so you can use their simple names.

The load() and loadWithNewGlobal() method can also load and evaluate a script in an object called a script object. A script object should contain two properties named name and script. The name property specifies a name for the script that is used as the script name when an error is thrown. You can give any name for your script you want. The script property contains the script to be loaded and evaluated. Both properties are mandatory. The following code creates a script object that prints the current date on the standard output, loads, and evaluates the script using the load() function. You may get a different output as the script prints the current date and time:

```
// Create a script object
var scriptObject = {
        name: "myscript",
        script: "var today = new Date; print('Today is', today);"
};

// Load and evaluate the script object
load(scriptObject);
```

Today is Wed Oct 08 2014 11:56:50 GMT-0500 (CDT)

Let's look at some examples to see the difference between the load() and loadWithNewGlobal() functions. I have used a script object in examples to keep the entire code short and at one place. You can load scripts from files or URLs as well.

The following code declares a global variable named x and assigns it a value of 100. It loads a script object that also declares a global variable with the same name x and assigns it a value of 200. When the script object is loaded using the load() function, it overwrites the value of the existing global variable x, as shown in the output:

```
// Declare and initialize a glocal variable named x
var x = 100;

print("Before loading the script object: x =", x);  // x is 100

// Create a script object that declares a global variable x
var scriptObject = {name: "myscript", script: "var x = 200;"};

// Load and evaluate the script object
load(scriptObject);

print("After loading the script object: x =", x); // x is 200
```

```
Before loading the script object: x = 100
After loading the script object: x = 200
```

The following code is the same as the previous one, except that it uses the loadWithNewGlobal() function to load the same script object. Because the loadWithNewGlobal() function creates a new global scope, its global variable x did not affect the existing global scope. The output confirms that the existing global variable x stays the same:

```
// Declare and initialize a glocal variable named x
var x = 100;

print("Before loading the script object: x =", x);  // x is 100

// Create a script object that declares a global variable x
var scriptObject = {name: "myscript", script: "var x = 200;"};

// Load and evaluate the script object
loadWithNewGlobal(scriptObject);

print("After loading the script object: x =", x); // x is 200
```

```
Before loading the script object: x = 100
After loading the script object: x = 100
```

The following code shows you how to pass arguments to the `loadWithNewGlobal()` function. The code simply prints the passed arguments:

```
// Create a script object prints the passed arguments
var scriptObject = {
        name: "myscript",
        script: "for each(var arg in arguments) {print(arg)}"
};

// Load and evaluate the script object passing three argumsnts
loadWithNewGlobal(scriptObject, 10, 20, 30);
```

```
10
20
30
```

You are not limited to passing only primitive values to the new global scope. You can also pass functions. You can communicate between two global scopes using functions. The following code passes a callback function to the new global scope. Notice that when the passed function is called from the new global scope, the function still uses the variable x defined in its creator global scope, not the new global scope:

```
var x = 100;

// Create a script object that prints the passed arguments
var scriptObject = {
        name: "myscript",
        script: "var x = 200; print('Inside new global. x =', x); " +
                "arguments[0]();"
};

// Load and evaluate the script object passing a function object
loadWithNewGlobal(scriptObject, function () {
        print("Called back from new global. x = " + x);
});
```

```
Inside new global. x = 200
Called back from new global. x = 100
```

Summary

Nashorn is a runtime implementation of the ECMAScript 5.1 specification on the JVM. ECMAScript defines its own syntax and constructs for declaring variables, writing statements and operators, creating and using objects and collections, iterating over collections of data, and so on. Nashorn is 100 percent compliant with the ECMAScript 5.1 specification, so you have a new set of language syntax to learn when you work with Nashorn.

Nashorn operates in two modes: strict mode and nonstrict mode. Typically, features that are error-prone are not allowed in strict mode. You can use the `"use strict"` directive at the start of a script or a function to execute the script or the function in strict mode.

Nashorn syntax supports two types of comments: single-line comments and multiline comments. They have the same syntax as single-line and multiline comments in Java. Single-line comments start with `//` and extend up to the end of the line. Multi-line comments start with `/*` and end with `*/`; they may extend to multiple lines.

Nashorn defines several keywords and reserved words. You cannot use them as an identifier to name variables and functions. The keyword `var` is used to declare a variable. The keyword `function` is used to declare a function.

Nashorn defines two types of data type: primitive types and object types. Undefined, Null, Number, Boolean, and String are primitive data types; everything else is of the object type. Functions in Nashorn are also objects. Primitive values are converted to objects automatically if needed.

Nashorn defines several operators and statements that let you write scripts. Most of them are the same as in Java. One of the biggest differences between Nashorn and Java is the way in which Nashorn works with Boolean expressions. Nashorn works with truthy and falsy values that can be converted to the Boolean values `true` or `false`. This makes it possible to use any value where a Boolean value is expected in Nashorn.

A function is a parameterized, named block of code that is defined once and executed on demand. A function is a first-class object. You can also define a function as a function expression or using a string that contains the code for the function. A function can also be used as a constructor with the `new` operator to create new objects. When a function is assigned as a value to an object's property, the function is known as a method.

An object in Nashorn is simply a map that is a collection of named properties. The properties of an object can have values that are simple data values, objects, or functions. Nashorn supports three ways to create a new object: using object literals, using constructors, and using the `Object.create()` method. Properties of an object may also have attributes that control how the properties can be used. For example, setting the `writable` attribute of a property to `false` makes the property read-only. You can access properties of an object using the dot notation or the bracket notation. Assigning a value to a nonexisting property of an object creates a new property with the name and assign the value to it. Nashorn supports prototype-based inheritance of objects.

Nashorn contains a built-in object called `JSON`, which supports the stringification and parsing of a Nashorn object to a string and a string to a Nashorn object, respectively.

In Nashorn, variable and function declarations do not have block scope. That is, declarations inside a block are visible outside the block as well. This is known as declaration hoisting. You can think of declaration hoisting as if all declarations are made at the top of the scope in which they are declared.

Nashorn contains several built-in global objects and functions. `Object`, `Function`, `String`, `Number`, and `Boolean` are examples of built-in objects. `parseInt()`, `parseFloat()`, `load()`, and `loadWithNewGlobal()` are examples of global functions.

A regular expression represents a pattern in text. Nashorn contains a `RegExp` built-in object whose instances represent regular expressions. You can also use regular expression literals to represent `RegExp` objects. A regular expression literal is enclosed in forward slashes and optionally followed by flags that define high-level text matching rules. `/Java/gi` is an example of a regular expression literal that will perform a global, case-insensitive match for the text `Java`. The `RegExp` object contains `test()` and `exec()` method to perform matches on input text. Several methods such as `replace()` and `match()` of the `String` object take regular expressions as arguments to perform operation such as match and find-and-replace.

■ ■ ■

CHAPTER 5

Procedures and Compiled Scripts

In this chapter, you will learn:

- How to invoke procedures written in scripts from Java programs
- How to implement Java interfaces in Nashorn script
- How to compile Nashorn scripts and execute them repeatedly

Invoking Procedures in Scripts

In previous chapters, you have seen how to invoke scripts using the eval() method of the ScriptEngine. It is also possible to invoke procedures written in a scripting language directly from the Java program, provided the ScriptEngine supports procedure invocation.

A scripting language may allow creating procedures, functions, and methods. The Java Scripting API lets you invoke such procedures, functions, and methods from a Java application. I will use the term "procedure" to mean procedure, function, and method in this section. I will use the specific term when the context of the discussion requires it.

Not all script engines are required to support procedure invocation. The Nashorn JavaScript engine supports procedure invocation. If a script engine supports it, the implementation of the script engine class must implement the Invocable interface. The Invocable interface contains the following four methods:

- `<T> T getInterface(Class<T> cls)`

- `<T> T getInterface(Object obj, Class<T> cls)`

- `Object invokeFunction(String name, Object... args)`
  `throws ScriptException, NoSuchMethodException`

- `Object invokeMethod(Object obj, String name, Object... args)`
  `throws ScriptException, NoSuchMethodException`

The two versions of the getInterface() method let you get an instance of a Java interface that is implemented in a scripting languages. I will discuss these functions in details in the next section. The invokeFunction() method lets you invoke a top-level function written in a scripting language. The invokeMethod() method lets you invoke methods of objects written in a scripting language.

It is the responsibility of the developer to check if a script engine implements the Invocable interface, before invoking a procedure. Invoking a procedure is a four-step process:

- Check if the script engine supports procedure invocation

- Cast the engine reference to the Invocable type

- Evaluate the script that contains the source code for the procedure, so the engine compiles and caches the script

- Use the invokeFunction() method of the Invocable interface to invoke procedures and functions; use the invokeMethod() method to invoke methods of the objects created in a scripting language

The following snippet of code performs the check that the script engine implementation class implements the Invocable interface:

```
// Get the Nashorn engine
ScriptEngineManager manager = new ScriptEngineManager();
ScriptEngine engine = manager.getEngineByName("JavaScript");

// Make sure the script engine implements the Invocable interface
if (engine instanceof Invocable) {
        System.out.println("Invoking procedures is supported.");
}
else {
        System.out.println("Invoking procedures is not supported.");
}
```

The second step is to cast the engine reference to the Invocable interface type:

```
if (engine instanceof Invocable) {
        Invocable inv = (Invocable)engine;

        // More code goes here
}
```

The third step is to evaluate the script, so the script engine compiles and stores the compiled form of the procedure for later invocation. The following snippet of code performs this step:

```
// Declare a function named add that adds two numbers
String script = "function add(n1, n2) { return n1 + n2; }";

// Evaluate the function. Call to eval() does not invoke the function.
// It just compiles it.
engine.eval(script);
```

The last step is to invoke the procedure, as shown:

```
// Invoke the add function with 30 and 40 as the function's arguments.
// It is as if you called add(30, 40) in the script.
Object result = inv.invokeFunction("add", 30, 40);
```

The first argument to the invokeFunction() is the name of the procedure. The second argument is a varargs that is used to specify arguments to the procedure. The invokeFunction() method returns the value returned by the procedure.

Listing 5-1 shows how to invoke a function. It invokes a function written in Nashorn JavaScript. It loads the scripts in the files named factorial.js and avg.js. These files contain the Nashorn code for the functions named factorial() and avg(). Later, the program invokes these function using the invokeFunction() of the Invocable interface.

Listing 5-1. Invoking a Function Written in Nashorn JavaScript

```
// InvokeFunction.java
package com.jdojo.script;

import javax.script.Invocable;
import javax.script.ScriptEngine;
import javax.script.ScriptEngineManager;
import javax.script.ScriptException;

public class InvokeFunction {
        public static void main(String[] args) {
                ScriptEngineManager manager = new ScriptEngineManager();
                ScriptEngine engine = manager.getEngineByName("JavaScript");

                // Make sure the script engine implements the Invocable
                // interface
                if (!(engine instanceof Invocable)) {
                        System.out.println(
                            "Invoking procedures is not supported.");
                        return;
                }
```

```
        // Cast the engine reference to the Invocable type
        Invocable inv = (Invocable) engine;

        try {
                String scriptPath1 = "factorial.js";
                String scriptPath2 = "avg.js";

                // Evaluate the scripts first, so the
                // factorial() and avg() functions are
                // compiled and are available to be invoked
                engine.eval("load('" + scriptPath1 + "');");
                engine.eval("load('" + scriptPath2 + "');");

                // Invoke the add function twice
                Object result1 = inv.invokeFunction("factorial", 10);
                System.out.println("factorial(10) = " + result1);

                Object result2 = inv.invokeFunction("avg", 10, 20, 30);
                System.out.println("avg(10, 20, 30) = " + result2);
        }
        catch (ScriptException | NoSuchMethodException e) {
                e.printStackTrace();
        }
    }
}
```

```
factorial(10) = 3628800.0
avg(10, 20, 30) = 20.0
```

An object-oriented or object-based scripting language may let you define objects and their methods. You can invoke methods of such objects using the invokeMethod(Object obj, String name, Object... args) method of the Invocable interface. The first argument is the reference of the object, the second argument is the name of the method that you want to invoke on the object, and the third argument is a varargs argument that is used to pass arguments to the method being invoked.

Listing 5-2 contains a Nashorn script that creates an object named calculator and adds four methods to add, subtract, multiply, and divide two numbers. Notice that I have used the Nashorn syntax extension to define the function expressions in which the braces and return statements are not specified.

Listing 5-2. A Calculator Object Created in Nashorn Script

```
// calculator.js

// Create an object
var calculator = new Object();

// Add four methods to the prototype to the calculator object
calculator.add = function (n1, n2) n1 + n2;
calculator.subtract = function (n1, n2) n1 - n2;
calculator.multiply = function (n1, n2) n1 * n2;
calculator.divide = function (n1, n2) n1 / n2;
```

Listing 5-3 demonstrates the invocation of a method on the `calculator` object that is created in Nashorn. Note that the object is created inside the Nashorn script. To invoke the method of the object from Java, you need to obtain the reference of the object through the script engine. The program evaluates the script in the `calculator.js` file that creates the `calculator` object and stores its reference in a variable named `calculator`. The `engine.get("calculator")` method returns the reference of the `calculator` object to the Java code.

Listing 5-3. Invoking a Method on an Object Created in Nashorn

```
// InvokeMethod.java
package com.jdojo.script;

import javax.script.Invocable;
import javax.script.ScriptEngine;
import javax.script.ScriptEngineManager;
import javax.script.ScriptException;

public class InvokeMethod {
        public static void main(String[] args) {
                // Get the Nashorn engine
                ScriptEngineManager manager = new ScriptEngineManager();
                ScriptEngine engine = manager.getEngineByName("JavaScript");

                // Make sure the script engine implements the Invocable
                // interface
                if (!(engine instanceof Invocable)) {
                        System.out.println(
                            "Invoking methods is not supported.");
                        return;
                }

                // Cast the engine reference to the Invocable type
                Invocable inv = (Invocable) engine;
```

```
            try {
                // Declare a global object with an add() method
                String scriptPath = "calculator.js";

                // Evaluate the script first
                engine.eval("load('" + scriptPath + "')");

                // Get the calculator object reference that was
                // created in the script
                Object calculator = engine.get("calculator");

                // Invoke the methods on the calculator object
                int x = 30;
                int y = 40;
                Object addResult = inv.invokeMethod(calculator,
                "add", x, y);
                Object subResult = inv.invokeMethod(calculator,
                "subtract", x, y);
                Object mulResult = inv.invokeMethod(calculator,
                "multiply", x, y);
                Object divResult = inv.invokeMethod(calculator,
                "divide", x, y);

                System.out.printf(
                    "calculator.add(%d, %d) = %s%n",
                    x, y, addResult);
                System.out.printf(
                    "calculator.subtract(%d, %d) = %s%n",
                    x, y, subResult);
                System.out.printf(
                    "calculator.multiply(%d, %d) = %s%n",
                    x, y, mulResult);
                System.out.printf(
                    "calculator.divide(%d, %d) = %s%n",
                    x, y, divResult);
            }
            catch (ScriptException | NoSuchMethodException e) {
                e.printStackTrace();
            }
        }
}
```

```
calculator.add(30, 40) = 70
calculator.subtract(30, 40) = -10.0
calculator.multiply(30, 40) = 1200.0
calculator.divide(30, 40) = 0.75
```

■ **Tip**   Use the `Invocable` interface to execute procedures, functions, and methods repeatedly. Evaluation of the script, having procedures, functions, and methods, stores the intermediate code in the engine that results in performance gain on their repeated execution.

Implementing Java Interfaces in Scripts

The Java Scripting API lets you implement Java interfaces in a scripting language. The advantage of implementing a Java interface in a scripting language is that you can use instances of the interface in Java code as if the interface was implemented in Java. You can pass instances of the interface as arguments to Java methods. Methods of the Java interface may be implemented in scripts using top-level procedures or methods of an object.

The `getInterface()` method of the `Invocable` interface is used to obtain the instances of a Java interface that is implemented in scripts. The method has two versions:

- `<T> T getInterface(Class<T> cls)`

- `<T> T getInterface(Object obj, Class<T> cls)`

The first version is used to obtain an instance of a Java interface whose methods are implemented as top-level procedures in scripts. The interface type is passed to this method as its argument. Suppose that you have a `Calculator` interface, as declared in Listing 5-4, that contains four methods called `add()`, `subtract()`, `multiply()` and `divide()`.

Listing 5-4.   A Calculator Interface

```
// Calculator.java
package com.jdojo.script;

public interface Calculator {
        double add (double n1, double n2);
        double subtract (double n1, double n2);
        double multiply (double n1, double n2);
        double divide (double n1, double n2);
}
```

Consider the top-level functions written in Nashorn as shown in Listing 5-5. The script contains four functions that correspond to the functions in the `Calculator` interface.

Listing 5-5. The Contents of the calculatorasfunctions.js File

```
// calculatorasfunctions.js

function add(n1, n2) {
        n1 + n2;
}

function subtract(n1, n2) {
        n1 - n2;
}

function multiply(n1, n2) {
        n1 * n2;
}

function divide(n1, n2) {
        n1 / n2;
}
```

These two functions provide the implementations for the four methods of the Calculator interface. After the functions are compiled by a JavaScript engine, you can obtain an instance of the Calculator interface, as shown:

```
// Cast the engine reference to the Invocable type
Invocable inv = (Invocable)engine;

// Get the reference of the Calculator interface
Calculator calc = inv.getInterface(Calculator.class);
if (calc == null) {
        System.err.println("Calculator interface implementation not found.");
}
else {
        // Use calc to call the methods of the Calculator interface
}
```

You can add two numbers, as shown:

```
int sum = calc.add(15, 10);
```

Listing 5-6 shows how to implement a Java interface using top-level procedures in Nashorn. Please consult the documentation of a scripting language (other than Nashorn) to learn how it supports this functionality.

Listing 5-6. Implementing a Java Interface Using Top-Level Functions in Script

```java
// UsingInterfaces.java
package com.jdojo.script;

import javax.script.Invocable;
import javax.script.ScriptEngine;
import javax.script.ScriptEngineManager;
import javax.script.ScriptException;

public class UsingInterfaces {
        public static void main(String[] args) {
                // Get the Nashorn engine
                ScriptEngineManager manager = new ScriptEngineManager();
                ScriptEngine engine = manager.getEngineByName("JavaScript");

                // Make sure the script engine implements Invocable
                // interface
                if (!(engine instanceof Invocable)) {
                        System.out.println(
                                "Interface implementation in script" +
                                "is not supported.");
                        return;
                }

                // Cast the engine reference to the Invocable type
                Invocable inv = (Invocable) engine;

                // Create the script for add() and subtract() functions
                String scriptPath  = "calculatorasfunctions.js";

                try {
                        // Compile the script that will be stored in the
                        // engine
                        engine.eval("load('" + scriptPath + "')");

                        // Get the interface implementation
                        Calculator calc =
                                inv.getInterface(Calculator.class);
                        if (calc == null) {
                                System.err.println("Calculator interface " +
                                        "implementation not found.");
                                return;
                        }
```

```
                        double x = 15.0;
                        double y = 10.0;
                        double addResult = calc.add(x, y);
                        double subResult = calc.subtract(x, y);
                        double mulResult = calc.multiply(x, y);
                        double divResult = calc.divide(x, y);

                        System.out.printf(
                            "calc.add(%.2f, %.2f) = %.2f%n",
                            x, y, addResult);
                        System.out.printf(
                            "calc.subtract(%.2f, %.2f) = %.2f%n",
                            x, y, subResult);
                        System.out.printf(
                            "calc.multiply(%.2f, %.2f) = %.2f%n",
                            x, y, mulResult);
                        System.out.printf(
                            "calc.divide(%.2f, %.2f) = %.2f%n",
                            x, y, divResult);
                }
                catch (ScriptException e) {
                        e.printStackTrace();
                }
        }
}
```

```
calc.add(15.00, 10.00) = 25.00
calcr.subtract(15.00, 10.00) = 5.00
calcr.multiply(15.00, 10.00) = 150.00
calc.divide(15.00, 10.00) = 1.50
```

How did the Nashorn engine find the implementation for the Calculator interface? When you call the getInterface(Class<T> cls) of Invocable, the engine looks for compiled functions with the matching names as the abstract methods in the specified class. In our case, the engine looks for compiled functions named add, subtract, multiply, and divide in the engine. Note that it is necessary to call the eval() method of the engine to compile the functions in the calculatorasfunctions.js file. The Nashorn engine does not match the number of formal parameters in the Java interface methods and script functions in the engine.

The second version of the getInterface() method is used to obtain an instance of a Java interface whose methods are implemented as instance methods of an object. Its first argument is the reference of the object that is created in the scripting language. The instance methods of the object implement the interface type passed in as the second argument. The code in Listing 5-2 creates an object named calculator whose instance methods implement the Calculator interface. You will the methods of the calculator object as an implementation of the Calculator interface in Java.

When instance methods of a script object implements methods of a Java interface, you need to perform an extra step. You need to get the reference of the script object before you can get the instance of the interface, as shown:

```
// Load the calculator object in the engine
engine.load('calculator.js');

// Get the reference of the global script object calculator
Object calc = engine.get("calculator");

// Get the implementation of the Calculator interface
Calculator calculator = inv.getInterface(calc, Calculator.class);
```

Listing 5-7 shows how to implement methods of a Java interface as instance methods of an object using Nashorn.

Listing 5-7. Implementing Methods of a Java Interface as Instance Methods of an Object in a Script

```
// ScriptObjectImplInterface.java
package com.jdojo.script;

import javax.script.Invocable;
import javax.script.ScriptEngine;
import javax.script.ScriptEngineManager;
import javax.script.ScriptException;

public class ScriptObjectImplInterface {
        public static void main(String[] args) {
                // Get the Nashorn engine
                ScriptEngineManager manager = new ScriptEngineManager();
                ScriptEngine engine = manager.getEngineByName("JavaScript");

                // Make sure the engine implements the Invocable interface
                if (!(engine instanceof Invocable)) {
                        System.out.println("Interface implementation in " +
                                        "script is not supported.");
                        return;
                }

                // Cast the engine reference to the Invocable type
                Invocable inv = (Invocable)engine;

                String scriptPath  = "calculator.js";

                try {
                        // Compile and store the script in the engine
                        engine.eval("load('" + scriptPath + "')");
```

```java
                // Get the reference of the global script object calc
                Object scriptCalc = engine.get("calculator");

                // Get the implementation of the Calculator interface
                Calculator calc = inv.getInterface(scriptCalc,
                Calculator.class);
                if (calc == null) {
                        System.err.println("Calculator interface " +
                                "implementation not found.");
                        return;
                }

                double x = 15.0;
                double y = 10.0;
                double addResult = calc.add(x, y);
                double subResult = calc.subtract(x, y);
                double mulResult = calc.multiply(x, y);
                double divResult = calc.divide(x, y);

                System.out.printf(
                    "calc.add(%.2f, %.2f) = %.2f%n",
                    x, y, addResult);
                System.out.printf(
                    "calc.subtract(%.2f, %.2f) = %.2f%n",
                    x, y, subResult);
                System.out.printf(
                    "calc.multiply(%.2f, %.2f) = %.2f%n",
                    x, y, mulResult);
                System.out.printf(
                    "calc.divide(%.2f, %.2f) = %.2f%n",
                    x, y, divResult);
            }
            catch (ScriptException e) {
                        e.printStackTrace();
            }
        }
}
```

```
calc.add(15.00, 10.00) = 25.00
calcr.subtract(15.00, 10.00) = 5.00
calcr.multiply(15.00, 10.00) = 150.00
calc.divide(15.00, 10.00) = 1.50
```

Using Compiled Scripts

A script engine may allow compiling a script and executing it repeatedly. Executing compiled scripts may increase the performance of an application. A script engine may compile and store scripts in the form of Java classes, Java class files, or in a language-specific form.

Not all script engines are required to support script compilation. Script engines that support script compilation must implement the Compilable interface. Nashorn engine supports script compilation. The following snippet of code checks if a script engine implements the Compilable interface:

```
// Get the script engine reference
ScriptEngineManager manager = new ScriptEngineManager();
ScriptEngine engine = manager.getEngineByName("YOUR_ENGINE_NAME");

if (engine instanceof Compilable) {
        System.out.println("Script compilation is supported.");
}
else {
        System.out.println("Script compilation is not supported.");
}
```

Once you know that a script engine implements the Compilable interface, you can cast its reference to a Compilable type, like so:

```
// Cast the engine reference to the Compilable type
Compilable comp = (Compilable)engine;
```

The Compilable interface contains two methods:

- CompiledScript compile(String script) throws ScriptException

- CompiledScript compile(Reader script) throws ScriptException

The two versions of the method differ only in the type of the source of the script. The first version accepts the script as a String and the second one as a Reader.

The compile() method returns an object of the CompiledScript class. CompiledScript is an abstract class. The provider of the script engine provides the concrete implementation of this class. A CompiledScript is associated with the ScriptEngine that creates it. The getEngine() method of the CompiledScript class returns the reference of the ScriptEngine to which it is associated.

To execute a compiled script, you need to call one of the following eval() methods of the CompiledScript class:

- Object eval() throws ScriptException

- Object eval(Bindings bindings) throws ScriptException

- Object eval(ScriptContext context) throws ScriptException

The eval() method without any arguments uses the default script context of the script engine to execute the compiled script. The other two versions work the same as the eval() method of the ScriptEngine interface when you pass a Bindings or a ScriptContext to them.

■ **Tip** When you evaluate scripts using the eval() method of the CompiledScript class, changes in the state of the engine made during the execution of the compiled script may be visible in the subsequent execution of the scripts by the engine.

Listing 5-8 shows how to compile a script and execute it. It executes the same compiled script twice with different parameters.

Listing 5-8. Using Compiled Scripts

```java
// CompilableTest .java
package com.jdojo.script;

import javax.script.Bindings;
import javax.script.Compilable;
import javax.script.CompiledScript;
import javax.script.ScriptEngine;
import javax.script.ScriptEngineManager;
import javax.script.ScriptException;

public class CompilableTest {
        public static void main(String[] args) {
                // Get the Nashorn engine
                ScriptEngineManager manager = new ScriptEngineManager();
                ScriptEngine engine = manager.getEngineByName("JavaScript");

                if (!(engine instanceof Compilable)) {
                        System.out.println(
                                "Script compilation not supported.");
                        return;
                }
```

```java
        // Cast the engine reference to the Compilable type
        Compilable comp = (Compilable)engine;

        try {
                // Compile a script
                String script = "print(n1 + n2)";
                CompiledScript cScript = comp.compile(script);

                // Store n1 and n2 script variables in a Bindings
                Bindings scriptParams = engine.createBindings();
                scriptParams.put("n1", 2);
                scriptParams.put("n2", 3);
                cScript.eval(scriptParams);

                // Execute the script again with different values
                // for n1 and n2
                scriptParams.put("n1", 9);
                scriptParams.put("n2", 7);
                cScript.eval(scriptParams);
        }
        catch (ScriptException e) {
                e.printStackTrace();
        }
    }
}
```

5
16

Summary

The Java Scripting API supports invoking procedures, functions, and methods written in a scripting language directly from Java. This is made possible through the Invocable interface. If a script engine supports procedure invocation, it implements the Invocable interface. Nashorn engine supports procedure invocation. The procedure being invoked may be implemented as top-level functions or methods of an object. The invokeFunction() method of the Invocable interface is used to invoke top-level functions in scripts. The invokeMethod() method of the Invocable interface is used to invoke a method of an object. The top-level functions and the objects whose methods are invoked must be evaluated by the engine before invoking them.

The Java Script API also lets you implement Java interfaces in scripting languages. The methods of a Java interface may be implemented as top-level functions or methods of an object. The getInterface() method of the Invocable interface is used to get the implementation of a Java interface.

The Java scripting API also let you compile a script once, store it in the script engine, and execute the script multiple times. It is supported through the `Compilable` interface. A script engine supporting script compilation needs to implement the `Compilable` interface. You need to call the `compile()` method of the `Compilable` interface to compile a script. The `compile()` method returns an instance of the `CompiledScript` whose `eval()` method is called to execute the script.

Note that implementing the `Invocable` and `Compilable` interfaces by a script engine is optional. Before invoking procedures and compiling scripts, you need to check if the script engine is an instance of these interfaces, cast the engine to these types, and, then, execute methods of these interfaces.

CHAPTER 6

■ ■ ■

Using Java in Scripting Languages

In this chapter, you will learn:

- How to import Java classes into scripts
- How to create Java objects and use them in scripts
- How to call overloaded methods of Java objects
- How to create Java arrays
- How to extend a Java class and implement Java interfaces in scripts
- How to invoke superclass methods of an object from scripts

Scripting languages allow using Java class libraries in scripts. Each scripting language has its own syntax for using Java classes. It is not possible, and is outside the scope of this book, to discuss the syntax of all scripting languages. In this chapter, I will discuss the syntax of using Java constructs in Nashorn.

Importing Java Types

There are four ways to import Java types into Nashorn script:

- Using the Packages global object
- Using the type() method of the Java global object
- Using the importPackage() and importClass() functions
- Using a JavaImporter in a with clause

Of the four types of importing Java types, the second type, using the type() method of the global Java object, is preferred. The following sections will describe the four ways of importing Java type in script in detail.

Using the Packages Global Object

Nashorn defines all Java packages as properties of a global variable named Packages. For example, the java.lang and javax.swing packages may be referred to as Packages. java.lang and Packages.javax.swing, respectively. The following snippet of code uses the java.util.List and javax.swing.JFrame in Nashorn:

```
// Create a List
var list1 = new Packages.java.util.ArrayList();

// Create a JFrame
var frame1 = new Packages.javax.swing.JFrame("Test");
```

Nashorn declares java, javax, org, com, edu, and net as global variables that are aliases for Packages.java, Packages.javax, Packages.org, Packages.com, Packages.edu, and Packages.net, respectively. Class names in examples in this book start with the prefix com, for example, com.jdojo.script.Test. To use this class name inside the JavaScript code, you may use Packages.com.jdojo.script.Test or com.jdojo.script.Test. However, if a class name does not start with one of these predefined prefixes, you must use the Packages global variable to access it; for example, if your class name is p1.Test, you need to access it using Packages.p1.Test inside JavaScript code. The following snippet of code uses the java and javax aliases for Packages.java and Packages.javax:

```
// Create a List
var list = new java.util.ArrayList();

// Create a JFrame
var frame = new javax.swing.JFrame("Test");
```

Using the Java Global Object

Accessing packages as the properties of the Packages object was also supported in Rhino JavaScript in Java 7. Using the Packages object is slower and error-prone. Nashorn defines a new global object called Java that contains many useful functions to work with Java packages and classes. If you are using Java 8 or later, you should prefer using the Java object. The type() function of the Java object imports a Java type into the script. You need to pass the fully qualified name of the Java type to import. In Nashorn, the following snippet of code imports the java.util.ArrayList class and creates its object:

```
// Import java.util.ArrayList type and call it ArrayList
var ArrayList = Java.type("java.util.ArrayList");

// Create an object of the ArrayList type
var list = new ArrayList();
```

You can also combine the two statements into one. Make sure to add the call to Java.type() method in a pair of parentheses; otherwise, the statement will generate an error thinking that Java.type is a constructor function and you are trying to create a Nashorn object using a constructor function:

```
// Create an object of the java.util.ArrayList type
var list = new (Java.type("java.util.ArrayList"));
```

In the code, you call the imported type returned from the Java.type() function as ArrayList that is also the name of the class that is imported. You do it to make the next statement read as if it was written Java. Readers of the second statement will know that you are creating an object of the ArrayList class. However, you can give the imported type any name you want. The following snippet of code imports java.util.ArrayList and calls it MyList:

```
// Import java.util.ArrayList type and call it MyList
var MyList = Java.type("java.util.ArrayList");

// Create an object of the MyList type
var list2 = new MyList();
```

Using the importPackage() and importClass() Functions

Rhino JavaScript allowed using the simple names of the Java types in script. Rhino JavaScript had two built-in functions called importPackage() and importClass() to import all classes from a package and a class from a package, respectively. For compatibility reasons, Nashorn keeps these functions. To use these functions in Nashorn, you need to load the compatibility module from mozilla_compat.js file using the load() function. The following snippet of code rewrites the above logic in the previous section these functions:

```
// Load the compatibility module. It is needed in Nashorn, not in Rhino.
load("nashorn:mozilla_compat.js");

// Import ArrayList class from the java.util package
importClass(java.util.ArrayList);

// Import all classes from the javax.swing package
importPackage(javax.swing);

// Use simple names of classes
var list = new ArrayList();
var frame = new JFrame("Test");
```

JavaScript does not import all classes from the java.lang package automatically because JavaScript classes with the same names, for example, String, Object, Number, and so on, will conflict with class names in the java.lang package. To use a class from the java.lang package, you can import it or use the Packages or Java global object to use its fully qualified name. You cannot import all classes from the java.lang package. The following snippet of code generates an error because the String class name is already defined in JavaScript:

```
// Load the compatibility module. It is needed in Nashorn, not in Rhino.
load("nashorn:mozilla_compat.js");

// Will cause a conflict with String object in Nashorn
importClass(java.lang.String);
```

If you want to use the java.lang.String class, you need to use its fully qualified name. The following snippet of code uses the built-in JavaScript String class and the java.lang.String class:

```
var javaStr = new java.lang.String("Hello"); // Java String class
var jsStr = new String("Hello");             // JavaScript String class
```

If a class name in the java.lang package does not conflict with a JavaScript top-level class name, you can use the importClass() function to import the Java class. For example, you can use the following snippet of code to use the java.lang.System class:

```
// Load the compatibility module. It is needed in Nashorn, not in Rhino.
load("nashorn:mozilla_compat.js");

importClass(java.lang.System);

var jsStr = new String("Hello");
System.out.println(jsStr);
```

In this snippet of code, jsStr is a JavaScript String that has been passed to the System.out.println() Java method that accepts a java.lang.String type. JavaScript takes care of the conversion from a JavaScript type to a Java type automatically in such cases.

Using the JavaImporter Object

In JavaScript, you can use the simple names of classes using a JavaImporter object in a with statement. Please refer to Chapter 4 for more details in the with statement. JavaImporter is a Nashorn function object that can be used as a function or a constructor. It accepts a list of Java packages and classes. You can create a JavaImporter object as shown:

```
// Import all classes from the java.lang package
var langPkg = new JavaImporter(Packages.java.lang);

// Import all classes from the java.lang and java.util packages and the
// JFrame class from the javax.swing package
var pkg2 = JavaImporter(java.lang, java.util, javax.swing.JFrame);
```

Notice the use of the new operator in the first statement. The second statement does not use the new operator; it used JavaImporter as a function. Both statements do the same thing.

The following snippet of code creates a JavaImporter object and uses it in a with statement:

```
// Create a Java importer for java.lang and java.util packages
var javaLangAndUtilPkg = JavaImporter(java.lang, java.util);

// Use the imported types in the with clause
with (javaLangAndUtilPkg) {
        var list = new ArrayList();
        list.add("one");
        list.add("two");
        System.out.println("Hello");
        System.out.println("List is " + list);
}
```

```
Hello
List is [one, two]
```

Creating and Using Java Objects

Use the new operator with a constructor to create a new Java object in scripts. The following snippet of code creates a String object in Nashorn:

```
// Create a Java String object
var JavaString = Java.type("java.lang.String");
var greeting = new JavaString("Hello");
```

Accessing methods and properties of Java objects is similar in most scripting languages. Some scripting languages let you invoke getter and setter methods on an object using the property name. The following code in Nashorn creates a java.util.Date object and accesses the object's method using both the property names and the method names. You may get a different output because the code operates on the current date:

```
var LocalDate = Java.type("java.time.LocalDate");
var dt = LocalDate.now();
var year = dt.year;              // Use as a property
var month = dt.month;            // Use as a property
var date = dt.getDayOfMonth();   // Use as a method
print("Date:" + dt);
print("Year:" + year + ", Month:" + month + ", Day:" + date);
```

```
Date:2014-10-12
Year:2014, Month:OCTOBER, Day:12
```

In JavaScript, you can use the methods of Java objects as if they are properties. When you are reading the property named xxx, JavaScript will automatically call the getXxx() method. When you are setting the property named xxx, the setXxx() method will be called. The JavaBeans method convention is used to find the corresponding method. For example, if you read the leapYear property of a LocalDate object, the object's isLeapYear() method will be called because the property is of the boolean type.

When using JavaScript, it is important to understand the different types of String objects. A String object may be a JavaScript String object or a Java java.lang.String object. JavaScript defines a length property for its String object, whereas Java has a length() method for its java.lang.String class. The following snippet of code shows the difference in creating and accessing the length of a JavaScript String and a Java java.lang.String objects:

```
// JavaScript String
var jsStr = new String("Hello JavaScript String");
print("JavaScript String: " + jsStr);
print("JavaScript String Length: " + jsStr.length);

// Java String
var javaStr = new java.lang.String("Hello Java String");
print("Java String: " + javaStr);
print("Java String Length: " + javaStr.length());
```

```
JavaScript String: Hello JavaScript String
JavaScript String Length: 23
Java String: Hello Java String
Java String Length: 17
```

Using Overloaded Java Methods

Java resolves the method call for an overloaded method at compile time. That is, the Java compiler determines the signature of the method that will be called when the code is run. Consider the code for a `PrintTest` class shown in Listing 6-1. You may get a different output in the second line.

Listing 6-1. Using Overloaded Methods in Java

```java
// PrintTest.java
package com.jdojo.script;

public class PrintTest {
        public void print(String str) {
                System.out.println("print(String): " + str);
        }

        public void print(Object obj) {
                System.out.println("print(Object): " + obj);
        }

        public void print(Double num) {
                System.out.println("print(Double): " + num);
        }

        public static void main(String[] args) {
                PrintTest pt = new PrintTest();
                Object[] list = new Object[]{"Hello", new Object(), 10.5};

                for(Object arg : list) {
                        pt.print(arg);
                }
        }
}
```

```
print(Object): Hello
print(Object): java.lang.Object@affc70
print(Object): 10.5
```

When the `PrintTest` class is run, all three calls to the `print()` method call the same version, `print(Object)` of the `PrintTest` class. When the code is compiled, the Java compiler sees the call `pt.print(arg)` as a call to the `print()` method with an `Object` type argument (which is the type of arg) and therefore binds this call to `print(Object)` method.

In a scripting language, the type of a variable is known at runtime, not at compile time. The interpreters of scripting languages resolve an overloaded method call appropriately depending on the runtime type of the arguments in a method call. The output of the following JavaScript code shows that the call to the print() method of the PrintTest class is resolved at runtime depending on the type of the argument. You may get a bit different output in the second line:

```
// JavaScript Code
// Create an object of the Java class called PrintTest
var PrintTest = Java.type("com.jdojo.script.PrintTest");
var pt = new PrintTest();

// Create a JavaScript array with three elements
var list = ["Hello", new Object(), 10.5];

// Call the overloaded method print() of the PrintTest class
// passing each object in an array at time
for each(var element in list) {
    pt.print(element);
}
```

```
print(String): Hello
print(Object): jdk.nashorn.internal.scripts.JO@405818
print(Double): 10.5
```

JavaScript lets you select a specific version of the overloaded method explicitly. You can pass the signature of the overloaded method to be invoked with the object reference. The following snippet of code selects the print(Object) version:

```
// JavaScript Code
var PrintTest = Java.type("com.jdojo.script.PrintTest");
var pt = new PrintTest();
pt["print(java.lang.Object)"](10.5); // Calls print(Object)
pt["print(java.lang.Double)"](10.5); // Calls print(Double)
```

```
print(Object): 10.5
print(Double): 10.5
```

Using Java Arrays

The way Java arrays can be created in JavaScript differs in Rhino and Nashorn. In Rhino, you need to create a Java array using the newInstance() static method of the java.lang.reflect.Array class. This syntax is also supported in Nashorn. The following snippet of code shows how to create and access Java arrays using the Rhino syntax:

```
// Create a java.lang.String array of 2 elements, populate it, and print
// the elements. In Rhino, you were able to use java.lang.String as
// the first argument, but in Nashorn, you need to use
// java.lang.String.class instead.
var strArray = java.lang.reflect.Array.newInstance(java.lang.String.class, 2);
strArray[0] = "Hello";
strArray[1] = "Array";
for(var i = 0; i < strArray.length; i++) {
        print(strArray[i]);
}
```

```
Hello
Array
```

To create primitive type arrays such as int, double, and so on, you need to use their TYPE constants for their corresponding wrapper classes, as shown:

```
// Create an int array of 2 elements, populate it, and print the elements
var intArray = java.lang.reflect.Array.newInstance(java.lang.Integer.TYPE, 2);
intArray[0] = 100;
intArray[1] = 200;
for(var i = 0; i < intArray.length; i++) {
        print(intArray[i]);
}
```

```
100
200
```

Nashorn supports a new syntax to create Java arrays. First, create the appropriate Java array type using the Java.type() method, and then use the familiar new operator to create the array. The following snippet of code shows how to create a String[] of two elements in Nashorn:

```
// Get the java.lang.String[] type
var StringArray = Java.type("java.lang.String[]");

// Create a String[] array of 2 elements
var strArray = new StringArray(2);
strArray[0] = "Hello";
strArray[1] = "Array";
for(var i = 0; i < strArray.length; i++) {
        print(strArray[i]);
}
```

```
Hello
Array
```

Nashorn supports creating the arrays of primitive types the same way. The following snippet of code creates an int[] of two elements in Nashorn:

```
// Get the int[] type
var IntArray = Java.type("int[]");

// Create a int[] array of 2 elements
var intArray = new IntArray(2);
intArray[0] = 100;
intArray[1] = 200;
for(var i = 0; i < intArray.length; i++) {
        print(intArray[i]);
}
```

```
100
200
```

I will discuss working with Java and JavaScript arrays in Chapter 7 in details.

Extending Java Classes Implementing Interfaces

JavaScript lets you extend Java classes and implement Java interfaces in JavaScript. The following sections describe different ways of achieving this.

Using a Script Object

You need to create a script object that contains implementations of the methods of the interface and pass it to the constructor of the Java interface using the new operator. In Java, an interface does not have a constructor and it cannot be used with the new operator, except when creating an anonymous class. However, JavaScript lets you do that.

In Chapter 5, we had created the Calculator interface with four abstract methods. The code for the interface is shown again in Listing 6-2 for your reference.

Listing 6-2. The Calculator Interface in Java

```java
// Calculator.java
package com.jdojo.script;

public interface Calculator {
        double add (double n1, double n2);
        double subtract (double n1, double n2);
        double multiply (double n1, double n2);
        double divide (double n1, double n2);
}
```

In Chapter 5, we have created a calculator JavaScript object whose script is shown again in Listing 6-3.

Listing 6-3. The Calculator Interface in Java

```javascript
// calculator.js

// Create an object
var calculator = new Object();

// Add four methods to the prototype to the calculator object
calculator.add = function (n1, n2) n1 + n2;
calculator.subtract = function (n1, n2) n1 - n2;
calculator.multiply = function (n1, n2) n1 * n2;
calculator.divide = function (n1, n2) n1 / n2;
```

Notice that the `calculator` object in JavaScript contains the implementation of all abstract methods of the Java `Calculator` interface. The following statement creates an implementation of the `Calculator` interface:

```
// Load the calculator object
load("calculator.js");

// Get the Java interface type
var Calculator = Java.type("com.jdojo.script.Calculator");

// Create an instance of the com.jdojo.script.Calculator interface
// passing its constructor a calculator JavaScript object
var calc = new Calculator(calculator);
```

Now you can start using the `calc` object as if it were an implementation of the `Calculator` interface, as shown:

```
// Use the instance of teh Calculator interface
var x = 15.0, y = 10.0;

var addResult = calc.add(x, y);
var subResult = calc.subtract(x, y);
var mulResult = calc.multiply(x, y);
var divResult = calc.divide(x, y);

printf("calc.add(%.2f, %.2f) = %.2f", x, y, addResult);
printf("calc.subtract(%.2f, %.2f) = %.2f", x, y, subResult);
printf("calc.multiply(%.2f, %.2f) = %.2f", x, y, mulResult);
printf("calc.divide(%.2f, %.2f) = %.2f", x, y, divResult);
```

```
calc.add(15.00, 10.00) = 25.00
calc.subtract(15.00, 10.00) = 5.00
calc.multiply(15.00, 10.00) = 150.00
calc.divide(15.00, 10.00) = 1.50
```

Using the Anonymous Class–Like Syntax

This method uses a syntax that is very similar to the syntax of creating an anonymous class in Java. The following statement implements the Java `Calculator` interface and creates an instance of that implementation:

```
// Get the Java interface type
var Calculator = Java.type("com.jdojo.script.Calculator");

// Create an instance of the com.jdojo.script.Calculator interface
// using an anonymous class-like syntax
var calc = new Calculator() {
                add: (function (n1, n2) n1 + n2),
                subtract: (function (n1, n2) n1 - n2),
                multiply: (function (n1, n2) n1 * n2),
                divide: (function (n1, n2) n1 / n2)
            };
```

Now you can use the `calc` object the same way as you did before.

Using the JavaAdapter Object

JavaScript lets you implement multiple interfaces and extend a class using the JavaAdapter class. However, the Rhino JavaScript implementation that is bundled with JDK has overridden the implementation of `JavaAdapter`, which allows you to implement only one interface; it does not let you extend a class. The first argument to the JavaAdapter constructor is the interface to implement and the second argument is the script object that implements the interface's abstract methods. To use the `JavaAdapter` object in Nashorn, you need to load the Rhino compatibility module. The following snippet of code implements the `Calculator` interface using `JavaAdapter`:

```
// Need to load the compatibility module in Nashorn.
// You do not need to the following load() call in Rhino.
load("nashorn:mozilla_compat.js");

// Load the script that creates the calculator JavaScript object
load("calculator.js");

var calc = new JavaAdapter(com.jdojo.script.Calculator, calculator);
```

Now you can use the `calc` object the same way as you did before. It is an instance of the `com.jdojo.script.Calculator` interface whose implementation has been provided by the methods declared in the `calculator` object as defined in script in the `calculator.js` file.

Using the Java.extend() Method

Nashorn provides a better way to extend a class and implement multiple interfaces using the Java.extend() method. In the Java.extend() method, you can pass maximum one class type and multiple interface types. It returns a type that combines all passed in types. You need to use the previously discussed anonymous class-like syntax to provide the implementation for the abstract methods of the new type or override the existing method of the types being extended. The following snippet of code uses the Java.extend() method to implement the Calculator interface:

```
// Get the Calculator interface type
var Calculator = Java.type("com.jdojo.script.Calculator");

// Get a type that extends the Calculator type
var CalculatorExtender = Java.extend(Calculator);

// Implement the abstract methods in CalculatorExtender
// using an anonymous class like syntax
var calc = new CalculatorExtender() {
                add: (function (n1, n2) n1 + n2),
                subtract: (function (n1, n2) n1 - n2),
                multiply: (function (n1, n2) n1 * n2),
                divide: (function (n1, n2) n1 / n2)
            };

// Use the instance of teh Calculator interface
var x = 15.0, y = 10.0;
var addResult = calc.add(x, y);
var subResult = calc.subtract(x, y);
var mulResult = calc.multiply(x, y);
var divResult = calc.divide(x, y);

printf("calc.add(%.2f, %.2f) = %.2f", x, y, addResult);
printf("calc.subtract(%.2f, %.2f) = %.2f", x, y, subResult);
printf("calc.multiply(%.2f, %.2f) = %.2f", x, y, mulResult);
printf("calc.divide(%.2f, %.2f) = %.2f", x, y, divResult);
```

```
calc.add(15.00, 10.00) = 25.00
calc.subtract(15.00, 10.00) = 5.00
calc.multiply(15.00, 10.00) = 150.00
calc.divide(15.00, 10.00) = 1.50
```

You can use the Java.extend() method to extends concrete classes, abstract classes, and interfaces. The following code extends the concrete class java.lang.Thread and implements the Calculator interface. The new implementation overrides the run() method of the Thread class:

```
// Get the Calculator interface type
var Calculator = Java.type("com.jdojo.script.Calculator");
var Thread = Java.type("java.lang.Thread");

// Get a type that extends the Calculator type
var ThreadCalcExtender = Java.extend(Thread, Calculator);

// Implement the abstract methods in CalculatorExtender
// using an anonymous class like syntax
var calcThread = new ThreadCalcExtender() {
                    add: (function (n1, n2) n1 + n2),
                    subtract: (function (n1, n2) n1 - n2),
                    multiply: (function (n1, n2) n1 * n2),
                    divide: (function (n1, n2) n1 / n2),
                    run: function () {
                        var n1 = Math.random();
                        var n2 = Math.random();
                        printf("n1 = %.2f, n2 = %.2f", n1, n2);
                        var addResult = this.add(n1, n2);
                        printf("calc.add(%.2f, %.2f) = %.2f", n1, n2, addResult);
                    }
                };

// Start the thread
calcThread.start();
```

```
n1 = 0.61, n2 = 0.66
calc.add(0.61, 0.66) = 1.27
```

Using a JavaScript Function

Sometimes a Java interface has only one method. In those cases, you can pass a JavaScript function object in place of an implementation of the interface. The Runnable interface in Java has only one method run(). When you need to use an instance of the Runnable interface in JavaScript, you can pass a JavaScript function object. The following snippet of code shows how to create a Thread object and start it. In the constructor of the Thread class, a JavaScript function object myRunFunc is passed instead of an instance of the Runnable interface:

```
function myRunFunc() {
        print("A thread is running.");
}

// Call Thread(Runnable) constructor and pass the myRunFunc function
// object that will serve as an implementation for the run() method of
// the Runnable interface.
var thread = new java.lang.Thread(myRunFunc);
thread.start();
```

```
A thread is running.
```

Accessing Methods of a Superclass

In Java, when you can access the methods of a superclass using the keyword super. When you extend a class in JavaScript, you can also access the methods of the superclass using the Java.super() method. The method takes the JavaScript object that has been extended in JavaScript and it returns a reference that can be used to call the method of the superclass. Consider the code for a Person class as shown in Listing 6-4.

Listing 6-4. A Person Class

```
// Person.java
package com.jdojo.script;

public class Person {
        private String firstName;
        private String lastName;

        public Person(String firstName, String lastName){
                this.firstName = firstName;
                this.lastName = lastName;
        }
```

```java
        public String getFirstName() {
                return firstName;
        }

        public void setFirstName(String firstName) {
                this.firstName = firstName;
        }

        public String getLastName() {
                return lastName;
        }

        public void setLastName(String lastName) {
                this.lastName = lastName;
        }

        public String getFullName() {
                return firstName + " " + lastName;
        }
}
```

Consider the code in Listing 6-5. It extends the Person class and override the getFullName() method.

Listing 6-5. Using the Java.super() Method to Access Superclass Methods

```javascript
// supermethod.js

var Person = Java.type("com.jdojo.script.Person");
var PersonExtender = Java.extend(Person);

// Extend the Person class and override the getFullName() method
var john = new PersonExtender("John", "Jacobs") {
        getFullName: function () {
                // You can use the variable john here that is declared outside.
                var _super_ = Java.super(john);
                var fullName = _super_.getFullName();
                return fullName.toUpperCase();
    }
}

// Get john's full name using the extended class implementation
var johnFullName = john.getFullName() ;

// Get the reference of john's super
var johnSuper = Java.super(john);
```

```
// Get john's full name from the Person class
var johnSuperFullName = johnSuper.getFullName();

// Print Names
print("Extended full name:", johnFullName);
print("Super full name:", johnSuperFullName);
```

```
Extended full name: JOHN JACOBS
Super full name: John Jacobs
```

Notice that the getFullName() method of the extended Person class refers to the variable named john that has been declared outside the function. The following statement assigns the reference of an object that can be used to call the methods of the superclass of the john object.

```
var _super_ = Java.super(john);
```

The overridden method calls the Person class' getFullName() method, converts the name to uppercase, and returns it. The code get the superclass reference again, as shown:

```
// Get the reference of john's super
var johnSuper = Java.super(john);
```

Finally, the code prints the returned value from the Person class and the extended Person class to show that you were really able to call the superclass method.

■ **Tip** Instead of using Java.super(obj) method to get the superclass object reference of obj and call methods on it, you can also use obj.super$MethodName(args) syntax to call the method of the superclass of the object named obj. For example, in the example, you could have used john.super$getFullName() to call the getFullName() method of the Person class on the object john.

Using Lambda Expressions

JavaScript supports anonymous functions that can be used as lambda expressions. The following is an anonymous function that takes a number as an argument and returns its square:

```
function (n) {
        return n * n;
}
```

The following is an example of creating a Runnable object in JavaScript using an anonymous function as a lambda expression. The Runnable object is used in the constructor of the Thread class.

```
var Thread = Java.type("java.lang.Thread");

// Create a Thread using a Runnable object. The Runnable object is
// created using an anonymous function as a lambda expressions.
var thread = new Thread(function () {
    print("Hello Thread");
});

// Start the thread
thread.start();
```

The Java equivalent of the JavaScript code using a lambda expression is as follows:

```
// Create a Thread using a Runnable object. The Runnable object is
// created using a lambda expression.
Thread thread = new Thread(() -> {
        System.out.println("Hello Thread");
});

// Start the thread
thread.start();
```

Summary

You will need to import Java types into scripts before you can use create objects of that Java in scripts. There are four ways to import a type in a script: using the Packages global object, using the Java.type() method, using the importPackage() and importClass() functions, and using JavaImporter in a with clause. Nashorn declares java, javax, org, com, edu, and net as global variables that are aliases for Packages.java, Packages.javax, Packages.org, Packages.com, Packages.edu, and Packages.net, respectively. Therefore, you can use the fully qualified names of any types in these packages to refer to the type.

You need to use the new operator along with the Java type to create Java objects in scripts. Using the Java.type() method lets you import the Java types including array type in uniform way. You can create an array object the same way you can create an object of any other type.

Most of the time, calling overloaded Java methods are resolved by Nashorn. If you want to call a specific version of an overloaded method from script, you can use the bracket notation to specify the specific method signature. For example, pt["print (java.lang.Object)"](10.5) calls the print(java.lang.Object) method on the object reference named pt passing 10.5 as the argument to the method.

Nashorn lets you extends interfaces, abstract classes, and concrete classes in scripts using the Java.extend() method. It lets you invoke the superclass methods on an object using the Java.super() method.

CHAPTER 7

■ ■ ■

Collections

In this chapter, you will learn:

- What arrays in Nashorn are
- How to create arrays in Nashorn using array literals and the Array object
- How to use different methods of the Array object
- How to work with array-like objects
- How to create and use typed arrays in Nashorn
- How to use Java collections in Nashorn
- How to create Java arrays in Nashorn
- How to convert Java arrays to Nashorn arrays and vice versa

What Is an Array in Nashorn?

An array in Nashorn is a specialized object, called an Array object, which is used to represent an ordered collection of values. An Array object treats certain property names in a special way. If a property name can be converted to an integer that is between 0 and $2^{32}-2$ (inclusive), such a property name is known as an array *index* and the property is known as an *element*. In other words, an element in an array is a special property whose name is an array index. Apart from adding elements to an array, you can add any other properties as you have been doing to Nashorn objects. Notice that, in an Array object, every array index is a property, but every property is not an array index. For example, you can add two properties named "0" and "name" to an array where "0" is an array index because it can be converted to an integer, whereas "name" is simply a property.

Every Array object has a property named length whose value is greater than the index of all elements. When elements are added, length is automatically adjusted. If length is changed, the elements whose indexes are greater than or equal to the new length are deleted. Note that, unlike Java arrays, Nashorn arrays are variable-length arrays. That is, Nashorn arrays are not fix-length arrays; they can expand and shrink when elements are added and removed, or the length property is changed.

211

There are two types of arrays: dense and sparse. In a dense array, the indexes of all elements are contiguous. Java arrays are always dense arrays. In a sparse array, indexes of all elements may not be contiguous. Nashorn arrays are sparse arrays. For example, you can have an array in Nashorn that has an element at index 1000 without having any elements from indexes 0 to 999.

Unlike in Java, arrays in Nashorn does not have a type. The elements in an array can be of mixed types—one element can be a Number, another a String, another an Object, and so on. Nashorn also supports typed-arrays, but they work quite differently than Java arrays. I will discuss typed arrays in the *Typed Arrays* section in this chapter.

Creating an Array

There are two ways to create an array in Nashorn:

- Using an array literal
- Using the Array object

Using an Array Literal

An *array literal* is an expression that represents an Array object. An array literal is also known as an *array initializer*. It is a comma-separated list of expressions enclosed in brackets; each expression in the list represents an element of the array. The following are examples of using array literals:

```
// An array with no elements, also called an empty array
var emptyArray = [];

// An array with two elements
var names = ["Ken", "Li"];

// An array with four element. Elements are of mixed types.
var misc = [1001, "Ken", 1003, new Object()];

// Print the array length and its elements
print("Array's length: " + emptyArray.length + ", elements: " + emptyArray);
print("Array's length: " + names.length + ", elements: " + names);
print("Array's length: " + misc.length + ", elements: " + misc);
```

```
Array's length: 0, elements:
Array's length: 2, elements: Ken,Li
Array's length: 4, elements: 1001,Ken,1003,[object Object]
```

Every Array object contains a toString() method that returns a comma-separated list of array elements as a string. Before adding to the list, each element is converted to a string. The toString() method of all arrays are called in the example to print their contents.

A trailing comma in the array literal is ignored. The following two array literals are considered the same. Both have three elements:

```
var empIds1 = [10, 20, 30];  // Without a trailing comma. empIds1.length is 3
var empIds2 = [10, 20, 30,]; // Same as [10, 20, 30]. empIds2.length is 3
```

The elements in the array literal are indexed properties of the array object. For a dense array, the first element is assigned an index of 0, the second an index of 1, the third an index of 3, and so on. I will discuss the indexing scheme for sparse arrays shortly. Consider the following dense array with three elements. Figure 7-1 shows the element's values and their indexes in the array.

```
var names = ["Fu", "Li", "Ho"]
```

Indexes	0	1	2
Values	Fu	Li	Ho

Figure 7-1. *Array elements and their indexes in a three-element dense array*

You can access the elements of an array the same way you access properties of an object. The only difference will be that the property name for the element is an integer. For example, in the names array, names[0] refers to the first element "Fu", names[1] refers to the second element "Li", and names[2] refers to the third element "Ho". The following code creates a dense array and uses a for loop to access and print all elements of the array:

```
// Create an array with three elements
var names = ["Fu", "Li", "Ho"]

// Print all array elements
for(var i = 0, len = names.length; i < len; i++) {
    print("names[" + i + "] = " + names[i]);
}
```

```
names[0] = Fu
names[1] = Li
names[2] = Ho
```

213

Adding an element to an array is the same as assigning a value at a nonexisting index. The following code creates an array with three elements and adds the fourth and fifth elements. Finally, the code prints all elements in the array:

```
// Create an array with three elements
var names = ["Fu", "Li", "Ho"]

// Add fourth element
names[3] = "Su"; // Adds an element at index 3

// Add fifth element
names[4] = "Bo"; // Adds an element at index 4

// Print all array elements
for(var i = 0, len = names.length; i < len; i++) {
    print("names[" + i + "] = " + names[i]);
}
```

```
names[0] = Fu
names[1] = Li
names[2] = Ho
names[3] = Su
names[4] = Bo
```

Recall that an array is an object, so you can add properties to an array just as you add properties to any other objects. If the property name is not an index, the property will be simply a property, not an element. A nonelement property does not contribute to length of the array. The following code creates an array, adds an element and a nonelement property, and prints the details:

```
// Create an array with three elements
var names = ["Fu", "Li", "Ho"]

// Add fourth element
names[3] = "Su"; // Adds an element at index 3

// Add a non-element property to the array. The property name is
// "nationality" that is not an index, so it does not define an element.
// Rather, it is a simply property.
names["nationality"] = "Chinese";

print("names.length = " + names.length);
```

```
// Print all array elements using a for loop
print("Using a for loop:");
for(var i = 0, len = names.length; i < len; i++) {
    print("names[" + i + "] = " + names[i]);
}

// Print all properties of the array using a for..in loop
print("Using a for..in loop:");
for(var prop in names) {
    print("names[" + prop + "] = " + names[prop]);
}
```

```
names.length = 4
Using a for loop:
names[0] = Fu
names[1] = Li
names[2] = Ho
names[3] = Su
Using a for..in loop:
names[0] = Fu
names[1] = Li
names[2] = Ho
names[3] = Su
names[nationality] = Chinese
```

Here are a few points to note about this example:

- It created an array with three elements with at indexes 0, 1, and 2. At this point, the length of the array is 3.

- It added an element with the value of "Su" at index 3. By adding this element, the length of the array is automatically increased to 4.

- It adds a property named "nationality." This property is simply a property, not an element, because its name is a string that is not convertible to an index. Adding this property does not affect the length of the array. That is, the length stays at 4.

- When it uses the for loop to print the array, the property named "nationality" is not printed because the code loops though the indexes, not all properties.

- When it uses the for..in loop all elements along with the "nationality" property is printed, because the for..in loop iterates over all properties of the object. This proves that all elements of an array are properties, but all properties are not elements.

Notice that a property name is considered an index if it can be converted to an integer between 0 and 2^{32}-2 (inclusive). The real test to check whether a property name is an index is to apply the following condition. Suppose property name is prop and it is a string. If the following expression returns true, the property name is an index; otherwise, it is just a property name:

```
ToString(ToUint32(prop)) = prop
```

Here, assume that ToUint32() is function to convert the property name to an unsigned 32-bit integer and ToString() is a function to convert the integer to a string. In other words, if a string property name converted to an unsigned 32-bit integer and back to a string results in the original property name, such a property name is an index. If the property name is simply a number in the valid range, it is an index if does not contain a fractional part. The following code demonstrates this rule:

```
// Create an array with two elements
var names = ["Fu", "Li"]

// Adds an element at the index 2
names[2.0] = "Su";

// Adds a property named "2.0", not an element at index 2
names["2.0"] = "Bo";

// Adds an element at index 3
names["3"] = "Do";

print("names.length = " + names.length);

// Print all properties of the array using a for..in loop
print("Using a for..in loop:");
for(var prop in names) {
    print("names[" + prop + "] = " + names[prop]);
}
```

```
names.length = 4
Using a for..in loop:
names[0] = Fu
names[1] = Li
names[2] = Su
names[3] = Do
names[2.0] = Bo
```

You can add a property to an array that is a negative number. Notice that a negative number as a property name does not qualify to be an index, so it will simply add a property, not an element:

```
// Create an array with two elements
var names = ["Fu", "Li"]

// Adds property with the name "-1", not an element.
names[-1] = "Do"; // names.length is still 2

print("names.length = " + names.length);
```

```
names.length = 2
```

You can also create a sparse array using an array literal. Using commas without specifying the elements in the element's list creates a sparse array. Note that in a sparse array, the index of elements are not contiguous. The following code creates a sparse array:

```
var names = ["Fu",,"Lo"];
```

The names array contains two elements. They are at index 0 and 2. The element at index 1 is missing and that is indicated by two consecutive commas. What is the length of the names array? It is 3, not 2. Recall that the length of an array is always greater than the maximum index of all elements. The maximum index in the array is 2, so the length is 3. What happens when you try reading names[1], which is a nonexisting element? Reading names[1] is simply treated as reading a property named "1" from the names object where the property named "1" does not exist. Recall from Chapter 4 that reading a non-existing property of an object returns undefined. Therefore, names[1] will simply return undefined, without causing any errors. If you assign a value to names[1], you are creating a new element at index 1 and the array will no longer be a sparse array. The following code shows this rule:

```
// Create a sparse array with 2 existing and 1 missing elements
var names = ["Fu",,"Lo"]; // names.length is 3
print("names.length = " + names.length);

for(var prop in names) {
    print("names[" + prop + "] = " + names[prop]);
}

// Add an element at index 1.
names[1] = "Do";  // names.length is still 3
```

```
print("names.length = " + names.length);
for(var prop in names) {
    print("names[" + prop + "] = " + names[prop]);
}
```

```
names.length = 3
names[0] = Fu
names[2] = Lo
names.length = 3
names[0] = Fu
names[1] = Do
names[2] = Lo
```

The following are more examples of sparse arrays. The comments explains the arrays:

```
var names = [,];      // A sparse array. length = 1 and no elements
names = [,,];         // A sparse array. length = 2 and no elements
names = [,,,];        // A sparse array. length = 3 and no elements
names = [,,,7,,2];    // A sparse array. length = 6 and 2 elements
```

Can you tell the difference between the following two arrays?

```
var names1 = [,,];
var names2 = [undefined,undefined];
```

Both arrays have length 2. The array named names1 is a sparse array. The elements at index 0 and 1 in names1 do not exist. Reading names1[0] and names1[1] will return undefined. The array named names2 is a dense array. The elements at index 0 and 1 in names2 exist and both are set to undefined. Reading names2[0] and names2[1] will return undefined.

How do you know whether an array is sparse? There is no built-in method in the Array object to check for a sparse array. You will need to check it yourself keeping in mind that if a property name that is an index (from 0 to length) does not exist in the array, it is a sparse array. I will discuss few ways to check for a sparse array in the section *Iterating Over Array Elements*.

Using the Array Object

Nashorn contains a built-in function object called Array. It is used to create and initialize an array. It can be called as a function or a constructor. Its use as a function or a constructor works the same way. Its signature is:

```
Array(arg1, arg2, arg3,...)
```

The `Array` object can take zero or more number of arguments. Its initialization behavior depends on the number and types of passed arguments that can be classified in three categories:

- No arguments are passed
- One argument is passed
- Two or more arguments are passed

Passing No Arguments

When no arguments are passed to the `Array` constructor, it creates an empty array, setting the `length` of the array to zero:

```
var names1 = new Array(); // Same as: var names = [];
```

Passing One Argument

When one argument is passed to the `Array` constructor, the type of the argument determines how the new array is created:

- If the argument is a Number and it is an integer in the range from 0 to $2^{32}-1$ (inclusive), the argument is considered the `length` of the array. Otherwise, a `RangeError` exception is throw.

- If the argument is not a Number, an array with the passed argument as the sole element of the array is created. The `length` of the array is set to 1.

The following code creates the biggest possible array in Nashorn:

```
var names = new Array(Math.pow(2, 32) -1); // The biggest possible array
print("names.length = " + names.length);
```

```
names.length = 4294967295
```

The following statement creates an array with `length` as 10. No elements exist in the array yet:

```
var names = new Array(10);
```

The following array creation expressions throws a `RangeError` exception, because the argument is a Number and it is either not an integer in the valid range or out of range:

```
var names1 = new Array(34.89);          // Not an integer
var names1 = new Array(Math.pow(2, 32)); // Out of range
var namess = new Array(-10);             // Out of range
```

The following code passes a nonnumeric argument to the Array constructor that creates an array with the passed argument as its sole element and sets the length of the array to 1:

```
var names1 = new Array("Fu"); // Creates an array with one element "Fu"
var names2 = new Array(true); // Creates an array with one element true
```

Passing Two or More Arguments

When two or more arguments are passed to the Array constructor, it creates a dense array with the specified arguments. The length is set to the number of arguments passed. The following statement creates an array with three passed arguments and sets the length to 3:

```
var names = new Array("Fu", "Li". "Do");
```

You cannot create a sparse array using the Array constructor. Using consecutive commas or trailing commas in the Array constructor throws a SyntaxError exception:

```
var names1 = new Array("Fu", "Li",, "Do");  // A SyntaxError
var names2 = new Array("Fu", "Li", "Do", ); // A SyntaxError
```

You can create a sparse array by adding elements at noncontiguous indexes or deleting the existing elements, so the indexes become noncontiguous. I will discuss deleting the elements of an array in the next section. The following code creates a dense array and adds a noncontiguous element to make it a sparse array:

```
// Creates a dense array with elements at indexes 0 and 1.
var names = new Array("Fu", "Li");  // names.length is set to 2

print("After creating the array: names.length = " + names.length);

// Add an element at index 4, skipping index 2 and 3.
names[4] = "Do"; // names.length is set to 5, making names a sparse array

print("After adding an element at index 4: names.length = " + names.length);

for(var prop in names) {
    print("names[" + prop + "] = " + names[prop]);
}
```

```
After creating the array: names.length = 2
After adding an element at index 4: names.length = 5
names[0] = Fu
names[1] = Li
names[4] = Do
```

Deleting Array Elements

Deleting an array element or nonelement properties of an array is the same as deleting properties of an object. Use the delete operator to delete an array element. If you delete an element from middle or beginning of a dense array, the array becomes sparse. The following code shows how to delete elements from an array:

```
// Creates a dense array with elements at indexes 0, 1, and 2.
var names = new Array("Fu", "Li", "Do");

print("Before deleting:");
print("names.length = " + names.length + ", Elements = " + names);

// Delete the element at index 1
delete names[1]; // names.length remains 3

print("AFter deleting:");
print("names.length = " + names.length + ", Elements = " + names);
```

```
Before deleting:
names.length = 3, Elements = Fu,Li,Do
AFter deleting:
names.length = 3, Elements = Fu,,Do
```

You can make elements of an array nonconfigurable and nonwritable, so they cannot be deleted and modified. Deleting a nonconfigurable element does not have any effect. In strict mode, deleting a nonconfigurable element generates an error. The following code demonstrates this:

```
var names = new Array("Fu", "Li", "Do");

// Make the element at index 1 non-configurable
Object.defineProperty(names, "1", {configurable: false});

print("Before deleting:");
print("names.length = " + names.length + ", Elements = " + names);

delete names[1]; // Will not delete "Li" as it is non-configurable.

print("AFter deleting:");
print("names.length = " + names.length + ", Elements = " + names);
```

```
Before deleting:
names.length = 3, Elements = Fu,Li,Do
AFter deleting:
names.length = 3, Elements = Fu,Li,Do
```

Length of an Array

Every Array object has a property named length that is maintained automatically when elements are added and removed from the array. The length property makes an array different from other types of objects. For a dense array, length is one more than the largest index in the array. For a sparse array, it is guaranteed to be greater than the largest index of all elements (existing and missing).

The length property of an array is writable. That is, you can also change it in code. If you set length to a value greater than the current value, length is changed to the new value, creating a sparse array towards the end. If you set length to a value less than its current value, all elements from the end are deleted until a nondeletable element is found that is greater than or equal to the new length value. That is, setting length to a smaller value make the array shrink up to a nondeletable element. The following examples will make this rule clear:

```
var names = new Array("Fu", "Li", "Do", "Ho");
print("names.length = " + names.length + ", Elements = " + names);

print("Setting length to 10...");
names.length = 10;
print("names.length = " + names.length + ", Elements = " + names);

print("Setting length to 0...");
names.length = 0;
print("names.length = " + names.length + ", Elements = " + names);

print("Recreating the array...");
names = new Array("Fu", "Li", "Do", "Ho");
print("names.length = " + names.length + ", Elements = " + names);

print('Making "Do" non-configurable...');
// Makes "Do" non-configurable (non-deletable)
Object.defineProperty(names, "2", {configurable:false});

print("Setting length to 0...");
names.length = 0; // Will delete only "Ho" as "Do" is non-deletable
print("names.length = " + names.length + ", Elements = " + names);
```

```
names.length = 4, Elements = Fu,Li,Do,Ho
Setting length to 10...
names.length = 10, Elements = Fu,Li,Do,Ho,,,,,,
Setting length to 0...
names.length = 0, Elements =
Recreating the array...
names.length = 4, Elements = Fu,Li,Do,Ho
Making "Do" non-configurable...
Setting length to 0...
names.length = 3, Elements = Fu,Li,Do
```

The `length` property of an `Array` object is writable, nonenumerable, and nonconfigurable. If you do not want someone to change it in code, you can make it nonwritable. The nonwritable `length` property will still be automatically changed when you add and remove elements from the array. The following code shows this rule:

```
var names = new Array("Fu", "Li", "Do", "Ho");

// Make the length property non-writable.
Object.defineProperty(names, "length", {writable:false});

// The length property cannot be changed directly anymore
names.length = 0; // No effects

// Add a new element
names[4] = "Nu"; // names.length changes from 4 to 5
```

Iterating Over Array Elements

If you are interested in iterating all properties, including elements, of an array, you can simply use the `for..in` and `for..each..in` statements. These statements are not supposed to iterate arrays in any specific order. As the title of this section suggests, I am going to discuss how to iterate over only the elements of arrays, particularly when arrays are sparse. If you add only elements to an array (not any nonelement properties), which you will do in most cases, using the `for..in` and `for..each..in` statements work fine for both dense and sparse.

Using the for Loop

If you know that the array is dense, you can use the simple `for` loop to iterate the array, like so:

```
// Create a dense array
var names = new Array("Fu", "Li", "Do");

// Use a for loop to iterate all elements of an array
for(var i = 0, len = names.length; i < len; i++) {
        print("names[" + i + "]=" + names[i]);
}
```

```
names[0]=Fu
names[1]=Li
names[2]=Do
```

The for loop does not work if you have a sparse array. If you try accessing the missing elements in the sparse array, it will return undefined that does not tell you whether the element is missing or the value for the existing element is undefined. You can get rid of this limitation by using the in operator to check if the index being iterated exists. If the index exists, the element exists; if the index does not exist, it is a missing element in a sparse array. The following code demonstrates this approach:

```
// Create a sparse array with an element set to undefined
var names = ["Fu", "Li", , "Do", undefined, , "Lu"];

// Use a for lop to iterate all elements of an array
for (var i = 0, len = names.length; i < len; i++) {
        // Check if the index being visited exists in the array
        if (i in names) {
                print("names[" + i + "]=" + names[i]);
        }
}
```

```
names[0]=Fu
names[1]=Li
names[3]=Do
names[4]=undefined
names[6]=Lu
```

Consider the following code. It creates a sparse array with only one element. The array is the biggest possible array in Nashorn and the element is added at the last index in the array. In practice, you will never have this big array. I used it just to prove the point that using the for loop is not the most efficient way to access all elements in a sparse array:

```
// Create an empty array
var names = new Array();

// Add one element to the end of the biggest possible  array
names[4294967294] = "almost lost";

// Use a for loop to iterate all elements of an array
for (var i = 0, len = names.length; i < len; i++) {
        // Check if the index being visited exists in the array
        if (i in names) {
                print("names[" + i + "]=" + names[i]);
        }
}
```

Using the `for` loop in this example is very inefficient, because it has to visit 4294967293 indexes, before it can get to the last one that has the value. It takes too long to get to just one element of the array. I will solve this slow performing `for` loop problem shortly using the `for..in` loop.

Using the forEach() Method

The `Array.prototype` object contains a method named `forEach()` that invokes a callback function for each element in the array in ascending order. It visits only the existing elements in the sparse array. Its signature is:

```
forEach (callbackFunc [, thisArg])
```

Here, `callbackFunc` is a function that is called once for each element in the array in ascending order. It is passed three arguments: the value of the element, the index of the element, and the object being iterated. The `thisArg` is optional; if it is specified, it is used as the `this` value for each invocation to `callbackFunc`.

The `forEach()` method sets the range of indexes it will visit before it starts executing. If elements are added beyond that range during its execution, those elements are not visited. If elements in the initially set range are deleted, those elements are not visited either:

```
// Create a sparse array with an element set to undefined
var names = ["Fu", "Li", , "Do", undefined, , "Lu"];

// Define the callback function
var visitor = function (value, index, array) {
        print("names[" + index + "]=" + value);
};

// Print all elements
names.forEach(visitor);
```

```
names[0]=Fu
names[1]=Li
names[3]=Do
names[4]=undefined
names[6]=Lu
```

If you use the `forEach()` method to visit a big sparse array, you will have the same problem as using the `for` loop that I discussed in the previous section.

Using the for-in Loop

Let us solve the inefficiency in accessing the elements in long sparse array using the `for..in` loop. Using the `for..in` loop brings in another problem that it iterates over all properties of the array, not just the elements. It does not iterate over the missing elements though. You will need a way to differentiate between a simple property and an existing element. You can do this by simply using the definition of an array index. An array index is an integer between 0 and 2^{32}-2. If the property is an array index, it is an element; otherwise, it is simply a property, not an element. Listing 7-1 contains the code for a function named isValidArrayIndex(). The function takes a property name as an argument. It returns true if the property name is a valid array index; otherwise, it returns false.

Listing 7-1. The Code for the isValidArrayIndex( ) Function

```
// arrayutil.js

var UPPER_ARRAY_INDEX = Math.pow(2, 32) - 2;
Object.defineProperty(this, "UPPER_ARRAY_INDEX", {writable: false});

function isValidArrayIndex(prop) {
        // Convert the prop to a Number
        var numericProp = Number(prop);

        // Check if prop is a number
        if (String(numericProp) === prop) {
                // Check if is an integer
                if (Math.floor(numericProp) === numericProp) {
                        // Check if it is in the valid array index range
                        if (numericProp >= 0 &&
                            numericProp <= UPPER_ARRAY_INDEX) {
                                return true;
                        }
                }
        }

        return false;
}
```

The following code uses the `for..in` loop to iterate over only the elements of a sparse array. It makes use of the isValidArrayIndex() function to determine if a property is a valid array index. Note that the code adds an element at the largest possible index in the array. The `for..in` loop gets to all elements of the array very quickly.

```
// load the script that contains isValidArrayIndex() function
load("arrayutil.js");

// Create a sparse array with an element set to undefined
var names = ["Fu", "Li", , "Do", undefined, , "Lu"];

// Add some properties to the array
names["nationality"] = "Chinese"; // A property
names[4294967294] = "almost lost"; // An element at the largest
                                   // possible array index
names[3.2] = "3.2";   // A property
names[7.00] = "7.00"; // An element

// Print all elements, ignoring the non-element properties
for(var prop in names) {
        if (isValidArrayIndex(prop)) {
                // It is an element
                print("names[" + prop + "]=" + names[prop]);
        }
}
```

```
names[0]=Fu
names[1]=Li
names[3]=Do
names[4]=undefined
names[6]=Lu
names[7]=7.00
names[4294967294]=almost lost
```

Checking for an Array

The Array object contains an isArray() static method that can be used to check whether an object is an array. The following code demonstrates its use:

```
var obj1 = [10, 20];     // An array
var obj2 = {x:10, y:20}; // An object, but not an array
print("Array.isArray(obj1) =",  Array.isArray(obj1));
print("Array.isArray(obj2) =",  Array.isArray(obj2));
```

```
Array.isArray(obj1) = true
Array.isArray(obj2) = false
```

Multidimensional Arrays

Nashorn does have any special construct to support multidimensional arrays. You need to use an array of arrays (a zagged array) to create a multidimensional arrays in which elements of an array can be arrays. Typically, you will need nested for loops to populate and access the elements of a multidimensional array. The following code demonstrates how to create, populate, and print the elements of a 3x3 matrix. The code uses the join() method of the Array object to concatenate elements of the array using a tab as a separator:

```
var ROWS = 3;
var COLS = 3;

// Create a 3x3 array, so you pre-allocate the memory
var matrix = new Array(ROWS);
for(var i = 0; i < ROWS; i++) {
        matrix[i] = new Array(COLS);
}

// Populate the array
for(var i = 0; i < ROWS; i++) {
        for(var j = 0; j < COLS; j++) {
                matrix[i][j] = i + "" + j;
        }
}

// Print the array elements
for(var i = 0; i < ROWS; i++) {
        var rowData = matrix[i].join("\t");
        print(rowData);
}
```

```
00      01      02
10      11      12
20      21      22
```

Methods of the Array Object

The Array.prototype object defines several methods that are available as an instance methods for all Array objects. In this section, I will discuss those methods. All array methods are intentionally generic, so they can be applied to not just arrays but to any array-like objects.

Concatenating Elements

The concat(arg1, arg2,...) method creates and returns a new array that contains the elements of the array object on which the method is invoked followed by the specified arguments in order. If an argument is an array, the array's elements are concatenated. If an argument is a nested array, it is flattened one level. The original array and arrays passed as arguments are not modified by this method. If the original array or arguments contain objects, a shallow copy of objects is made. Examples of using the concat() method are as follows:

```
var names = ["Fu", "Li"];

// Assigns ["Fu", "Li", "Do", "Su"] to names2
var names2 = names.concat("Do", "Su");

// Assigns ["Fu", "Li", "Do", "Su", ["Lu", "Zu"], "Yu"] to names3
var names3 = names.concat("Do", ["Su", ["Lu","Zu"]], "Yu");
```

Joining Array Elements

The join(separator) method converts all elements of the array to Strings, concatenates them using separator, and returns the resulting string. If separator is unspecified, a comma is used as the separator. The method works on all elements of the array starting from the index 0 to the index equal to length - 1. If an element is undefined or null, the empty string is used. Here are some examples of using the join() method:

```
var names = ["Fu", "Li", "Su"];
var namesList1 = names.join();     // Assigns "Fu,Li,Su" to namesList1
var namesList2 = names.join("-"); // Assigns "Fu-Li-Su" to namesList2

var ids = [10, 20, , 30, undefined, 40, null]; // A sparse array
var idsList1 = ids.join();     // Assigns "10,20,,30,,40," to idsList1
var idsList2 = ids.join("-"); // Assigns "10-20--30--40-" to idsList2
```

Reversing Array Elements

The reverse() method rearranges the elements of the array in reverse order and returns the array. Examples of using this method are as follows:

```
var names = ["Fu", "Li", "Su"];
names.reverse(); // Now, the names array contains ["Su","Li","Fu"]

// Assigns "Fu,Li,Su" to reversedList
var reversedList = names.reverse().join();
```

Slicing an Array

The slice(start, end) method returns an array containing a subarray of the original array from index between start and end (exclusive). If start and end are negative, they are treated as start + length and end + length, respectively, where length is the length of the array. Both start and end are capped between 0 and length (inclusive). If end is unspecified, it is assumed as length. If start and end (exclusive) include a sparse range, the resulting subarray will be sparse. Here are examples of using the slice() method:

```
var names = ["Fu", "Li", "Su"];

// Assigns ["Li","Su"] to subNames1. end = 5 will be replaced with end = 3.
var subNames1 = names.slice(1, 5);

// Assigns ["Li","Su"] to subNames2. start = -1 is used as start = 1 (-2 + 3).
var subNames12 = names.slice(-2, 3);

var ids = [10, 20,,,30, 40, 40]; // A sparse array

// Assigns [20,,,30,40] to idsSubList whose length = 5
var idsSubList = ids.slice(1, 6);
```

Splicing an Array

The splice() method can perform insertion, deletion, or both, depending on the arguments passed. Its signature is:

```
splice (start, deleteCount, value1, value2,...)
```

The method deletes deleteCount elements starting at index start and inserts the specified arguments (value1, value2, etc.) at index start. It returns an array that contains the deleted elements from the original array. The indexes of the existing elements after the deletion, insertion, or both are adjusted, so they are contiguous. If deleteCount is 0, specified values are inserted without deleting any elements. Here are examples of using the method:

```
var ids = [10, 20, 30, 40, 50];

// Replace 10 and 20 in the array with 100 and 200
var deletedIds  = ids.splice(1, 2, 100, 200);

print("ids = " + ids);
print("deletedIds = " + deletedIds);
```

```
// Keep the first 3 elements and delete the rest
var deletedIds2  = ids.splice(3, 2);

print("ids = " + ids);
print("deletedIds2 = " + deletedIds2);
```

```
ids = 10,100,200,40,50
deletedIds = 20,30
ids = 10,100,200
deletedIds2 = 40,50
```

Sorting an Array

The sort(compareFunc) method sorts the array in place and returns the sorted array. The compareFunc argument, which is a function with two arguments, is optional. If it is not specified, the array is sorted in alphabetical order, converting the elements to strings, if necessary, during comparison. Undefined elements are sorted to the end.

If compareFunc is specified, it is passed two elements and its returns value determines the order of the two elements. Suppose that it is passed x and y. It returns a negative value if x < y, zero if x = y, and a positive value if x > y. The following code sorts an integer array in ascending order by not specifying a compareFunc. Later, it sorts the same array in descending order by specifying a compareFunc:

```
var ids = [30, 10, 40, 20];
print("ids = " + ids);

// Sort the array
ids.sort();

print("Sorted ids = " + ids);

// A comparison function to sort ids in descending order
var compareDescending = function (x, y) {
        if (x > y) {
                return -1;
        }
        else if (x < y) {
                return 1;
        }
        else {
                return 0;
        }
};
```

```
ids.sort(compareDescending);
print("Sorted in descending order, ids = " + ids);
```

```
ids = 30,10,40,20
Sorted ids = 10,20,30,40
Sorted in descending order, ids = 40,30,20,10
```

Adding and Removing Elements at Ends

The following four methods let you add and remove elements at the beginning and end of an array:

- unshift(value1, value2,...): The unshift() method prepends the arguments to the array, so they appear in the beginning of the array in the same order they appear as arguments. It returns the new length of the array. Indexes of the existing elements are adjusted to make room for new elements.

- shift(): The shift() method removes and returns the first element of the array, shifting all other elements one position to the left.

- push(value1, value2,...): The push() method works the same as the unshift() method, except that it adds elements at the end of the array.

- pop(): The pop() method works the same as the shift() method, except it removes and returns the last element of the array

Here are examples of using these methods:

```
var ids = [10, 20, 30];
print("ids: " + ids);

ids.unshift(100, 200, 300);
print("After ids.unshift(100, 200, 300): " + ids);

ids.shift();
print("After ids.shift(): " + ids);

ids.push(1, 2, 3);
print("After ids.push(1, 2, 3): " + ids);

ids.pop();
print("After ids.pop(): " + ids);
```

```
ids: 10,20,30
After ids.unshift(100, 200, 300): 100,200,300,10,20,30
After ids.shift(): 200,300,10,20,30
After ids.push(1, 2, 3): 200,300,10,20,30,1,2,3
After ids.pop(): 200,300,10,20,30,1,2
```

Using these methods, you can implement a stack, a queue, and a doubly-ended queue. Let us implement a stack using the push() and pop() methods. Listing 7-2 contains the code for the Stack object. It holds the stack's data in a private Array object. It provides isEmpty(), push(), pop(), and peek() methods to perform stack operations. It override the toString() method of the Object.prototype to return the current elements in the stack as a string. Listing 7-3 contains the code to test the Stack object.

Listing 7-2. A Stack Object Declaration

```javascript
// stack.js

// Define the constructor for the Stack object
function Stack(/*varargs*/) {
        // Define a private array to keep the stack elements
        var data = new Array();

        // If any arguments were passed to the constructor, add them to the stack
        for (var i in arguments) {
                data.push(arguments[i]);
        }

        // Define methods
        this.isEmpty = function () {
                return (data.length === 0);
        };
        this.pop = function () {
                if (this.isEmpty()) {
                        throw new Error("Stack is empty.");
                }

                return data.pop();
        };
        this.push = function (arg) {
                data.push(arg);
                return arg;
        };
```

```
        this.peek = function () {
                if (this.isEmpty()) {
                        throw new Error("Stack is empty.");
                }
                else {
                        return data[data.length - 1];
                }
        };
        this.toString = function () {
                return data.toString();
        };
}
```

Listing 7-3. Testing the Stack Object

```
// stacktest.js

load("stack.js");

// Create a Stack with initial 2 elements
var stack = new Stack(10, 20);

print("Stack = " + stack);

// Push an element
stack.push(40);

print("After push(40), Stack = " + stack);

// Pop two elements
stack.pop();
stack.pop();

print("After 2 pops, Stack = " + stack);

print("stack.peek() = " + stack.peek());
print("stack.isEmpty() = " + stack.isEmpty());

// Pop the last element
stack.pop();
print("After another pop(), stack.isEmpty() = " + stack.isEmpty());
```

```
Stack = 10,20
After push(40), Stack = 10,20,40
After 2 pops, Stack = 10
stack.peek() = 10
stack.isEmpty() = false
After another pop(), stack.isEmpty() = true
```

Searching an Array

Two methods, indexOf() and lastIndexOf(), let you search an array for a specified element. Their signatures are:

- indexOf(searchElement, fromIndex)

- lastIndexOf(searchElement, fromIndex)

The indexOf() method searches for the specified searchElement in the array starting at fromIndex. If fromIndex is not specified, 0 is assumed, meaning that the entire array is searched. The method returns the index of the first element in the array that is equal to the searchElement using the === operator. If the searchElement is not found, -1 is returned.

The lastIndexOf() method works the same as the indexOf() method, except that it performs the search from the end to the beginning. That is, it returns the index of the last found element in the array that is equal to the searchElement. The following code shows how to use these methods:

```
var ids = [10, 20, 30, 20];
print("ids = " + ids);
print("ids.indexOf(20) = " + ids.indexOf(20));
print("ids.indexOf(20, 2) = " + ids.indexOf(20, 2));
print("ids.lastIndexOf(20) = " + ids.lastIndexOf(20));
print("ids.indexOf(25) = " + ids.lastIndexOf(25));
```

```
ids = 10,20,30,20
ids.indexOf(20) = 1
ids.indexOf(20, 2) = 3
ids.lastIndexOf(20) = 3
ids.indexOf(25) = -1
```

Evaluating Predicates

You can check if a predicate evaluates to true for all or some of the elements in an array. The following two methods let you perform this:

- every(predicate, thisArg)

- some(predicate, thisArg)

The first argument, predicate, is a function that is called once for every existing elements in the array. The function is passed three arguments: the value of the element, the index of the element, and the array object. The second argument, thisArg, if specified, is used as the this value for the function invocation specified by predicate.

The every() method returns true if the specified predicate function returns a truthy value for every existing elements in the array. Otherwise, it returns false. The method returns false as soon as predicate returns a falsy value for an element.

The some() method returns true if predicate returns a truthy value for at least one element. Otherwise, it returns false. The method returns true as soon as predicate returns a truthy value for an element. The following example shows how to check if an array of numbers contains any/all even/odd numbers:

```
var ids = [10, 20, 30, 20];
print("ids = " + ids);

var hasAnyEven = ids.some(function (value, index, array) {
                    return value %2 === 0;
                });
var hasAllEven = ids.every(function (value, index, array) {
                    return value %2 === 0;
                });
var hasAnyOdd = ids.some(function (value, index, array) {
                    return value %2 === 1;
                });
var hasAllOdd = ids.every(function (value, index, array) {
                    return value %2 === 1;
                });
print("ids has any even numbers: " + hasAnyEven);
print("ids has all even numbers: " + hasAllEven);
print("ids has any odd numbers: " + hasAnyOdd);
print("ids has all odd numbers: " + hasAllOdd);
```

```
ids = 10,20,30,20
ids has any even numbers: true
ids has all even numbers: true
ids has any odd  numbers: false
ids has all odd  numbers: false
```

Converting an Array to a String

You can convert an array to a string in any way you want. However, the `toString()` and `toLocaleString()` methods provide two built-in implementations to convert the array elements to a string. The `toString()` method returns a string that is returned by calling the `join()` method on the array without specifying any separator. That is, it returns the list of elements as a string where elements are separated by commas. The `toLocaleString()` method calls the `toLocaleString()` method of all array elements, concatenates the returned strings using a local-specific separator and return the final string. You have been using the `toString()` method of the `Array` object whenever you used the array object as an argument to the `print()` method or used it with the string concatenation operator.

Stream-Like Processing of Arrays

Java 8 introduced the Streams API that lets you process Java collections as stream using several patterns such as map-filter-reduce. The `Array` object in Nashorn provides methods to apply stream-like processing to arrays. Such methods are:

- `map()`
- `filter()`
- `reduce()`
- `reduceRight()`
- `forEach()`
- `some()`
- `every()`

I have already discussed the last three methods in detail in previous section. I will discuss other methods in this section.

The `map()` method maps elements of an array to another values and returns a new array containing the mapped values. The original array is not modified. Its signature is:

```
map(callback, thisArg)
```

The first argument, `callback`, is a function that is called for each element in the array; the function is passed three arguments: the value of the element, the index of the element, and the array itself. The returned value from the function is the element of the new (mapped) array. The second argument is used as the `this` value in the function invocation. The following is an example of using the `map()` method. It maps each element of a number array to their squares:

```
var nums = [1, 2, 3, 4, 5];

// Map each element in the nums array to their squares
var squaredNums = nums.map(function (value, index, data) value * value);

print(nums);
print(squaredNums);
```

```
1,2,3,4,5
1,4,9,16,25
```

The `filter()` method returns a new array containing the elements of the original array that pass a predicate. Its signature is:

```
filter(callback, thisArg)
```

The first argument, `callback`, is a function that is called for each element in the array; the function is passed three arguments: the value of the element, the index of the element, and the array itself. If the function returns a truthy value, the element is included in the returned array; otherwise, the element is excluded. The second argument is used as the `this` value in the function invocation. The following code shows how to use the `filter()` method to filter out even numbers from an array:

```
var nums = [1, 2, 3, 4, 5];

// Filter out even numbers, keep odd numbers only
var oddNums = nums.filter(function (value, index, data) (value % 2 !== 0));

print(nums);
print(oddNums);
```

```
1,2,3,4,5
1,3,5
```

The reduce() method applies a reduction operation on the array, reducing it to a single value such as computing the sum of all elements in a number array. It returns a computed value. Its signature is:

```
reduce(callback, initialValue)
```

The first argument, callback, is a function that is called with four arguments: the previous value, the current value, the current index, and the array itself.
If initialValue is unspecified:

- For the first call to callback, the first element of the array is passed as the previous value and the second element as the current value; the index of the second element is passed as the index

- For subsequent calls to callback, the value returned from the previous call is passed as the previous value. The current value and index are the value and index of the current element

If initialValue is specified:

- For the first call to callback, initialValue is passed as the previous value and the first element as the current value; the index of the first element is passed as the index

- For subsequent calls to callback, the value returned from the previous call is passed as the previous value; the current value and index are the value and index of the current element

The reduceRight() method works the same as the reduce() method, except that it processes the elements of the array from end to start. The following code shows how to use the reduce() and reduceRight() methods to compute the sum of all numbers in an array and to join elements of a string array:

```
var nums = [1, 2, 3, 4, 5];

// Defines a reducer function to compute sum of elements of an array
var sumReducer = function(previous, current, index, data) {
        return previous + current;
};

var sum = nums.reduce(sumReducer);
print("Numbers :" + nums);
print("Sum: " + sum);

// Defines a reducer function to concatenate elements of an array
var concatReducer = function(previous, current, index, data) {
        return previous + "-" + current;
};
```

```
var names = ["Fu", "Li", "Su"];
var namesList = names.reduce(concatReducer);
var namesListRight = names.reduceRight(concatReducer);

print("Names: " + names);
print("Names Reduced List: " + namesList);
print("Names Reduced Right List: " + namesListRight);
```

```
Numbers :1,2,3,4,5
Sum: 15
Names: Fu,Li,Su
Names Reduced List: Fu-Li-Su
Names Reduced Right List: Su-Li-Fu
```

You can also chain these methods to perform complex processing on arrays. The following code shows how to compute the sum of squares of all positive odd numbers in an array in one statement:

```
var nums = [-2, 1, 2, 3, 4, 5, -11];

// Compute the sum of squares of all positive odd numbers
var sum = nums.filter(function (value, index, data) value > 0 && value % 2
!== 0)
                .map(function (value, index, data) value * value)
                .reduce(function (prev, curr, index, data) prev + curr, 0);

print("Numbers: " + nums);
print("Sum of squares of positive odd elements: " + sum);
```

```
Numbers: -2,1,2,3,4,5,-11
Sum of squares of positive odd elements: 35
```

Array-Like Objects

Arrays have two features that make them distinct from regular objects:

- It has a length property

- Its elements have special property names that are integers

You can define any object with these two characteristics and call them array-like objects. The following code defines an object named list that is an array-like object:

```
// Creates an array-like object
var list = {"0":"Fu", "1":"Su", "2":"Li", length:3};
```

Nashorn contains few array-like objects such as the String and arguments objects. Most of the methods in the Array.prototype object are generic, meaning that they can be invoked on any array-like objects, not necessarily only on arrays. The following code shows how to call the join() method of the Array.prototype object on an array-like object:

```
// An array-like object
var list = {"0":"Fu", "1":"Su", "2":"Li", length:3};

var joinedList = Array.prototype.join.call(list, "-");
print(joinedList);
```

```
Fu-Su-Li
```

The String object is also an array-like object. It maintains a read-only length property and each character has an index as its property name. You can perform the following array-like operations on strings:

```
// A String obejct
var str = new String("ZIP");

print("str[0] = " + str[0]);
print("str[1] = " + str[1]);
print("str[2] = " + str[2]);
print('str["length"] = ' + str["length"]);
```

You could have achieved the same results using the charAt() and length() methods of the String object. The following code converts a string to uppercase, removes vowels of English alphabets, and joins all characters using a hyphen as the separator. All are done using the methods on the Array.prototype object as if the string is an array of characters:

```
// A String object
var str = new String("Nashorn");

// Use the map-filter-reduce patern on the string
var newStr = Array.prototype.map.call(str, (function (v, i, d)
v.toUpperCase()))
    .filter(function (v, i, d) (v !== "A" && v !== 'E' && v !== 'I' && v !==
'O' && v !== 'U'))
    .reduce(function(prev, cur, i, data) prev + "-" + cur);
print("Original string: " + str);
print("New string: " + newStr);
```

```
Original string: Nashorn
New string: N-S-H-R-N
```

Typed Arrays

Typed arrays in Nashorn are array-like objects. They provide views of raw binary data called the *buffer*. You can have multiple typed views of the same buffer. Suppose you have a buffer of 4 bytes. You can have an 8-bit signed integer typed array view of the buffer that will represent four 8-bit signed integers. At the same time, you can have a 32-bit unsigned integer typed array view of the same buffer that can represent one 32-bit unsigned integer.

■ **Tip** A typed array is an array-like object providing a typed view of raw binary data in memory. The specification for typed arrays implementation in Nashorn can be found at `https://www.khronos.org/registry/typedarray/specs/latest/`.

The buffer in a typed array is represented by an ArrayBuffer object. Using an ArrayBuffer object directly or indirectly, you can create a typed array view. Once you have a typed array view, you can write or read data of the specific type supported by the typed array view, using the array-like syntax. In the next section, I will discuss how to work with ArrayBuffer objects. In the subsequent sections, I will discuss different types of typed array views (or simply called typed arrays).

The ArrayBuffer Object

An ArrayBuffer object represents a fixed-length buffer of raw binary data. The contents of an ArrayBuffer does not have a type. You cannot directly modify the data in an ArrayBuffer; you must create and use one of the typed views on it to do so. It contains few properties and methods to copy its contents into another ArrayBuffer and to query its size.

The ArrayBuffer constructor takes one argument that is the length of the buffer in bytes. The length of an ArrayBuffer object cannot be changed, after it is created. The object has a read-only property named byteLength that represents the length of the buffer. The following statement creates a buffer of 32 bytes and prints its length:

```
// Create a ArrayBuffer of 32 bytes
var buffer = new ArrayBuffer(32);

// Assigns 32 to len
var len = buffer.byteLength;
```

■ **Tip** When you create an ArrayBuffer, its contents are initialized to zero. There is no way to initialize its contents with values other than zero, at the time of creation. Each byte in the ArrayBuffer uses a zero-based index. The first byte has indexed 0, second 1, third 2, and so on.

The specification for typed array implemented by Nashorn contains an isView(args) static method in the ArrayBuffer object. However, it does not seem to be implemented by Nashorn in Java 8u40. A bug has been filed at https://bugs.openjdk.java.net/browse/JDK-8061959. The method returns true if the specified argument represents an array buffer view. For example, if you pass an object like Int8Array, Int16Array, DataView, and so on to this method, it returns true, because these objects represent an array buffer view. If you pass a simple object or a primitive value to this method, it returns false. The following code shows how to use this method. Note that as of Java 8u40, this method does not exist in Nashorn and the code will throw an exception:

```
// Creates an array buffer view of length 4
var int8View = new Int8Array(4);

// Assigns true to isView1
var isView1 = ArrayBuffer.isView(int8View);

// Assigns false to isView2
var isView2 = ArrayBuffer.isView({});
```

The ArrayBuffer object contains a slice(start, end) method that creates and returns a new ArrayBuffer whose contents are a copy of the original ArrayBuffer from the index start, inclusive, up to end, exclusive. If start or end is negative, it refers to an index from the end of the buffer. If end is unspecified, it defaults to the byteLength property of the ArrayBuffer. Both start and end are clamped between 0 and byteLength–1. The following code shows how to use the slice() method:

```
// Create an ArrayBuffer of 4 bytes. Bytes have indexes 0, 1, 2, and 3
var buffer = new ArrayBuffer(4);

// Manipulate buffer using one of the typed views here...

// Copy the last 2 bytes from buffer to buffer2
var buffer2 = buffer.slice(2, 4);

// Copy the bytes from buffer from index 1 to the end (last 3 bytes)
// to buffer3
var buffer3 = buffer.slice(1);
```

Views of an ArrayBuffer

There are two types of views of an ArrayBuffer:

- Typed Array Views
- DataView Views

Typed Arrays

Typed array views are array-like objects that deal with a specific type of values such as 32-bit signed integers. They provides a means to read and write the specific type of data to the ArrayBuffer. In a typed array view, all data values are of the same size. Table 7-1 contains the list of typed array views, their sizes and descriptions. The size in the table is the size of one element of the typed array view. For example, Int8Array contains elements that are 1 byte in length each. You can think of the Int8Array as a byte array type in Java, the Int16Array as the short array type in Java, and Int32Array as the int array type in Java.

Table 7-1. *The List of Typed Array Views, Their Sizes, and Descriptions*

Typed Array View	Size in Byte	Description
Int8Array	1	8-bit 2's complement signed integer
Uint8Array	1	8-bit unsigned integer
Uint8ClampedArray	1	8-bit unsigned integer (clamped)
Int16Array	2	16-bit 2's complement signed integer
Uint16Array	2	16-bit unsigned integer
Int32Array	4	32-bit 2's complement signed integer
Uint32Array	4	32-bit unsigned integer
Float32Array	4	32-bit IEEE floating point
Float64Array	8	64-bit IEEE floating point

■ **Tip** A typed array is a fixed-length, dense array-like object, whereas an Array object is a variable-length array that may be sparse or dense.

Let us differentiate between two array types: Uint8Array and Uint8ClampedArray. Elements in both arrays contain 8-bit unsigned integers ranging from 0 to 255. Uint8Array uses modulo 256 to store values in the array whereas Uint8ClampedArray clamps the values between 0 and 255 (inclusive). For example, if you store 260 in a UInt8array, 4 is stored because 260 modulo 256 is 4. If you store 260 in a Uint8ClampedArray, 255 is stored because 260 is greater than 255 and the upper limit is clamped at 255. Similarly, storing -2 stores 254 in a Uint8Array and 0 in a Uint8ClampedArray.

Each of the typed array view object defined the following two properties:

- BYTES_PER_ELEMENT
- name

The BYTES_PER_ELEMENT property contains the size of the elements of the types array in bytes. Its value for a view type is the same as in the "Size in Bytes" column in Table 0-1. The name property contains a string that is the name of the view and it is the same as the "Typed array View" column in the table. For example, Int16Array.BYTES_PR_ELEMNET is 2 and Int16Array.name is "Int16Array".

All typed array views provide four constructors. The following are four constructors for Int8Array. You can replace the name Int8Array with the name of other typed array views to get their constructors:

- Int8Array(arrayBuffer, byteOffset, elementCount)

- Int8Array(length)

- Int8Array(typedArray)

- Int8Array(arrayObject)

The first constructor creates a typed array view from an ArrayBuffer. You can create a full or a partial view of the specified ArrayBuffer. If byteOffset and elementCount are unspecified, it creates a full view of the ArrayBuffer. byteOffset is the byte offset in the buffer from beginning and the elementCount is the number of elements of the array that will occupy the buffer.

The second constructor takes the length of the typed array an argument and creates an ArrayBuffer of the appropriate size and returns a view of the full ArrayBuffer.

The third and fourth constructors let you create a typed array from another typed array and an Array object; the contents of the new typed array are initialized from the contents of the specified array. A new ArrayBuffer of the appropriate size to hold the copied contents is created.

The following code shows how to create Int8Array objects (arrays of bytes) using different constructors:

```
// Create an ArrayBuffer of 8 bytes
var buffer = new ArrayBuffer(8);

// Create an Int8Array that is a full view of buffer
var fullView = new Int8Array(buffer);

// Create an Int8Array that is the first half view of buffer
var firstHalfView = new Int8Array(buffer, 0, 4);

// Create an Int8Array that is the copy of the firstHalfView array
var copiedView = new Int8Array(firstHalfView);

// Create an Int8Array using elements from an Array object
var ids = new Int8Array([10, 20, 30]);
```

All typed array objects have the following properties:

- length: It is the number of elements in the array
- byteLength: It is the length of the array in bytes
- buffer: It is the reference of the underlying ArrayBuffer object used by the typed array
- byteOffset: It is the offset in bytes from the start of its ArrayBuffer

Once you create a typed array, you can use it as a simple array object. You can set and read its elements using the bracket notation using indexes. If you set a value that is not of the type of the typed array type, the value is converted appropriately. For example, setting 23.56 to an element in an Int8Array will set 23 as the value. The following code shows how to read and write contents of a typed array:

```
// Create an Int8Array of 3 elements. Each element is an 8-bit sign integer.
var ids = new Int8Array(3);

// Populate the array
ids[0] = 10;
ids[1] = 20.89; // 20 will be stored
ids[2] = 140;   // -116 is stored as byte's range is -128 to 127.

// Read the elements
print("ids[0] = " + ids[0]);
print("ids[1] = " + ids[1]);
print("ids[2] = " + ids[2]);
```

```
ids[0] = 10
ids[1] = 20
ids[2] = -116
```

The following code creates an Int32Array from an Array object and reads all elements:

```
// An Array object
var ids = [10, 20, 30];

// Create an Int32Array from ids
var typedIds = new Int32Array(ids);

// Read elements from typedids
for(var i = 0, len = typedIds.length; i < len; i++) {
        print("typedIds[" + i + "] = " + typedIds[i]);
}
```

```
typedIds[0] = 10
typedIds[1] = 20
typedIds[2] = 30
```

It is also possible to use the same ArrayBuffer to store different types of values. Recall that the views on the ArrayBuffer are typed, not the ArrayBuffer itself; it simply contains raw binary data. The following code creates an 8-byte ArrayBuffer to store a 32-bit signed integer in the first 4 bytes and a 32-bit signed floating point number in the last 4 bytes:

```
// Create an 8=byte buffer
var buffer = new ArrayBuffer(8);

// Create an Int32Array view for the first 4 bytes. byteOffset is 0
// and element count is 1
var id = new Int32Array(buffer, 0, 1);

// Create a Float32Array view for the second 4 bytes. The first 4 bytes
// will be used for integer value. byteOffset is 4 and element count is 1
var salary = new Float32Array(buffer, 4, 1);

// Use the Int32Array view to store an integer
id[0] = 1001;

// Use the Float32Array view to store a floating-point number
salary[0] = 129019.50;

// Read and print the two values using the two views
print("id = " + id[0]);
print("salary = " + salary[0]);
```

```
id = 1001
salary = 129019.5
```

When you create a typed array by supplying the length of an ArrayBuffer, the length or the size of the ArrayBuffer must be a multiple of element's size. For example, when you are creating an Int32Array, the size of its buffer must be a multiple of 4 (32-bit is 4 bytes). The following code will throw an exception:

```
var buffer = new ArrayBuffer(15);

// Throws an exception because an element of Int32Array takes 4 bytes and
// 15, which is the buffer size for the view, is not a multiple of 4
var id = new Int32Array(buffer);
```

The following code shows how to copy part of an ArrayBuffer using its slice() method and create a new view on the copied buffer:

```
// Create an ArrayBuffer of 4 bytes
var buffer = new ArrayBuffer(4);

// Create an Int8Array from buffer
var int8View1 = new Int8Array(buffer);

// Populate the array
int8View1[0] = 10;
int8View1[1] = 20;
int8View1[2] = 30;
int8View1[3] = 40;

print("In original buffer:")
for(var i = 0; i < int8View1.length; i++) {
        print(int8View1[i]);
}

// Copy the last two bytes from buffer to buffer2
var buffer2 = buffer.slice(2, 4);

// Create an Int8Array from buffer2
var int8View2 = new Int8Array(buffer2);

print("In copied buffer:");
for(var i = 0; i < int8View2.length; i++) {
        print(int8View2[i]);
}
```

```
In original buffer:
10
20
30
40
In copied buffer:
30
40
```

Because typed arrays are array-like objects, you can use most of the methods of the Array object on typed arrays. The following code shows how to use the join() method to concatenate elements of an Int32Array:

```
// Create an Int32Array of 4 elements
var ids = new Int32Array(4);

// Populate the array
ids[0] = 101;
ids[1] = 102;
ids[2] = 103;
ids[3] = 104;

// Call the join() method of the Array.prototype object and print the result
var idsList = Array.prototype.join.call(ids);
print(idsList);
```

```
101,102,103,104
```

DataView View

The DataView view provides low-level interface to read and write different types of data from an ArrayBuffer. Typically, you use a DataView when the data in an ArrayBuffer contains different types of data in different regions of the same ArrayBuffer. Notice that DataView is not a typed array; it is simply a view of an ArrayBuffer. The signature of the DataView constructor is:

```
DataView(arrayBuffer, byteOffset, byteLength)
```

It creates a view of the specified arrayBuffer referencing byteLength bytes from byteOffset index. If byteLength is unspecified, it references arrayBuffer starting at byteOffset and to the end. If both byteOffset and byteLength are unspecified, it references the entre arrayBuffer.

Unlike typed array view types, the DataView object can use mixed data types values, so it does not have a length property. Like typed arrays, it has buffer, byteOffset, and byteLength properties. It contains the following getter and setter methods for reading and writing different types of values:

- getInt8(byteOffset)
- getUint8(byteOffset)
- getInt16(byteOffset, littleEndian)
- getUint16(byteOffset, littleEndian)
- getInt32(byteOffset, littleEndian)

- getUint32(byteOffset, littleEndian)
- getFloat32(byteOffset, littleEndian)
- getFloat64(byteOffset, littleEndian)
- setInt8(byteOffset, value)
- setUint8(byteOffset, value)
- setInt16(byteOffset, value, littleEndian)
- setUint16(byteOffset, value, littleEndian)
- setInt32(byteOffset, value, littleEndian)
- setUint32(byteOffset, value, littleEndian)
- setFloat32(byteOffset, value, littleEndian)
- setFloat64(byteOffset, value, littleEndian)

The getters and setters for multibyte value types have a Boolean, optional last parameter named littleEndian. It specifies whether the value being read and set is in little-endian or big-endian format, If it is unspecified, the value is assumed to be big-endian. It is useful if the data you read come from different sources in different endian-ness. The following code uses a DataView to write and read a 32-bit signed integer and a 32-bit floating-point number from an ArrayBuffer:

```
// Create an ArrayBuffer of 8 bytes
var buffer = new ArrayBuffer(8);

// Create a DataView from the ArrayBuffer
var data = new DataView(buffer);

// Use the first 4 bytes to store a 32-bit signed integer
data.setInt32(0, 1001);

// Use the second 4 bytes to store a 32-bit floating-point number
data.setFloat32(4, 129019.50);

var id = data.getInt32(0);
var salary = data.getFloat32(4);
print("id = " + id);
print("salary = " + salary);
```

```
id = 1001
salary = 129019.5
```

Using Lists, Maps, and Sets

Nashorn does not provide built-in objects to represent general-purpose maps and sets. You can use any object in Nashorn as a map whose keys are strings. It is possible to create objects in Nashorn to represent maps and sets. However, doing so will be like reinventing the wheel. The Java programming language provides many types of collections, including maps and sets. You can use those collections in Nashorn directly. Please refer to Chapter 6 for more details on how to use Java classes in Nashorn scripts. I will discuss Java Lists and Maps in this section that are given special treatment in Nashorn.

Using a Java List as a Nashorn Array

Nashorn allows you to treat a Java List as a Nashorn array to read and update elements of the List. Note that it does not let you add elements to the List using the array indexes. You can use indexes to access and update elements of the List. Nashorn adds a length property to instances of Java List, so you can treat the List as an array-like object. Listing 7-4 shows you an example of using Java List in a Nashorn script.

Listing 7-4. Accessing and Updating a java.util.List as an Array Object in Nashorn Script

```
// list.js

var ArrayList = Java.type("java.util.ArrayList");
var nameList = new ArrayList();

// Add few names using List.add() Java method
nameList.add("Lu");
nameList.add("Do");
nameList.add("Yu");

// Print the List
print("After adding names:");
for(var i = 0, len = nameList.size(); i < len; i++) {
        print(nameList.get(i));
}

// Update names using array indexes
nameList[0] = "Su";
nameList[1] = "So";
nameList[2] = "Bo";
```

```
// The following statement will throw an IndexOutOfBoundsException because
// it is trying to add a new element using teh array syntax. You can only
// update an element, not add a new element, using the array syntax.
// nameList[3] = "An";

print("After updating names:");
for(var i = 0, len = nameList.length; i < len; i++) {
        print(nameList[i]);
}

// Sort the list in natural order
nameList.sort(null);

// Use the Array.prototype.forEach() method to print the list
print("After sorting names:");
Array.prototype.forEach.call(nameList, function (value, index, data) {
        print(value);
});
```

```
After adding names:
Lu
Do
Yu
After updating names:
Su
So
Bo
After sorting names:
Bo
So
Su
```

The example performs several things:

- Creates an instance of the java.util.ArrayList

- Use the add() method of the Java List interface to add three elements to the list

- Prints the elements using the size() and get() method of the List interface

- Updates the elements and prints them using the Nashorn syntax for accessing array elements. It uses the Nashorn property length to get the size of the list

- Uses the Java `List.sort()` method to sort the elements in natural order

- Uses the `Array.prototype.forEach()` method to print the sorted elements

Using a Java Map as a Nashorn Object

You have seen that Nashorn objects are simply maps storing string-object pairs. Nashorn allows using a Java Map as a Nashorn object in which you can use keys in the Map as the properties of the object. Listing 7-5 shows how to use a Java Map as a Nashorn object.

Listing 7-5. Using a Java Map as a Nashorn Object

```
// map.js

// Create a Map instance
var HashMap = Java.type("java.util.HashMap");
var map = new HashMap();

// Add key-value pairs to the map using Java methods
map.put("Li", "999-11-0001");
map.put("Su", "999-11-0002");

// You can treat the Map as an object and add key-value pairs
// as if you are adding proeprties to the object
map["Yu"] = "999-11-0003";
map["Do"] = "999-11-0004";

// Access values using the Java Map.get() method and the bracket notation
var liPhone = map.get("Li");   // Java way
var suPhone = map.get("Su");   // Java way
var yuPhone = map["Yu"];       // Nashorn way
var doPhone = map["Do"];       // Nashorn way

print("Li's Phone: " + liPhone);
print("su's Phone: " + suPhone);
print("Yu's Phone: " + yuPhone);
print("Do's Phone: " + doPhone);
```

```
Li's Phone: 999-11-0001
su's Phone: 999-11-0002
Yu's Phone: 999-11-0003
Do's Phone: 999-11-0004
```

Using Java Arrays

You can use Java arrays in Nashorn scripts. The way that Java arrays can be created in JavaScript differs in Rhino and Nashorn. In Rhino, you need to create a Java array using the newInstance() static method of the java.lang.reflect.Array class, which is inefficient and limited. Nashorn supports a new way of creating Java arrays that I will discuss shortly. This syntax is also supported in Nashorn. The following code shows how to create and access Java arrays using the Rhino syntax:

```
// Create a java.lang.String array of 2 elements, populate it, and print the
// elements. In Rhino, you were able to use java.lang.String as the first
// argument; in Nashorn, you need to use java.lang.String.class instead.
var strArray = java.lang.reflect.Array.newInstance(java.lang.String.class, 2);

strArray[0] = "Hello";
strArray[1] = "Array";

for(var i = 0; i < strArray.length; i++) {
        print(strArray[i]);
}
```

```
Hello
Array
```

To create primitive type arrays such as arrays of int, double, and so on, you need to use their TYPE constants for their corresponding wrapper classes, as shown:

```
// Create an int array of 2 elements, populate it, and print the elements
var intArray = java.lang.reflect.Array.newInstance(java.lang.Integer.TYPE, 2);

intArray[0] = 100;
intArray[1] = 200;

for(var i = 0; i < intArray.length; i++) {
        print(intArray[i]);
}
```

```
100
200
```

Nashorn supports a new syntax to create Java arrays. First, create the appropriate Java array type using the Java.type() method, and then use the familiar new operator to create the array. The following code shows how to create a String[] of two elements in Nashorn:

```
// Get the java.lang.String[] type
var StringArray = Java.type("java.lang.String[]");

// Create a String[] array of 2 elements
var strArray = new StringArray(2);

// Populate the array
strArray[0] = "Hello";
strArray[1] = "Array";

for(var i = 0; i < strArray.length; i++) {
        print(strArray[i]);
}
```

```
Hello
Array
```

Nashorn supports creating the arrays of primitive types the same way. The following code creates an int[] of two elements in Nashorn:

```
// Get the int[] type
var IntArray = Java.type("int[]");

// Create a int[] array of 2 elements
var intArray = new IntArray(2);

intArray[0] = 100;
intArray[1] = 200;
for(var i = 0; i < intArray.length; i++) {
        print(intArray[i]);
}
```

```
100
200
```

> ▪ **Tip** If you want to create multidimensional Java arrays in Nashorn, the array type will
> be as you declare the array in Java. For example, `Java.type("int[][]")` will import a Java
> `int[][]` array type; using the new operator on the imported type will create the `int[][]` array.

You can use a Nashorn array when a Java array is expected. Nashorn will perform the
necessary conversion. Suppose that you have a `PrintArray` class, as shown in Listing 7-6,
that contains a `print()` method that accepts a `String` array as an argument.

Listing 7-6. A PrintArray Class

```
// PrintArray.java
package com.jdojo.script;

public class PrintArray {
        public void print(String[] list) {
                System.out.println("Inside print(String[] list):" + list.
                length);
                for(String s : list) {
                        System.out.println(s);
                }
        }
}
```

The following script passes a Nashorn array to the `PrintArray.print(String[])`
method. Nashorn takes care of converting the native array to a `String` array, as shown in
the output:

```
// Create a JavaScript array and populate it with three strings
var names = new Array();
names[0] = "Rhino";
names[1] = "Nashorn";
names[2] = "JRuby";

// Create an object of the PrintArray class
var PrintArray = Java.type("com.jdojo.script.PrintArray");
var pa = new PrintArray();
```

```
// Pass a JavaScript array to the PrintArray.print(String[] list) method
pa.print(names);
```

```
Inside print(String[] list):3
Rhino
Nashorn
JRuby
```

Nashorn supports array type conversions between Java and Nashorn arrays using the Java.to() and Java.from() methods. The Java.to() method converts a Nashorn array type to a Java array type; it takes the array object as the first argument and the target Java array type as the second argument. The target array type can be specified as a string or a type object. The following snippet of code converts a Nashorn array to a Java String[]:

```
// Create a JavaScript array and populate it with three integers
var personIds = [100, 200, 300];

// Convert the JavaScript integer array to Java String[]
var JavaStringArray = Java.to(personIds, "java.lang.String[]")
```

If the second argument in the Java.to() function is omitted, the Nashorn array is converted to a Java Object[].

The Java.from() method converts a Java array type to a Nashorn array. The method takes the Java array as an argument. The following snippet of code shows how to convert a Java int[] to a JavaScript array:

```
// Create a Java int[]
var IntArray = Java.type("int[]");
var personIds = new IntArray(3);
personIds[0] = 100;
personIds[1] = 200;
personIds[2] = 300;

// Convert the Java int[] array to a Nashorn array
var jsArray = Java.from(personIds);

// Print the elements in the Nashorn array
for(var i = 0; i < jsArray.length; i++) {
    print(jsArray[i]);
}
```

```
100
200
300
```

> ■ **Tip** It is possible to return a Nashorn array to Java code from a Nashorn function. You need to extract the elements of the native array in Java code, and therefore, you need to use Nashorn-specific classes in Java. This approach is not advised. You should convert the Nashorn array to a Java array and return the Java array from a Nashorn function instead, so the Java code deals only with Java classes.

Arrays to Java Collections Conversions

Whenever possible, Nashorn provides automatic conversion from Nashorn arrays to Java arrays, Lists, and Maps. Converting Nashorn arrays to Java arrays and Lists is straightforward. When a Nashorn array is converted to a Java Map, the indexes of array elements become keys in the Map and element's values become the values for the corresponding indexes. Consider a Java class named ArrayConversion as shown in Listing 7-7. It contains four methods that accept arrays, Lists, and Maps as arguments.

Listing 7-7. A Java Class Named ArrayConversion

```java
// ArrayConversion.java
package com.jdojo.script;

import java.util.Arrays;
import java.util.List;
import java.util.Map;

public class ArrayConversion {
        public static void printInts(int[] ids) {
                System.out.print("Inside printInts():");
                System.out.println(Arrays.toString(ids));
        }

        public static void printDoubles(double[] salaries) {
                System.out.print("Inside printDoubles(double[]):");
                System.out.println(Arrays.toString(salaries));
        }

        public static void printList(List<Integer> idsList) {
                System.out.print("Inside printList():");
                System.out.println(idsList);
        }
```

```
    public static void printMap(Map<?,?> phoneMap) {
        System.out.println("Inside printMap():");
        phoneMap.forEach((key, value) -> {
            System.out.println("key = " + key + ", value = " +
            value);
        });
    }
}
```

Consider the Nashorn script as shown in Listing 7-8. It passes Nashorn arrays to Java methods that expects arrays, Lists, and Maps. The output proves that all methods are called and Nashorn runtime provides automatic conversions. Notice that when a Nashorn array contains elements of types not matching Java types, those elements are converted to appropriate Java types according to Nashorn type conversion rules. For example, a string in Nashorn is converted to 0 as Java int.

Listing 7-8. A Nashorn Script to test the ArrayConversion Class

```
// arrayconversion.js

var ArrayConversion = Java.type("com.jdojo.script.ArrayConversion");

ArrayConversion.printInts([1, 2, 3]);
ArrayConversion.printInts([1, "Hello", 3]); // "hello" is converted to 0

// Non-integers will be converted to corresponding integers per Nashorn rules
// when a Nashorn array is converted to a Java array. true and false are
// converted to 1 and 0, and 10.3 is converted to 10.
ArrayConversion.printInts([1, true, false, 10.3]);

// Nashorn array to Java double[] conversion
ArrayConversion.printDoubles([10.89, "Hello", 3]);

// Nashorn array to Java List conversion
ArrayConversion.printList([10.89, "Hello", 3]);

// Nashorn array to Java Map conversion
ArrayConversion.printMap([10.89, "Hello", 3]);
```

```
Inside printInts():[1, 2, 3]
Inside printInts():[1, 0, 3]
Inside printInts():[1, 1, 0, 10]
Inside printDoubles(double[]):[10.89, NaN, 3.0]
Inside printList():[10.89, Hello, 3]
Inside printMap():
key = 0, value = 10.89
key = 1, value = Hello
key = 2, value = 3
```

Sometimes it is not possible for Nashorn to automatically convert a Nashorn array to a Java array automatically—particularly when Java methods are overloaded. Consider the following code that throws an exception:

```
var Arrays = Java.type("java.util.Arrays");
var str = Arrays.toString([0, 1, 2]); // Throws a java.lang.
NoSuchMethodException
```

The Arrays.toString() method is overloaded and Nashorn cannot make a decision which version of the method to call. In this case, you must either explicitly convert the Nashorn array to the specific Java array type or choose the specific Java method to call. The following code shows both approaches:

```
var Arrays = Java.type("java.util.Arrays");

// Explicitly convert Nashorn array to Java int[]
var str1 = Arrays.toString(Java.to([1, 2, 3], "int[]"));

// Explicitly choose the Arrays.toString(int[]) method to call
var str2 = Arrays["toString(int[])"]([1, 2, 3]);
```

Summary

An array in Nashorn is a specialized object, called an Array object, which is used to represent an ordered collection of values. An Array object treats certain property names in a special way. If a property name can be converted to an integer that is between 0 and 2^{32}-2 (inclusive), such a property name is known as an array *index* and the property is known as an *element*. An Array object has a special property called length that represents the number of elements in the array.

An array can be created using an array literal or using the constructor of the Array object. An array literal is a comma-separated list of expressions enclosed in brackets that constitute the elements of the array. Arrays in Nashorn are variable-length and may be dense or sparse. Elements in an array can also be of different types.

You can access the array elements using the bracket notation and the index of the array elements. You can delete an array element using the delete operator. You can iterate array elements using the for loop, for..in loop, and for..each..in loop. The for..in and for..each..in loops iterate over elements as well as nonelement properties of the array. The Array.prototype object contains a forEach() method that iterates over only array elements and calls back the passed function for each element.

The Array object contains several useful methods to work with array elements. The Array.isArray(object) static method returns true if the specified object is an array; otherwise, it returns false. Other methods such as concat(), join(), slice(), splice(), sort(), and so on are in the Array.prototype object.

An array-like object is a Nashorn object that has a length property and property names that are valid array indexes. String objects and arguments object are examples of array-like objects. Most of the methods in the Array object are generic and they can be used on any array-like object.

Nashorn supports typed arrays. A typed array is a typed view of an ArrayBuffer object that contains raw binary data. Different types of typed arrays are available such as Int8Array to deal with 8-bit signed integers, Int32Array to deal with 32-bit signed integers, etc. Once you create a typed array, you can use it like an array to deal with the specific types of values. The DataView object provides a low-level interface to deal with an ArrayBuffer object whose binary data may contain different types of numeric values.

All Nashorn objects are maps. Nashorn lets you treat Java Maps in a special way by allowing you to access their values using the bracket notation with keys as indexes. Nashorn lets you treat Java Lists like Nashorn arrays. You can read and update elements of Java Lists using the bracket notation where element's indexes are treated as indexes in the arrays. Nashorn creates a special property named length for Java List objects that represents the number of elements in the List. If you need any other types of collections in Nashorn, you can use the corresponding collections from Java.

Nashorn lets you use Java arrays in scripts. You need to use the Java.type() method to import the Java array type in the script. For example. Java.type("int[]") returns a Java type that represents a Java int[]. Once you get the Java array type, you need to use the new operator to create the array. Nashorn also supports Nashorn-to-Java and Java-to-Nashorn array conversions. The Java.to() method converts a Nashorn array to a Java array and the Java.from() method converts a Java array to a Nashorn array. Nashorn attempts to perform automatic conversion from Nashorn arrays to Java arrays, Lists, and Maps, provided the choice of type conversion is unique. In other cases, you will need to perform explicit conversion from Nashorn arrays to collections.

CHAPTER 8

■ ■ ■

Implementing a Script Engine

In this chapter, you will learn:

- The components of a script engine that need to be developed when implementing a new script engine

- How to implement the different components of a simple script engine that will perform addition, subtraction, multiplication, and division on two numbers

- How to package the code of the script engine

- How to deploy and test the script engine

Introduction

Implementing a full-blown script engine is no simple task and it is outside the scope of this book. This chapter is meant to give you a brief, but complete, overview of the setup needed to implement a script engine. In this section, you will implement a simple script engine called the JKScript engine. It will evaluate arithmetic expressions with the following rules:

- It will evaluate an arithmetic expression that consists of two operands and one operator

- The expression may have two number literals, two variables, or one number literal and one variable as operands. The number literals must be in decimal format. Hexadecimal, octal, and binary number literals are not supported

- The arithmetic operations in an expression are limited to add, subtract, multiply, and divide

- It will recognize +, -, *, and / as arithmetic operators

- The engine will return a Double object as the result of the expression

- Operands in an expression may be passed to the engine using global scope or engine scope bindings of the engine

- It should allow executing scripts from a String object and a java.io.Reader object. However, a Reader should have only one expression as its contents

- It will not implement the Invocable and Compilable interfaces

Using these rules, some valid expressions for your script engine are as follows:

- 10 + 90

- 10.7 + 89.0

- +10 + +90

- num1 + num2

- num1 * num2

- 78.0 / 7.5

You need to provide implementation for the following two interfaces when you implement a script engine:

- javax.script.ScriptEngineFactory

- javax.script.ScriptEngine

As part of your implementation for the JKScript script engine, you will develop three classes as listed in Table 8-1. In subsequent sections, you will develop these classes.

***Table 8-1.** The List of Classes to be Developed for the JKScript Script Engine*

Class	Description
Expression	The Expression class is the heart of your script engine. It performs the work of parsing and evaluating an arithmetic expression. It is used inside the eval() methods of the JKScriptEngine class.
JKScriptEngine	An implementation of the ScriptEngine interface. It extends the AbstractScriptEngine class that implements the ScriptEngine interface. The AbstractScriptEngine class provides a standard implementation for several versions of the eval() methods of the ScriptEngine interface. You need to implement the following two versions of the eval() method: Object eval(String, ScriptContext) Object eval(Reader, ScriptContext)
JKScriptEngineFactory	An implementation of the ScriptEngineFactory interface.

The Expression Class

The Expression class contains the main logic for parsing and evaluating an arithmetic expression. Listing 8-1 contains the complete code for the Expression class.

Listing 8-1. The Expression Class That Parses and Evaluates an Arithmetic Expression

```java
// Expression.java
package com.jdojo.script;

import java.util.regex.Matcher;
import java.util.regex.Pattern;
import javax.script.ScriptContext;

public class Expression {
        private String exp;
        private ScriptContext context;

        private String op1;
        private char op1Sign = '+';

        private String op2;
        private char op2Sign = '+';

        private char operation;

        private boolean parsed;

        public Expression(String exp, ScriptContext context) {
                if (exp == null || exp.trim().equals("")) {
                        throw new IllegalArgumentException(this.
                        getErrorString());
                }
                this.exp = exp.trim();

                if (context == null) {
                        throw new IllegalArgumentException(
                                "ScriptContext cannot be null.");
                }
                this.context = context;
        }

        public String getExpression() {
                return exp;
        }
```

```java
    public ScriptContext getScriptContext() {
            return context;
    }

    public Double eval() {
            // Parse the expression
            if (!parsed) {
                    this.parse();
                    this.parsed = true;
            }

            // Extract the values for the operand
            double op1Value = getOperandValue(op1Sign, op1);
            double op2Value = getOperandValue(op2Sign, op2);

            // Evaluate the expression
            Double result = null;
            switch (operation) {
                    case '+':
                            result = op1Value + op2Value;
                            break;
                    case '-':
                            result = op1Value - op2Value;
                            break;
                    case '*':
                            result = op1Value * op2Value;
                            break;
                    case '/':
                            result = op1Value / op2Value;
                            break;
                    default:
                            throw new RuntimeException(
                                    "Invalid operation:" + operation);
            }
            return result;
    }

    private double getOperandValue(char sign, String operand) {
            // Check if operand is a double
            double value;
            try {
                    value = Double.parseDouble(operand);
                    return sign == '-' ? -value : value;
            }
            catch (NumberFormatException e) {
                    // Ignore it. Operand is not in a format that can be
                    // converted to a double value.
            }
```

```java
        // Check if operand is a bind variable
        Object bindValue = context.getAttribute(operand);
        if (bindValue == null) {
                throw new RuntimeException(operand +
                        " is not found in the script context.");
        }

        if (bindValue instanceof Number) {
                value = ((Number) bindValue).doubleValue();
                return sign == '-' ? -value : value;
        }
        else {
                throw new RuntimeException(operand +
                        " must be bound to a number.");
        }
    }

    public void parse() {
        // Supported expressions are of the form v1 op v2,
        // where v1 and v2 are variable names or numbers,
        // and op could be +, -, *, or /

        // Prepare the pattern for the expected expression
        String operandSignPattern = "([+-]?)";
        String operandPattern = "([\\p{Alnum}\\p{Sc}_.]+)";
        String whileSpacePattern = "([\\s]*)";
        String operationPattern = "([+*/-])";
        String pattern = "^" + operandSignPattern + operandPattern +
                whileSpacePattern + operationPattern +
                whileSpacePattern +
                operandSignPattern + operandPattern + "$";

        Pattern p = Pattern.compile(pattern);
        Matcher m = p.matcher(exp);
        if (!m.matches()) {
                // The expression is not in the expected format
                throw new IllegalArgumentException(this.
                getErrorString());
        }

        // Get operand-1
        String temp = m.group(1);
        if (temp != null && !temp.equals("")) {
                this.op1Sign = temp.charAt(0);
        }
        this.op1 = m.group(2);
```

```java
                    // Get operation
                    temp = m.group(4);
                    if (temp != null && !temp.equals("")) {
                            this.operation = temp.charAt(0);
                    }

                    // Get operand-2
                    temp = m.group(6);
                    if (temp != null && !temp.equals("")) {
                            this.op2Sign = temp.charAt(0);
                    }
                    this.op2 = m.group(7);
            }

        private String getErrorString() {
                    return "Invalid expression[" + exp + "]" +
                    "\nSupported expression syntax is: op1 operation op2" +
                    "\n where op1 and op2 can be a number or a bind variable" +
                    " , and operation can be +, -, *, and /.";
            }

        @Override
        public String toString() {
                    return "Expression: " + this.exp + ", op1 Sign = " +
                            op1Sign + ", op1 = " + op1 + ", op2 Sign = " +
                            op2Sign + ", op2 = " + op2 + ", operation = " +
                            operation;
            }
}
```

The Expression class is designed to parse and evaluate an arithmetic expression of the form:

```
op1 operation op2
```

Here, op1 and op2 are two operands that can be numbers in decimal format or variables, and operation can be +, -, *, or /.

The suggested use of the Expression class is:

```java
Expression exp = new Expression(expression, scriptContext);
Double value = exp.eval();
```

Let's discuss important components of the Expression class in detail.

The Instance Variables

Instance variables named exp and context are the expression and the ScriptContext to evaluate the expression, respectively. They are passed to the constructor of this class.

The instance variables named op1 and op2 represent the first and the second operands in the expression, respectively. The instance variables op1Sign and op2Sign represent signs, which could be '+' or '-', for the first and the second operands in the expression, respectively. The operands and their signs are populated when the expression is parsed using the parse() method.

The instance variable named operation represents an arithmetic operation (+, -, *, or /)) to be performed on the operands.

The instance variable named parsed is used to keep track of the fact whether the expression has been parsed or not. The parse() method sets it to true.

The Constructor

The constructor of the Expression class accepts an expression and a ScriptContext. It makes sure that they are not null and stores them in the instance variables. It trims the leading and trailing whitespaces from the expression before storing it in the instance variable named exp.

The parse() Method

The parse() method parses the expression into operands and operations. It uses a regular expression to parse the expression text. The regular expression expects the expression text in the following form:

- An optional sign + or - for the first operand

- The first operand that may consist of a combination of alphanumeric letters, currency signs, underscores, and decimal points

- Any number of whitespaces

- An operation sign that may be +, -, *, or /

- An optional sign + or - for the second operand

- The second operand that may consist of a combination of alphanumeric letters, currency signs, underscores, and decimal points

The regular expression (([+-]?) will match the optional sign for the operand. The regular expression ([\\p{Alnum}\\p{Sc}_.]+) will match an operand, which may be a decimal number or a name. The regular expression ([\\s]*) will match any number of whitespaces. The regular expression ([+*/-]) will match an operation sign. All regular expressions are enclosed in parentheses to form groups, so you can capture the matched parts of the expression.

If an expression matches the regular expression, the parse() method stores the matched parts into respective instance variables.

Notice that the regular expression to match operands is not perfect. It will allow several invalid cases, such as an operand having multiple decimal points, and so on. However, for the purposes of this demonstration, it will do.

The getOperandValue() Method

The getOperandValue() method is used during an expression evaluation after the expression has been parsed. If the operand is a double number, it returns the value by applying the sign of the operand. Otherwise, it looks up the name of the operand in the ScriptContext. If the name of the operand is not found in the ScriptContext, it throws a RuntimeException. If the name of the operand is found in the ScriptContext, it checks if the value is a number. It the value is a number, it returns the value after applying the sign to the value; otherwise, it throws a RuntimeException.

The method does not support operands in hexadecimal, octal, and binary formats. For example, an expression like "0x2A + 0b1011" will not be treated as an expression having two operands with int literals. It is left to readers to enhance this method to support numeric literals in hexadecimal, octal, and binary formats.

The eval() Method

The eval() method evaluates the expression and returns a double value. First, it parses the expression if it has not already been parsed. Note that multiple calls to the eval() parses the expression only once.

It obtains values for both operands, performs the operation, and returns the value of the expression.

The JKScriptEngine Class

Listing 8-2 contains the implementation for the JKScript script engine. Its eval(String, ScriptContext) method contains the main logic, as shown:

```
Expression exp = new Expression(script, context);
Object result = exp.eval();
```

It creates an object of the Expression class. It calls the eval() method of the Expression object that evaluates the expression and returns the result.

The eval(Reader, ScriptContext) method reads all lines from the Reader, concatenates them, and passes the resulting String to the eval(String, ScriptContext) method to evaluate the expression. Notice that a Reader must have only one expression. An expression may be split into multiple lines. Whitespaces in the Reader are ignored.

Listing 8-2. An Implementation of JKScript Script Engine

```java
// JKScriptEngine.java
package com.jdojo.script;

import java.io.BufferedReader;
import java.io.IOException;
import java.io.Reader;
import javax.script.AbstractScriptEngine;
import javax.script.Bindings;
import javax.script.ScriptContext;
import javax.script.ScriptEngineFactory;
import javax.script.ScriptException;
import javax.script.SimpleBindings;

public class JKScriptEngine extends AbstractScriptEngine {
        private ScriptEngineFactory factory;

        public JKScriptEngine(ScriptEngineFactory factory) {
                this.factory = factory;
        }

        @Override
        public Object eval(String script, ScriptContext context)
                        throws ScriptException {
                try {
                        Expression exp = new Expression(script, context);
                        Object result = exp.eval();
                        return result;
                }
                catch (Exception e) {
                        throw new ScriptException(e.getMessage());
                }
        }

        @Override
        public Object eval(Reader reader, ScriptContext context)
                        throws ScriptException {
                // Read all lines from the Reader
                BufferedReader br = new BufferedReader(reader);

                String script = "";
                String str = null;
                try {
                        while ((str = br.readLine()) != null) {
                                script = script + str;
                        }
                }
```

```
                    catch (IOException e) {
                            throw new ScriptException(e);
                    }

                    // Use the String version of eval()
                    return eval(script, context);
            }

            @Override
            public Bindings createBindings() {
                    return new SimpleBindings();
            }

            @Override
            public ScriptEngineFactory getFactory() {
                    return factory;
            }
    }
```

The JKScriptEngineFactory Class

Listing 8-3 contains the implementation for the ScriptEngineFactory interface for the JKScript engine. Some of its methods return a "Not Implemented" string because you do not support features exposed by those methods. The code in the JKScriptEngineFactory class is self-explanatory. An instance of the JKScript engine may be obtained using ScriptEngineManager with a name of jks, JKScript, or jkscript as coded in the getNames() method.

Listing 8-3. A ScriptEngineFactory Implementation for JKScript Script Engine

```
// JKScriptEngineFactory.java
package com.jdojo.script;

import java.util.ArrayList;
import java.util.Arrays;
import java.util.Collections;
import java.util.List;
import javax.script.ScriptEngine;
import javax.script.ScriptEngineFactory;

public class JKScriptEngineFactory implements ScriptEngineFactory {
        @Override
        public String getEngineName() {
                return "JKScript Engine";
        }
```

```java
@Override
public String getEngineVersion() {
        return "1.0";
}

@Override
public List<String> getExtensions() {
        return Collections.unmodifiableList(Arrays.asList("jks"));
}

@Override
public List<String> getMimeTypes() {
        return Collections.unmodifiableList(Arrays.asList("text/
        jkscript") );
}

@Override
public List<String> getNames() {
        List<String> names = new ArrayList<>();
        names.add("jks");
        names.add("JKScript");
        names.add("jkscript");
        return Collections.unmodifiableList(names);
}

@Override
public String getLanguageName() {
        return "JKScript";
}

@Override
public String getLanguageVersion() {
        return "1.0";
}

@Override
public Object getParameter(String key) {
        switch (key) {
                case ScriptEngine.ENGINE:
                        return getEngineName();
                case ScriptEngine.ENGINE_VERSION:
                        return getEngineVersion();
                case ScriptEngine.NAME:
                        return getEngineName();
                case ScriptEngine.LANGUAGE:
                        return getLanguageName();
```

```java
            case ScriptEngine.LANGUAGE_VERSION:
                    return getLanguageVersion();
            case "THREADING":
                    return "MULTITHREADED";
            default:
                    return null;
        }
    }

    @Override
    public String getMethodCallSyntax(String obj, String m, String[] p) {
        return "Not implemented";
    }

    @Override
    public String getOutputStatement(String toDisplay) {
        return "Not implemented";
    }

    @Override
    public String getProgram(String[] statements) {
        return "Not implemented";
    }

    @Override
    public ScriptEngine getScriptEngine() {
        return new JKScriptEngine(this);
    }
}
```

Preparing for Deployment

Before you package the classes for the JKScript script engine, you need to perform one more step: Create a directory named META-INF. Under the META-INF directory, create a subdirectory named services. In the services directory, create a text file named javax.script.ScriptEngineFactory. Notice that the filename must be the way it is mentioned and should not have any extension such as .txt.

Edit the javax.script.ScriptEngineFactory file and enter the contents as shown in Listing 8-4. The first line in the file is a comment that starts with a # sign. The second line is the fully qualified name of the JKScript script engine factory class.

Listing 8-4. Contents of the File Named javax.script.ScriptEngineFactory

```
#The factory class for the JKScript engine
com.jdojo.script.JKScriptEngineFactory
```

Why do you have to perform this step? You will package the `javax.script.`
`ScriptEngineFactory` file along with the class files for the JKScript engine in a JAR
file. The discovery mechanism for script engines searches for this file in the `META-INF/`
`services` directory in all JAR files in the CLASSPATH. If this file is found, its contents are
read and all script factory classes in this file are instantiated and included in the list of
script engine factories. Therefore, this step is necessary to make your JKScript engine
autodiscoverable by the `ScriptEngineManager`.

Packaging the JKScript Files

You need to package all files for the JKScript script engine in a JAR file named `jkscript.`
`jar`. You can name the file anything else as well. The following is the list of files with their
directories. Note that an empty `manifest.mf` file will work in this case:

- `com\jdojo\script\Expression.class`
- `com\jdojo\script\JKScriptEngine.class`
- `com\jdojo\script\JKScriptEngineFactory.class`
- `META-INF\manifest.mf`
- `META-INF\services\javax.script.ScriptEngineFactory`

You can create the `jkscript.jar` file manually by copying all of these files, except
the `manifest.mf` file, into a directory, say `C:\build` on Windows, and then executing the
following command from the `C:\build` directory:

```
C:\build> jar cf jkscript.jar com\jdojo\script\*.class META-INF\services\*.*
```

The `jkscript.jar` file is available in the `src\JavaScripts` directory in the
downloadable package for this book. The downloadable source code contains a
NetBeans 8.0 project and the `jkscript.jar` file is added to the project's CLASSPATH.
If you run the engine from the included NetBeans IDE, you do not need to perform the
packaging and deploying steps to use the JKScript engine.

Using the JKScript Script Engine

It is time to test your JKScript script engine. The first and most important step is to
include the `jkscript.jar`, which you created the previous section, to the application
CLASSPATH. Once you have included the `jkscript.jar` file in your application
CLASSPATH, using JKScript is no different from using any other script engines.

The following snippet of code creates an instance of the JKScript script engine using JKScript as its name. You can also use its other names such as jks and jkscript:

```
// Create the JKScript engine
ScriptEngineManager manager = new ScriptEngineManager();
ScriptEngine engine = manager.getEngineByName("JKScript");

if (engine == null) {
        System.out.println("JKScript engine is not available. " +
                             "Add jkscript.jar to CLASSPATH.");
}
else {
        // Evaluate your JKScript
}
```

Listing 8-5 contains a program that uses the JKScript script engine to evaluate different types of expressions. Expressions stored in String objects and files are executed. Some expressions use numeric literals and some bind variables whose values are passed in bindings in engine scope and global scope of the default ScriptContext of the engine. Note that this program expects a file named jkscript.txt in the current directory that contains an arithmetic expression that can be understood by the JKScript script engine. If the script file does not exist, the program prints a message on the standard output with the path of the expected script file. You may get a different output in the last line.

Listing 8-5. Using the JKScript Script Engine

```
// JKScriptTest.java
package com.jdojo.script;

import java.io.FileNotFoundException;
import java.io.IOException;
import java.io.Reader;
import java.nio.file.Files;
import java.nio.file.Path;
import java.nio.file.Paths;
import javax.script.ScriptEngine;
import javax.script.ScriptEngineManager;
import javax.script.ScriptException;

public class JKScriptTest {
        public static void main(String[] args) throws FileNotFoundException,
        IOException {
                // Create JKScript engine
                ScriptEngineManager manager = new ScriptEngineManager();
                ScriptEngine engine = manager.getEngineByName("JKScript");
```

```
        if (engine == null) {
                System.out.println("JKScript engine is not
                available. " + "Add jkscript.jar to CLASSPATH.");
                return;
        }
        // Test scripts as String
        testString(manager, engine);

        // Test scripts as a Reader
        testReader(manager, engine);
}

public static void testString(ScriptEngineManager manager,
ScriptEngine engine) {
        try {
                // Use simple expressions with numeric literals
                String script = "12.8 + 15.2";
                Object result = engine.eval(script);
                System.out.println(script + " = " + result);

                script = "-90.0 - -10.5";
                result = engine.eval(script);
                System.out.println(script + " = " + result);

                script = "5 * 12";
                result = engine.eval(script);
                System.out.println(script + " = " + result);

                script = "56.0 / -7.0";
                result = engine.eval(script);
                System.out.println(script + " = " + result);

                // Use global scope bindings variables
                manager.put("num1", 10.0);
                manager.put("num2", 20.0);
                script = "num1 + num2";
                result = engine.eval(script);
                System.out.println(script + " = " + result);
```

```java
                        // Use global and engine scopes bindings. num1 from
                        // engine scope and num2 from global scope will be used.
                        engine.put("num1", 70.0);
                        script = "num1 + num2";
                        result = engine.eval(script);
                        System.out.println(script + " = " + result);
                        // Try mixture of number literal and bindings. num1
                        // from the engine scope bindings will be used
                        script = "10 + num1";
                        result = engine.eval(script);
                        System.out.println(script + " = " + result);
            }
            catch (ScriptException e) {
                    e.printStackTrace();
            }
    }

    public static void testReader(ScriptEngineManager manager,
    ScriptEngine engine) {
            try {
                    Path scriptPath = Paths.get("jkscript.txt").
                    toAbsolutePath();
                    if (!Files.exists(scriptPath)) {
                            System.out.println(scriptPath +
                                    " script file does not exist.");
                            return;
                    }

                    try(Reader reader = Files.
                    newBufferedReader(scriptPath);) {
                            Object result = engine.eval(reader);
                            System.out.println("Result of " +
                                    scriptPath + " = " + result);
                    }
            }
            catch(ScriptException | IOException e) {
                    e.printStackTrace();
            }
    }
}
```

```
12.8 + 15.2 = 28.0
-90.0 - -10.5 = -79.5
5 * 12 = 60.0
56.0 / -7.0 = -8.0
num1 + num2 = 30.0
num1 + num2 = 90.0
10 + num1 = 80.0
Result of C:\jkscript.txt = 190.0
```

Summary

You can implement a script engine using the Java Script API. You will need to provide the implementation for the ScriptEngine and the ScriptEngineFactory interfaces. You need to package your script engine code in a certain way, so the engine can be discovered by the ScriptManager at runtime. The JAR file for the engine should contain a file named META-INF\services\javax.script.ScriptEngineFactory that should contain the fully qualified names of all script engine factory classes; the Java Script API discovers those script engine factories automatically. Once you package and deploy the script engine code, you can access it the same way you have been accessing Nashorn and other script engines.

■ ■ ■

CHAPTER 9

The jrunscript Command-Line Shell

In this chapter, you will learn:

- What the jrunscript command-line shell is

- How to invoke the jrunscript command-line shell

- The different modes in which the jrunscript command-line shell can be invoked

- How to list the available script engines with the jrunscript command-line shell

- How to add a script engine to the jrunscript command-line shell

- How to pass arguments to the jrunscript command-line shell

- The global functions made available by the jrunscript command-line shell

The JDK includes a command-line script shell called jrunscript. It is script-engine-independent and it can be used to evaluate any script including your JKScript that you developed in Chapter 8. You can find this shell in the JAVA_HOME\bin directory, where JAVA_HOME is the directory in which you have installed the JDK. In this section, I will discuss how to use the jrunscript shell to evaluate scripts using different script engines.

The Syntax

The syntax to use the jrunscript shell is:

```
jrunscript [options] [arguments]
```

Both [options] and [arguments] are optional. However, if both are specified, [options] must precede [arguments]. Table 9-1 lists all available options for the jrunscript shell.

Table 9-1. *The List of Options for the jrunscript Shell*

Option	Description
-classpath <path>	Used to specify the CLASSPATH.
-cp <path>	The same as the -classpath option.
-D<name>=<value>	Sets a system property for Java runtime.
-J<flag>	Passes the specified <flag> to the JVM on which jrunscript is run.
-l <language>	Allows you to specify a scripting language that you want to use with the jrunscript. By default, Rhino JavaScript is used in JDK 6 and JDK 7. In JDK 8, Nashorn is the default. If you want to use a language other than JavaScript, say JKScript, you will need to use -cp or -classpath option to include the JAR file that contains the script engine.
-e <script>	Executes the specified script. Typically, it is used to execute a one-liner script.
-encoding <encoding>	Specifies the character encoding used while reading script files.
-f <script-file>	Evaluates the specified script-file in batch mode.
-f -	Allows you to evaluate scripts in interactive mode. It reads scripts from the standard input and executes it.
-help	Outputs the help message and exits.
-?	Outputs the help message and exits.
-q	Lists all available script engines and exits. Note that script engines other than JavaScript are available only when you include their JAR files using the -cp or -classpath option.

The [arguments] part of the command is a list of arguments, which are interpreted depending on whether the -e or -f option is used or not. Arguments that are passed to the script are available inside the script as an object named arguments. Please refer to Chapter 4 for more details on using the arguments object in scripts. Table 9-2 lists interpretations of the arguments when they are used with the -e or -f option.

Table 9-2. Interpretation of [arguments] in Combination of the -e or -f Option

-e or -f option	Arguments	Interpretation
Yes	Yes	If -e or -f option is specified, all arguments are passed to the script as script arguments.
No	Yes	If arguments are specified with no -e or -f option, the first argument is considered a script file to run. The rest of the arguments, if any, are passed to the script as script arguments.
No	No	If arguments and -e or -f option are missing, the shell works in interactive mode, where the shell executes the script entered in the standard input interactively.

Execution Modes of the Shell

You can use the jrunscript shell in the following three modes:

- One-liner mode
- Batch mode
- Interactive mode

One-liner Mode

The -e option lets you use the shell in one-liner mode. It executes one line of script. The following command prints a message on the standard output using the Nashorn engine:

```
C:\>jrunscript -e "print('Hello Nashorn!');"
Hello Nashorn!

C:\>
```

In one-liner mode, the entire script must be entered on one line. However, a one-liner script may contain multiple statements.

Batch Mode

The -f option lets you use the shell in batch mode. It executes a script file. Consider a script file named jrunscripttest.js as shown in Listing 9-1.

Listing 9-1. A jrunscripttest.js Script File Written in Nashorn JavaScript

```
// jrunscripttest.js

// Print a message
print("Hello Nashorn!");

// Add two integers and print the value
var x = 10;
var y = 20;
var z = x + y;
printf("x + y = z", x, y, z);
```

The following command runs the script in the jrunscripttest.js file in a batch mode. You may need to specify the full path of the jrunscripttest.js file if it is not in the current directory.

```
C:\>jrunscript -f jrunscripttest.js
Hello Nashorn!
10 + 20 = 30

C:\>
```

Interactive Mode

In interactive mode, the shell reads and evaluates a script as it is entered on the standard input. There are two ways to use the shell in interactive mode:

- Using no -e or -f options and no arguments

- Using the "-f -" option

The following command uses no options and arguments to enter into interactive mode. Pressing the Enter key makes the shell evaluate the entered script. Notice that you will need to execute the exit() or quit() function to exit from the interactive mode:

```
c:\>jrunscript
nashorn> print("Hello Interactive mode!");
Hello Interactive mode!
nashorn> var num = 190;
nashorn> print("num is " + num);
num is 190
nashorn> exit();

C:\>
```

Listing Available Script Engines

The jrunscript shell is a scripting-language-neutral shell. You can use it to run scripts in any scripting language for which the script engine JAR files are available. By default, the Nashorn JavaScript engine is available. To list all available script engines, use the -q option as shown:

```
c:\>jrunscript -q
Language ECMAScript ECMA - 262 Edition 5.1 implementation
"Oracle Nashorn" 1.8.0_05
```

Please refer to the next section on how to add a script engine to the shell.

Adding a Script Engine to the Shell

How do you make script engines other than the Nashorn engine available to the shell? To make a script engine available to the shell, you need to provide the list of JAR files for the script engine using the -classpath or -cp option. The following command makes JKScript and jython script engines available to the shell by providing the list of JAR files for Jython and JKScript engines. Notice that the Nashorn engine is always available by default. The command uses the -q option to list all available script engines:

```
c:\> jrunscript -cp C:\jython-standalone-2.5.3.jar;C:\jkscript.jar -q
Language python 2.5 implementation "jython" 2.5.3
Language ECMAScript ECMA - 262 Edition 5.1 implementation
"Oracle Nashorn" 1.8.0_05
Language JKScript 1.0 implementation "JKScript Engine" 1.0
```

■ **Tip** The CLASSPATH set using the -cp or -classpath option is effective only for the command in which the option is used. If you run the shell in interactive mode, the CLASSPATH is effective for the entire interactive session.

Using Other Script Engines

You can use other script engines by specifying the script engine name with the -l option. You must use the -cp or -classpath option to specify the JAR files for the script engine, so the shell has access to the engine. The following command uses the JKScript engine in interactive mode:

```
C:\>jrunscript -cp C:\jkscript.jar -l JKScript
jks> 10 + 30
40.0
jks> +89.7 + -9.7
80.0
jks>
```

Passing Arguments to Scripts

The jrunscript shell allows passing arguments to scripts. The arguments are made available to the script in an array-like object named arguments. You can access the arguments array inside the script in a language-specific way. The following command passes three arguments of 10, 20, and 30, and prints the value of the first argument:

```
C:\>jrunscript -e "print('First argument is ' + arguments[0])" 10 20 30
First argument is 10
```

Consider the Nashorn JavaScript file nashornargstest.js shown in Listing 9-2, which prints the number of arguments and their values that are passed to the script.

Listing 9-2. A nashornargstest.js File Written in Nashorn JavaScript to Print Command-Line Arguments

```
// nashornargstest.js

print("Number of arguments:" + arguments.length);
print("Arguments are ") ;

for(var i = 0; i < arguments.length; i++) {
        print(arguments[i]);
}
```

The following commands run the nashornargstest.js file using the jrunscript shell:

```
C:\>jrunscript nashornargstest.js
Number of arguments:0
Arguments are

C:\>jrunscript nashornargstest.js 10 20 30
Number of arguments:3
Arguments are
10
20
30
```

If you want to run the nashornargstest.js file from a Java application, you need to pass an argument named arguments to the engine. The argument named arguments is passed to the script by the shell automatically, not by a Java application.

Global Functions

The jrunscript command-line shell makes several global functions available for use as listed in Table 9-3.

Table 9-3. *The List of Global Objects Loaded by the jrunscript Command-Line Shell*

Function	Description
cat(path, pattern)	Shows the content of a file, URL, or InputStream specified by path. Optionally, you can specify pattern to show only the matching contents.
cd(target)	Changes the present working directory to the target directory.
cp(from, to)	Copies a file, URL, or stream to another file or stream.
date()	Prints the current date using the current locale.
del(pathname)	A synonym for the rm command.
dir(d, filter)	A synonym for the ls command.
dirname(pathname)	Returns the directory part of the specified pathname.
echo(str)	Echoes the specified string arguments.
exec(cmd)	Starts a child process, executes the specified command, waits for completion, and returns the exit code.
exit(code)	Exit the shell program with the specified code as the exit code.
find(dir, pattern, callback)	Find files in dir with file names matching the specified pattern. When a match is found, the callback function is called passing the found file. Search is performed recursively in all subdirectories. You can pass some functions listed in this table as callback. If callback is not specified, the default is to print the found files path. If pattern is not specified, all files are printed.
grep(pattern, files)	Unix-like grep, but accepts JavaScript regex patterns.
ip(name)	Prints the IP addresses of a given domain name.
load(path)	Loads and evaluates JavaScript code from a stream, file, or URL.
ls(dir, filter)	Lists the files in dir matching the filter regular expression.
mkdir(dir)	Creates a new directory with the name dir.

(continued)

287

Table 9-3. (*continued*)

Function	Description
mkdirs(dir)	Creates a directory named dir, including any necessary but nonexistent parent directories.
mv(from, to)	Moves a file to another directory.
printf(format, args)	A C-like printf.
pwd()	Prints the working directory.
quit(code)	A synonym for exit(code).
read(prompt, multiline)	Reads and returns one or more lines from standard input after printing the specified prompt. The default prompt is a >. If multiline is 0, it reads one line. If multiline is other than 0, it reads multiple lines. You need to press Enter to stop entering text.
ren(from, to)	A synonym for mv.
rm(filePath)	Removes the file with the specified filePath.
rmdir(dirPath)	Removes the directory with the specified dirPath.
which(cmd)	Unix-like which command to print the path of the specified cmd command based on the PATH environment variable.
XMLDocument(input)	Converts input that can be a filepath or a Reader to DOM Document object. If input is not specified, an empty DOM document is returned.
XMLResult(input)	Convert an arbitrary stream or file to an XMLResult. If input is an instance of javax.xml.transform.Result, input is returned; if input is an instance of org.w3c.dom.Document, a javax.xml.transform.dom.DOMResult is returned; otherwise, a javax.xml.transform.stream.StreamResult is returned.
XMLSource(input)	Converts an arbitrary stream, file, URL to an XMLSource. If input is an instance of javax.xml.transform.Source, input is returned; if input is an instance of org.w3c.dom.Document, a javax.xml.transform.dom.DOMSource is returned; otherwise, a javax.xml.transform.stream.StreamSource is returned.
XSLTransform(input, style, output)	Perform an XSLT transform; input is the input XML; style is the XML stylesheet; output is the output XML. Input and style can be a URL, a File or an InputStream; output can be a File or an OutputStream.

The following is the output of using some of the utility functions provided by jrunscript:

```
C:\>jrunscript
nashorn> cat("http://jdojo.com/about", "ksharan")
68       : <p>You can contact Kishori Sharan by email at <a
href="mailto:ksharan@jdojo.com">ksharan@jdojo.com</a>.</p>

nashorn> var addr = read("Please enter your address: ", 1);
Please enter your address: 9999 Main St.
Please enter your address: Dreamland, HH 11111
Please enter your address:
nashorn> print(addr)
9999 Main St.
Dreamland, HH 11111

nashorn> which("jrunscript.exe");
c:\JAVA8\BIN\jrunscript.exe

nashorn>pwd()
C:\

nashorn>
```

Most of these utility functions have been written as Nashorn scripts taking advantage of the Java class libraries. The best way to learn about how these functions work is to read the source code. You can print the source of nonnative functions by simply entering the function name at the nashorn command prompt. The following sequence of commands shows you how to print the source code for the exec(cmd) function. The output shows that the function uses the Java Runtime class internally to run the command:

```
c:\>jrunscript
nashorn> exec
function exec(cmd) {
    var process = java.lang.Runtime.getRuntime().exec(cmd);
    var inp = new DataInputStream(process.getInputStream());
    var line = null;
    while ((line = inp.readLine()) != null) {
        println(line);
    }
    process.waitFor();
    $exit = process.exitValue();
}
nashorn> exit()

c:\>
```

There are three other global functions provided by `jrunscript` that are worth mentioning. These functions can be used as functions and constructors:

- `jlist(javaList)`
- `jmap(javaMap)`
- `JSInvoker(object)`

The `jlist()` function takes an instance of `java.util.List` and returns a JavaScript object that you can use to access the `List` as if it is an array. You can use the bracket notation with indexes to access the elements of the `List`. The returned object contains a length property that gives you the size of the `List`. Listing 9-3 contains the code showing how to use the `jlist()` function.

Listing 9-3. Using the jlist() Function

```
// jlisttest.js

// Create an ArrayList and add two elements to it
var ArrayList = Java.type("java.util.ArrayList");
var list = new ArrayList();
list.add("Ken");
list.add("Li");

// Convert the ArrayList into a Nashorn array
var names = jlist(list);
print("Accessing an ArrayList as a Nashorn array...");
for(var i = 0; i < names.length; i++) {
    printf("names[%d] = %s", i, names[i]);
}
```

The following command executes the code in Listing 9-3 using the `jrunscript` command-line shell:

```
C:\>jrunscript -f jlisttest.js
Accessing an ArrayList as a Nashorn array...
names[0] = Ken
names[1] = Li
```

The `jmap()` function takes an instance of `java.util.Map` and returns a JavaScript object that you can use to access the Map. The keys in the Map becomes the properties of the JavaScript object. Listing 9-4 contains the code showing how to use the `jmap()` function.

Listing 9-4. Using the jmap() Function

```
// jmaptest.js

// Create an HashMap and add two elements to it
var HashMap = Java.type("java.util.HashMap");
var map = new HashMap();
map.put("Ken", "(999) 777-3331");
map.put("Li", "(888) 444-1111");

// Convert the HashMap into a Nashorn object
var phoneDir = jmap(map);

print("Accessing a HashMap as a Nashorn object...");
for(var prop in phoneDir) {
    printf("phoneDir['%s'] = %s", prop, phoneDir[prop]);
}

// Use dot notation to access the proeprty
var kenPhone = phoneDir.Ken; // Same as phoneDir["Ken"]
printf("phoneDir.Ken = %s", kenPhone)
```

The following command executes the code in Listing 9-4 using the jrunscript command-line shell:

```
C:\>jrunscript -f jmaptest.js
Accessing a HashMap as a Nashorn object...
phoneDir['Ken'] = (999) 777-3331
phoneDir['Li'] = (888) 444-1111
phoneDir.Ken = (999) 777-3331
```

The JSInvoker() function takes a delegate object as an argument. When a function is invoked on the JSInvoker object, the invoke(name, args) method is called on the delegate object. The name of the function being called is passed as the first argument to the invoke() method; the passed argument to the function call is passed as the second argument to the invoke() method. Listing 9-5 shows how to use the JSInvoker object.

Listing 9-5. Using the JSInvoker Object

```
// jsinvokertest.js
var calcDelegate = { invoke: function(name, args) {
                    if (args.length !== 2) {
                        throw new Error("Must pass 2 arguments to " + name);
                    }

                    var value = 0;
                    if (name === "add")
                        value = args[0] + args[1];
```

```
            else if (name === "subtract")
                value = args[0] - args[1];
            else if (name === "multiply")
                value = args[0] * args[1];
            else if (name === "divide")
                value = args[0] / args[1];
            else
                throw new Error("Operation " + name +
                " not supported.");

            return value;
        }
    };

var calc = new JSInvoker(calcDelegate);
var x = 20.44, y = 30.56;
var addResult = calc.add(x, y); // Will call calcDelegate.invoke("add", [x, y])
var subResult = calc.subtract(x, y);
var mulResult = calc.multiply(x, y);
var divResult = calc.divide(x, y);
printf("calc.add(%.2f, %.2f) = %.2f%n", x, y, addResult);
printf("calc.sub(%.2f, %.2f) = %.2f%n", x, y, subResult);
printf("calc.mul(%.2f, %.2f) = %.2f%n", x, y, mulResult);
printf("calc.div(%.2f, %.2f) = %.2f", x, y, divResult);
```

The code creates an object named calcDelegate that contains an invoke() method. The JSInvoker object wraps the calcDelegate object. When a function is called on the calc object, the invoke() method of the calcDelegate object is called with the function name as its first argument and function arguments passed as an array as the second argument. The invoke() function performs addition, subtraction, multiplication, and division on the arguments. The following command shows how to execute the code:

```
c:\>jrunscript -f jsinvokertest.js
calc.add(20.44, 30.56) = 51.00
calc.sub(20.44, 30.56) = -10.12
calc.mul(20.44, 30.56) = 624.65
calc.div(20.44, 30.56) = 0.67
```

The JSInvoker object works in Java 7 but generates the following error in Java 8 when you run this example. It seems to be a bug introduced in Java 8:

```
c:\>jrunscript -f jsinvokertest.js
script error in file jsinvoker.js : TypeError: [object JSAdapter] has no
such function "add" in jsinvoker.js at line number 25
```

The jrunscript shell also creates aliases for several Java classes such as java.io.File, java.io.Reader, java.net.URL, and so on, so you can refer to them by their simple names. Several other objects are also exposed as global objects by jrunscript. You can get the entire list of global objects and their types printed on the command-line using the following command. Only partial output has been shown. Notice that the output will also include a property named p, which is the variable name declared in the for loop.

```
c:\>jrunscript
nashorn> for(var p in this) print(p, typeof this[p]);
engine object
JSInvoker function
jmap function
jlist function
inStream function
outStream function
streamClose function
javaByteArray function
pwd function
...

nashorn>exit()

c:\
```

Summary

The JDK includes a script-engine-independent command-line shell called jrunscript. It can be used to evaluate scripts entered on the command-line or from files. You can find this shell in the JAVA_HOME\bin directory, where JAVA_HOME is the directory in which you have installed the JDK.

The jrunscript command-line shell can run scripts written in any scripting language supported by Java. By default, it runs Nashorn scripts. To use a scripting language other than Nashorn, you need to include the language's JAR file with jrunscript using the -cp or -classpath option. The -l option lets you choose the scripting language you want to use.

You can use jrunscript in one-liner mode, batch mode, and interactive mode. The one-liner mode lets you execute one line of script. You invoke the one-liner mode using the -e option. The batch mode lets you execute scripts stored in a file. You invoke the batch mode using the -f option. The interactive mode lets you execute scripts entered on the command-line interactively. You invoke interactive mode by not using the -e and -f options, or by using the -f - option (note a following - after -f).

You can list all of the available script engines with jrunscript using the -q option. Notice that you must include the script engine's JAR files for languages other than Nashorn to make them available with jrunscript. Several useful global functions and objects are made available by the jrunscript shell. For example, the cat() function can be used to print the contents of a file or URL, optionally applying a filter.

■ ■ ■

CHAPTER 10

The jjs Command-Line Tool

In this chapter, you will learn:

- What the jjs command-line tool is
- How to invoke the jjs command-line tool
- How to pass arguments to the jjs command-line tool
- How to use the jjs command-line tool in interactive and scripting mode

To work with the Nashorn script engine, JDK 8 includes a new command-line tool called jjs. If you wonder what jjs stands for, it stands for Java JavaScript. The command is located in the JDK_HOME\bin directory. The command can be used to run scripts in files or scripts entered on the command-line in interactive mode. It can also be used to execute shell scripts.

The Syntax

The syntax to invoke the command is:

jjs [options] [script-files] [-- arguments]

Here:

- [options] are options for the jjs command. Multiple options are separated by a space
- [script-files] is the list of script files to be interpreted by the Nashorn engine
- [-- arguments] is the list of arguments to be passed to the scripts or the interactive shell as arguments. Arguments are specified after double hyphens and they can be accessed using the arguments property inside the script

The Options

The jjs tool supports several options. Table 10-1 lists all the options for the jjs tool. Some of the options have a variant that work the same way; for example, the options -classpath and -cp are synonymous. Both are used to set CLASSPATH. Notice that some of the options start with two hyphens. To print the list of all options, run the tool on the command prompt with the -xhelp option:

```
jjs -xhelp
```

Table 10-1. Options for the jjs Comand-Line Tool

Option	Description
-D<name>=<value>	Sets a system property for the Java runtime. This option can be repeated to set multiple runtime property values.
-ccs=<size> --class-cache-size=<size>	Sets the class cache size (in bytes). By default, the class cache size is set to 50 bytes. You can use k/K, m/M and g/G with the size to mean KB, MB, and GB in size. The options -ccs=200 and -ccs=2M set the class cache size to 200 bytes and 2 MB, respectively.
-classpath <path> -cp <path>	Specifies CLASSPATH.
-co --compile-only	Compiles the script without running. By default, it is disabled, which means that scripts are compiled and run.
--const-as-var	Replaces the keyword const in scripts with the keyword var. This option is available if a script uses the const keyword, which is not recognized by Nashorn. By default, it is disabled.
-d=<path> --dump-debug-dir=<path>	Specifies a destination directory to dump class files for scripts.
--debug-lines	Generates a line number table in .class files. By default, it is enabled. Specify --debug-lines=false to disable this feature.
--debug-locals	Generates a local variable table in .class files. By default, it is set to false.
-doe --dump-on-error	When this is specified, a full stack trace of the error is printed. By default, a brief error message is printed.

(continued)

Table 10-1. *(continued)*

Option	Description
--early-lvalue-error	Reports invalid lvalue expressions as early errors when the code is parsed. By default, it is set to true. When set to false, invalid lvalue expressions are reported when the code is executed.
--empty-statements	Preserves empty statements in the Java abstract syntax tree (AST). By default, it is set to false.
-fv -fullversion	Prints the full version of the Nashorn engine.
--function-statement-error	Prints an error message when a function declaration is used as a statement. The default is set to false.
--function-statement-warning	Prints a warning message when a function declaration is used as a statement. The default is set to false.
-fx	Launches the script as a JavaFX application.
--global-per-engine	Uses a single global instance per script engine instance. The default is false.
-help -h	Outputs the help message and exits.
-J<flag>	Passes the specified <flag> to the JVM.
-language	Specifies the ECMAScript language version. Valid values are es5 and es6. The default is es5.
--lazy-compilation	Enables lazy code generation strategies by not compiling the entire script at once. The default is true.
--loader-per-compile	Creates a new class loader per compile. The default is true.
-l --locale	Sets the locale for script execution. The default is en-US.
--log=subsystem:lebel	Enables logging of a given level for a given number of subsystems, for example, --log=fields:finest, codegen:info. Logging for multiple subsystems are separated by commas.
-nj --no-java	Disables Java support. The default is false, meaning that using Java classes in scripts are allowed.
-nse --no-syntax-extensions	Disallows nonstandard syntax extensions. The default is false.

(continued)

297

Table 10-1. (*continued*)

Option	Description
-nta --no-typed-arrays	Disables typed arrays support. The default is false.
--optimistic-types	Uses optimistic type assumptions with deoptimizing recompilation. The default is true.
--parse-only	Parses the code without compiling. The default is false.
-pcc --persistent-code-cache	Enables disk cache for compiled scripts. The default is false.
--print-ast	Prints the abstract syntax tree. The default is false.
-pc --print-code	Prints the generated bytecode on standard error or to the specified directory. You can specify a function name for which to print the bytecode. The syntax to specify directory and function is: -pc=dir:<output-directory-path>, function:<function-name>
--print-lower-ast	Prints the lowered abstract syntax tree. The default is false.
-plp --print-lower-parse	Prints the lowered parse tree. The default is false.
--print-mem-usage	Prints the memory usage of instruction register (IR) after each compile stage. The default is false.
--print-no-newline	The print() function will not print a newline character after printing its arguments. The default is false.
-pp --print-parse	Prints the parse tree. The default is false.
--print-symbols	Prints the symbol table. The default is false.
-pcs --profile-callsites	Dumps callsite profile data. The default is false.
-scripting	Enables shell scripting features. The default is false.
--stderr= <filename|stream|tty>	Redirects stderr to the specified filename, stream, or text terminal.
--stdout= <filename|stream|tty>	Redirects stdout to the specified filename, stream, or text terminal.

(*continued*)

Table 10-1. (*continued*)

Option	Description
-strict	Enables strict mode where the scripts are executed using the ECMAScript Edition 5.1 standards. The default is false.
-t=<timezone> -timezone=<timezone>	Sets the time zone for the script execution. The default time zone is Chicago/America.
-tcs=<option> --trace-callsites=<option>	Enables the callsite trace mode. Valid options are miss (traces callsite misses), enterexit (traces callsite enter/exit), and objects (prints object properties). Specify multiple options by separating them with commas: -tcs=miss,enterexit,objects
--verify-code	Verifies the bytecode before running. The default is false.
-v -version	Prints the version of the Nashorn engine. The default is false.
-xhelp	Prints extended help. The default is false.

Using jjs in Interactive Mode

If you run jjs without specifying any options or script files, it is run in interactive mode. The script is interpreted as you enter it. Recall that strings in Nashorn can be enclosed in single quotes or double quotes.

The following are some examples of using the jjs tool in interactive mode. It is assumed that you have included the path to the jjs tool in the PATH environment variable on your machine. If you have not done so, you can replace jjs with JDK_HOME\bin\jjs in the following command. Remember to execute the quit() or exit() function to exit the jjs tool:

```
c:\>jjs
jjs> "Hello Nashorn"
Hello Nashorn
jjs> "Hello".toLowerCase();
hello
jjs> var list = [1, 2, 3, 4, 5]
jjs> var sum = 0;
jjs> for each (x in list) { sum = sum + x};
15
jjs> quit()

c:\>
```

Passing Arguments to jjs

The following is an example of passing arguments to the jjs tool. The first five natural numbers are passed to the jjs tool as arguments and they are accessed using the arguments property later. Notice that you must add a space between the two hyphens and the first argument:

```
c:\>jjs -- 1 2 3 4 5
jjs> for each (x in arguments) print(x)
1
2
3
4
5
jjs> quit()

c:\>
```

Consider the script in Listing 10-1. The script has been saved in a file named stream.js. The script works on a list of integers. The list can be passed to the script as the command-line arguments. If the list is not passed as arguments, it uses the first five natural numbers as the list. It computes the sum of the squares of odd integers in the list. It prints the list and the sum.

Listing 10-1. A Script to Compute the Sum of the Squares of Odd Integers in a List

```
// stream.js

var list;
if (arguments.length == 0) {
    list = [1, 2, 3, 4, 5];
}
else {
  list = arguments;
}

print("List of numbers: " + list);

var sumOfSquaredOdds = list.filter(function(n) {return n % 2 == 1;})
                  .map(function(n) {return n * n;})
                  .reduce(function(sum, n) {return sum + n;}, 0);

print("Sum of the squares of odd numbers: " + sumOfSquaredOdds);
```

Using the jjs tool, you can run the script in the stream.js file as follows. It is assumed that the stream.js file is in the current directory. Otherwise, you need to specify the full path of the file:

```
c:\>jjs stream.js
List of numbers: 1,2,3,4,5
Sum of the squares of odd numbers: 35

c:\>jjs stream.js -- 10 11 12 13 14 15
List of numbers: 10,11,12,13,14,15
Sum of the squares of odd numbers: 515

c:\>
```

Using jjs in Scripting Mode

The jjs tool can be invoked in scripting mode, which allows you to run shell commands. You can start the jjs tool in scripting mode using the -scripting option. The shell commands are enclosed in back quotes, not single/double quotes. The following are examples of using the date and ls shell commands using the jjs tool in scripting mode:

```
c:\>jjs -scripting
jjs> `date`
Wed Oct 15 15:27:07 CDT 2014

jjs> `ls -l`
total 3102
drwxr-xr-x  4 ksharan Administrators      0 Jan 11  2014 $AVG
drwxr-xr-x  5 ksharan Administrators      0 Jan 22  2014 $Recycle.Bin
-rw-r--r--  1 ksharan Administrators      1 Jun 18  2013 BOOTNXT
-rw-r--r--  1 ksharan Administrators     94 May 23  2013 DBAR_Ver.txt
More output goes here...
jjs> exit()

c:\>
```

Nashorn defines several global objects and functions in scripting mode, as listed in Table 10-2.

Table 10-2. *Global Objects and Functions Available in Scripting Mode*

Global Object	Description
$ARG	Stores the arguments passed to the script. Works the same way as arguments.
$ENV	Maps all environment variables to an object.
$EXEC(cmd, input)	A global function used to run a command in a new process passing input to cmd. Both arguments can be commands, and in that case, the output of input will be passed as input Io cmd.
$OUT	Stores the latest standard output of the process. For example, the result of executing the $EXEC() is saved in $OUT.
$ERR	Stores the latest standard output of the process.
$EXIT	Stores the exit code of the process. A nonzero value indicates that the process failed.
echo(arg1, arg2,...)	The echo() function works the same as the print() function, but it is available only in scripting mode.
readLine(prompt)	Reads one line of input from standard input. The specified argument is displayed as a prompt. By default, the read input is displayed on the standard output. The function returns the read input.
readFully(filePath)	Reads the entire contents of the specified file. The contents are displayed on the standard output by default. You can assign the returned value of the function to a variable.

The following script shows how to use the $ARG global object:

```
c:\>jjs -scripting -- 10 20 30
jjs> for each(var arg in $ARG) print(arg);
10
20
30
jjs>
```

The following script shows how to use the $ENV global object. It prints the value of the OS environment variable on Windows, and lists all environment variables:

```
jjs> print($ENV.OS);
Windows_NT
jjs> for(var x in $ENV) print(x);
LOCALAPPDATA
PROCESSOR_LEVEL
```

```
FP_NO_HOST_CHECK
USERDOMAIN
LOGONSERVER
PROMPT
OS
...
```

The following script uses the $EXEC() global function to list all files with the extension txt, which contains the ksharan:

```
jjs> $EXEC("grep -l ksharan *.txt");
test.txt
```

You can capture the output of the shell command in a variable. Scripting mode allows for expression substitution in strings enclosed in double quotes. Notice that the expression substitution feature is not available in strings enclosed in single quotes. The expression is specified as ${expression}. The following commands capture the value of the date shell command in a variable and embed the date value in a string using the expression substitution. Notice that in the example the expression substitution does not work when the string is enclosed in single quotes:

```
c:\ >jjs -scripting
jjs> var today = `date`
jjs> "Today is ${today}"
Today is Mon Jul 14 22:48:26 CDT 2014

jjs> 'Today is ${today}'
Today is ${today}
jjs> quit()

c:\>
```

You can also execute the shell script stored in a file using the scripting mode:

```
C:\> jjs -scripting myscript.js
```

The jjs tool supports heredocs in script files that can be run in scripting mode. A heredoc is also known as a *here document, here-string,* or *here-script.* It is a multiline string in which whitespaces are preserved. A heredoc starts with a double angle bracket (<<) and a delimiting identifier. Typically, EOF or END is used as the delimiting identifier. However, you can use any other identifier that is not used as an identifier elsewhere in the script. The multiline string starts at the end line. The string ends with the same delimiting identifier. The following is an example of using a heredoc in Nashorn:

```
var str = <<EOF
This is a multi-line string using the heredoc syntax.
Bye Heredoc!
EOF
```

Listing 10-2 contains the script that uses a heredoc in Nashorn. The $ARG property is defined only in scripting mode, and its value is the arguments passed to the script using the jjs tool:

Listing 10-2. The Contents of the heredoc.js File That Using Heredoc Style a Multiline String

```
// heredoc.js
var str = <<EOF
This is a multiline string.
Number of arguments passed to this
script is ${$ARG.length}
Arguments are ${$ARG}

Bye Heredoc!
EOF

print(str);
```

You can execute the heredoc.js script file as shown:

```
c:\> jjs -scripting heredoc.js
This is a multi-line string.
Number of arguments passed to this
script is 0
Arguments are

Bye Heredoc!

c:\> jjs -scripting heredoc.js -- Kishori Sharan
This is a multi-line string.
Number of arguments passed to this
script is 2
Arguments are Kishori,Sharan

Bye Heredoc!
```

In addition to two styles of comments (// and /* */) supported by Nashorn, the jjs tool supports an additional single-line comment style that starts with a number sign (#). If a script file run by the jjs tool starts with the sign #, the jjs tool automatically enables the scripting mode and executes the entire script in scripting mode. Consider the script shown in Listing 10-3.

Listing 10-3. Special Comments for the jjs Tool. Contents Are Stored in jjscomments.js File

```
# This script will run in scripting mode by the jjs tool
# because it starts with a number sign

// Set the current directory to C:\kishori
$ENV.PWD = "C:\\kishori";

// Get the list of files and directories in the current directory
var str = `ls -F`;

print(str);
```

The following command runs the script in the `jjscomments.js` file. The script starts with the # sign, so the `jjs` tool will automatically enable the scripting mode:

```
c:\>jjs jjscomments.js
books/
ejb/
hello.txt
important/
programs/
rmi.log
rmi.policy
scripts/

c:\>
```

With the `jjs` tool interpreting a script file with the first # sign as a shell executable, you can use a shebang (#!) at the beginning of the script file to run it as a script executable. Notice that a shebang is directly supported on Unix-like operating systems. You will need to include the path to the jjs tool in the shebang, so the script will be executed by the `jjs` tool. The script file will be passed to the jjs tool to execute. Because the script file starts with a # sign (part of the shebang #!), the `jjs` tool will automatically enable the scripting mode. The following is an example of a script using a shebang, assuming that the `jjs` tool is located at /usr/bin directory:

```
#!/usr/bin/jjs
var str = `ls -F`;
print(str);
```

Summary

The Java 8 ships a command-line tool called jjs. It is located in the JDK_HOME\bin directory. It is used to run Nashorn scripts on a command line. The jjs tool supports many options. It can be invoked to run scripts in a file, in interactive mode, and in scripting mode.

If you do not specify any options or script files, jjs is run in interactive mode. In interactive mode, scripts are interpreted as they are entered.

If you invoke jjs using the -scripting option, it is run in scripting mode, allowing you to use any operating system-specific shell commands. Shell commands are enclosed in back quotes. In scripting mode, the jjs tool supports heredocs in script files. If a script file starts with the # sign, running the script file automatically enables scripting mode. This supports executing scripts that contains a shebang (#! at the beginning of the script).

■ ■ ■

CHAPTER 11

Using JavaFX in Nashorn

In this chapter, you will learn:

- The JavaFX support in the jjs command-line tool

- Providing an implementation for the init(), start(), and stop() methods of the JavaFX Application class in scripts

- How to load and use JavaFX packages and classes using the predefined scripts

- Creating and launching a simple JavaFX application using a Nashorn script

Throughout this chapter, it is assumed that you have beginner-level experience in JavaFX 8. If you do not have experience in JavaFX, please learn JavaFX before reading this chapter.

JavaFX Support in jjs

The jjs command-line tool lets you launch JavaFX applications created in Nashorn scripts. You need to use the -fx option with the jjs tool to run a script as a JavaFX application. The following command runs a script stored in the myfxapp.js file as a JavaFX application:

```
jjs -fx myfxapp.js
```

Structure of JavaFX Applications in Scripts

In a JavaFX application, you override the following three methods of the Application class to manage the lifecycle of the application:

- The init() method

- The start() method

- The stop() method

In a Nashorn script, you can manage the lifecycle of a JavaFX application the same way as you do in Java. You can have three functions named init(), start(), and stop() in the script. Notice that all three functions are optional in a Nashorn script. These functions correspond to the three methods in the Java class and they are called as follows, in order:

1. The init() function is called. You can initialize the application in this function.

2. The start() function is called. As is the case in a Java application, the start() function is passed the reference to the primary stage of the application. You need to populate the scene, add the scene to the primary stage, and show the stage.

3. The stop() function is called when the JavaFX application exits.

■ **Tip** If you do not have the start() function in a script for a JavaFX application, the entire script in the global scope is considered the code for the start() function. You can have functions other than these three functions. They will be treated as functions without assigning any special meaning to them. Those functions will not be called automatically; you will need to call them in your script.

Listing 11-1 contains code for a simple JavaFX application in Java. It displays a window with a Text node in a StackPane. The HelloFX class contains the init(), start(), and stop() methods. Figure 11-1 shows the window displayed by the HelloFX application. When you exit the application the stop() method displays a message on the standard output.

Listing 11-1. The HelloFX Application in Java

```java
// HelloFX.java
package com.jdojo.script;

import javafx.application.Application;
import javafx.scene.Scene;
import javafx.scene.layout.StackPane;
import javafx.scene.text.Font;
import javafx.scene.text.Text;
import javafx.stage.Stage;

public class HelloFX extends Application {
        private Text msg;
        private StackPane sp;

        public static void main(String[] args) {
                Application.launch(HelloFX.class);
        }
```

```
@Override
public void init() {
        msg = new Text("Hello JavaFX from Nashorn!");
        msg.setFont(Font.font("Helvetica", 18));
        sp = new StackPane(msg);
}

@Override
public void start(Stage stage) throws Exception {
        stage.setTitle("Hello FX");
        stage.setScene(new Scene(sp, 300, 100));
        stage.sizeToScene();
        stage.show();
}

@Override
public void stop() {
        System.out.println("Hello FX application is stopped.");
}
}
```

Hello FX application is stopped.

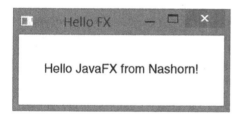

Figure 11-1. *The Windows Displayed by the HelloFX Application*

Listing 11-2 contains the Nashorn script for the HelloFX application. It is a one-to-one translation of the Java code in Listing 11-1. Notice that the code for the same application is much shorter when written in Nashorn. The script is stored in the hellofx.js file. You can run the script using the command prompt as follows and it will display the same window as shown in Figure 11-1:

```
jjs -fx hellofx.js
```

Listing 11-2. The Nashorn Script for the HelloFX Application Stored in hellofx.js

```
// hellofx.js

var msg;
var sp;

function init() {
        msg = new javafx.scene.control.Label("Hello JavaFX from Nashorn!");
        msg.font = javafx.scene.text.Font.font("Helvetica", 18);
        sp = new javafx.scene.layout.StackPane(msg);
}

function start(stage) {
        stage.setTitle("Hello FX");
        stage.setScene(new javafx.scene.Scene(sp, 300, 100));
        stage.sizeToScene();
        stage.show();
}

function stop() {
        java.lang.System.out.println("Hello FX application is stopped.");
}
```

You are not required to have any of the init(), start(), and stop() functions in the script. Listing 11-3 contains another version of the HelloFX application. The init() and stop() functions are not included. The code from the init() function has been moved to global scope. The stop() method has been removed, so you will not see a message on the standard output when the application is exited. Nashorn will execute the code in the global scope first, and then call the start() method. The script is stored in the hellofx2.js file. Running it displays the same window as shown in Figure 11-1. You can run the script:

```
jjs -fx hellofx2.js
```

Listing 11-3. Another Version of the HelloFX Application without init() and stop() Methods

```
// hellofx2.js

var msg = new javafx.scene.control.Label("Hello JavaFX from Nashorn!");
msg.font = javafx.scene.text.Font.font("Helvetica", 18);
var sp = new javafx.scene.layout.StackPane(msg);

function start(stage) {
        stage.setTitle("Hello FX");
        stage.setScene(new javafx.scene.Scene(sp, 300, 100));
        stage.sizeToScene();
        stage.show();
}
```

You can simplify the script for the HelloFX application a bit more. You can remove the start() function from the script. The JavaFX runtime creates and passes the reference of the primary stage to the start() function. How will you get the reference to the primary stage if you do not have the start() function? Nashorn creates a global object named $STAGE, which is the reference to the primary stage. You can use this global object to work with the primary stage. You do not even need to show the primary stage; Nashorn will automatically show it for you.

Listing 11-3 contains the script that is another version for the same HelloFX application. It uses the global object $STAGE to reference the primary stage. I have removed the init() function. This time, you are not even calling the show() method of the primary stage. You are letting Nashorn show the primary stage automatically for you. The script is saved in the hellofx3.js file. You can run the script:

```
jjs -fx hellofx3.js
```

Listing 11-4. Another Version of the HelloFX Application without init(), start(), and stop() Functions

```
// hellofx3.js

var msg = new javafx.scene.control.Label("Hello JavaFX from Nashorn!");
msg.font = javafx.scene.text.Font.font("Helvetica", 18);
var sp = new javafx.scene.layout.StackPane(msg);
$STAGE.setTitle("Hello FX");
$STAGE.setScene(new javafx.scene.Scene(sp, 300, 100));
$STAGE.sizeToScene();
// $STAGE.show(); // No need to show the primary stage. Nashorn will
// automatically show it.
```

Let's try one more combination of functions. You will provide the init() function but not the start() function. Listing 11-5 contains the code for the same HelloFX application. It contains the init() method that creates the controls, but the start() method is removed.

Listing 11-5. Incorrect Implementation of JavaFX Application in a Nashorn Script

```
// incorrectfxapp.js

var msg;
var sp;

function init() {
    msg = new javafx.scene.control.Label("Hello JavaFX from Nashorn!");
    msg.font = javafx.scene.text.Font.font("Helvetica", 18);
    sp = new javafx.scene.layout.StackPane(msg);
}
```

```
$STAGE.setTitle("Hello FX");
$STAGE.setScene(new javafx.scene.Scene(sp, 300, 100));
$STAGE.sizeToScene();
```

When you run the script in Listing 11-5, it throws an exception, as shown:

```
jjs -fx incorrectfxapp.js
```

```
Exception in Application start method
Exception in thread "main" java.lang.RuntimeException: Exception in
Application start method
        at com.sun.javafx.application.LauncherImpl.
launchApplication1(LauncherImpl.java:875)
        at com.sun.javafx.application.LauncherImpl.lambda$launchApplication
$149(LauncherImpl.java:157)
        at com.sun.javafx.application.LauncherImpl$$Lambda$1/23211803.
run(Unknown Source)
        at java.lang.Thread.run(Thread.java:745)
Caused by: java.lang.ClassCastException: Cannot cast
jdk.nashorn.internal.runtime.Undefined to javafx.scene.Parent
        at java.lang.invoke.MethodHandleImpl.newClassCastException
(MethodHandleImpl.java:364)
...
```

The exception is thrown when you try to create the scene using the global variable sp, which is a reference to a StackPane. Contrary to expectations, the init() method is not called before running the code in the global scope. The code in the global scope is called before the init() function is automatically called. In the script, the init() method creates the controls to be added to the scene. When the scene is being created, the variable sp is still undefined, which causes the exception. If you show the primary stage in the script, the init() function is called after the primary stage is already shown. If you let Nashorn show the primary stage for you, the init() function is called before the primary stage.

■ **Tip** If you do not provide a start() function in a JavaFX script, providing the init() function is almost useless because such an init() function will be called after the primary stage has been constructed. If you want to use the init() function to initialize your JavaFX application, you should provide both init() and start() methods so that they are called in order.

Finally, I will show you the simplest JavaFX application, which can be written in just one line of script. It will show a message in a window. The window will not have title text, however. Listing 11-6 contains the one-liner script. It shows the beauty of Nashorn, which shrinks 10 to 15 lines of Java code into 1 line of script! The following command runs the script that displays a window, as shown in Figure 11-2:

```
jjs -fx simplestfxapp.js
```

Listing 11-6. The Simplest JavaFX Application in Nashorn

```
// simplestfxapp.js

$STAGE.scene = new javafx.scene.Scene(new javafx.scene.control.Label
("Hello JavaFX Scripting"));
```

Figure 11-2. *The simplest JavaFX application using Nashorn script*

It was an understatement that you need to write one line of code for the simplest JavaFX application in Nashorn. The true statement is that you do not need to write even one line of code in Nashorn to display a window. Create a script file named empty.js and do not write any code in it. You can name the file anything else. Use the following command to run the empty.js file:

```
jjs -fx empty.js
```

The command will display a window as shown in Figure 11-3. How did Nashorn display a window without you writing even one line of code? Recall that Nashorn creates the primary stage and a global object $STAGE to represent that primary stage. If it sees that you have not shown the primary stage, it shows it for you. That is what happened in this case. The script file is empty and Nashorn automatically displayed the empty primary stage.

Figure 11-3. *The simplest JavaFX application using a Nashorn script without writing even one line of code*

Importing JavaFX Types

You can use the fully qualified name of the JavaFX classes or import them using the Java.type() function. In the previous section, you used the fully qualified names of all JavaFX classes. The following snippet of code shows the two approaches to create a Label in JavaFX:

```
// Using the fully qualified name of the Label class
var msg = new javafx.scene.control.Label("Hello JavaFX!");

// Using Java.type() function
var Label = Java.type("javafx.scene.control.Label");
var msg = new Label("Hello JavaFX!");
```

It may be cumbersome to type the fully qualified names of all JavaFX classes. Aren't scripts supposed to be shorter than Java code? Nashorn has a way to make your JavaFX script shorter. It includes several script files that import the JavaFX types as their simple names. You will need to load those script files using the load() method before using the simple names of JavaFX classes in your script. For example, Nashorn includes a fx:controls.js script file that imports all JavaFX control classes as their simple class names. Table 11-1 contains the list of script files and the classes/packages that they import.

Table 11-1. *The List of Nashorn Script Files and the Classes/Packages That They Import*

Nashorn Script File	Imported Classes/Packages
fx:base.js	javafx.stage.Stage javafx.scene.Scene javafx.scene.Group javafx/beans javafx/collections javafx/events javafx/util
fx:graphics.js	javafx/animation javafx/application javafx/concurrent javafx/css javafx/geometry javafx/print javafx/scene javafx/stage
fx:controls.js	javafx/scene/chart javafx/scene/control
fx:fxml.js	javafx/fxml
fx:web.js	javafx/scene/web
fx:media.js	javafx/scene/media
fx:swing.js	javafx/embed/swing
fx:swt.js	javafx/embed/swt

The following snippet of code shows how to load this script file and use the simple name of the javafx.scene.control.Label class:

```
// Import all JavaFX control class names
load("fx:controls.js")

// Use the simple name of the Label control
var msg = new Label("Hello JavaFX!");
```

Listing 11-7 contains the code for a JavaFX greeter application that is saved in a file named greeter.js. You can run the script as follows:

```
jjs -fx greeter.js
```

Listing 11-7. A JavaFX Application Using Nashorn Script

```
// greeter.js

// Load Nashorn predefined scripts to import JavaFX specific classes
// and packages
load("fx:base.js");
load("fx:controls.js");
load("fx:graphics.js");

// Define the start() method of the JavaFX application class
function start(stage) {
        var nameLbl = new Label("Enter your name:");
        var nameFld = new TextField();
        var msg = new Label();
        msg.style = "-fx-text-fill: blue;";

        // Create buttons
        var sayHelloBtn = new Button("Say Hello");
        var exitBtn = new Button("Exit");

        // Add the event handler for the Say Hello button
        sayHelloBtn.onAction = sayHello;

        // Call the same fucntion sayHello() when the user
        nameFld.onAction = sayHello;

        // Add the event handler for the Exit button
        exitBtn.onAction = function() {
                Platform.exit();
        };

        // Create the root node
        var root = new VBox();
        root.style = "-fx-padding: 10;" +
                     "-fx-border-style: solid inside;" +
                     "-fx-border-width: 2;" +
                     "-fx-border-insets: 5;" +
                     "-fx-border-radius: 5;" +
                     "-fx-border-color: blue;";

        // Set the vertical spacing between children to 5px
        root.spacing = 5;

        // Add children to the root node
        root.children.addAll(msg, new HBox(nameLbl, nameFld,
        sayHelloBtn, exitBtn));
```

```
        // Set the scene and title for the stage
        stage.scene = new Scene(root);
        stage.title = "Greeter";

        // Show the stage
        stage.show();

        // A nested function to say hello based on the entered name
        function sayHello(evt) {
                var name = nameFld.getText();
                if (name.trim().length() > 0) {
                        msg.text = "Hello " + name;
                }
                else {
                        msg.text = "Hello there";
                }
        }
}
```

The greeter application displays a window, as shown in Figure 11-4. Enter a name and press the Enter key or click the Say Hello button. A message with a greeting will be displayed.

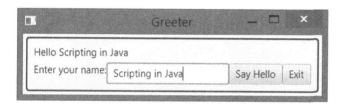

Figure 11-4. The greeter JavaFX aplication in action

Developing a JavaFX application is much easier in Nashorn. In the script, you are able to call the getters and setters of Java objects using properties. You can access properties directly for all Java objects, not just for JavaFX objects. For example, instead of writing root.setSpacing(5) in Java, you can write root.spacing = 5 in Nashorn.

Adding the event handler for buttons is also easier. You can set an anonymous function as the event handler for the buttons. Notice that you are able to use onAction property to set the event handler rather than calling the setOnAction() method of the Button class. The following snippet of code shows how to set the ActionEvent handler for a button using a function reference sayHello:

```
// Add the event handler for the Say Hello button
sayHelloBtn.onAction = sayHello
```

Notice that, in the example, you used a nested function sayHello() inside the start() function. The reference to the function is used as the event handler. An event handler takes an argument and the evt formal parameter in the sayHello() function is that event object.

Summary

The jjs command-line tool in Nashorn supports launching a JavaFX application written in scripts. The -fx option is used with jjs to launch a JavaFX application. The script for a JavaFX application can have init(), start(), and stop() functions that correspond to the init(), start(), and stop() methods of the JavaFX Application class. Nashorn calls these functions in the same order as they are called in a JavaFX application.

The start() function is passed a reference to the primary stage. If you do not provide a start() function, the entire script is considered the start() function. Nashorn provides a global object named $STAGE, which is the reference to the primary stage. If you do not provide a start() function, you need to use the $STAGE global variable to access the primary stage. If you do not provide a start() method and do not show the primary stage, Nashorn will call the $STAGE.show() method for you.

■ ■ ■

CHAPTER 12

Java APIs for Nashorn

In this chapter, you will learn:

- What Java APIs for Nashorn are
- How to instantiate the Nashorn engine directly
- How to pass options to the Nashorn engine in Java code and on the command-line
- How to share globals among script contexts in a Nashorn engine
- How to add, update, delete, and read properties of script objects in Java code
- How to create script objects and invoke their methods in Java code
- How to invoke script functions from Java code
- How to convert script dates to Java dates

What Are Java APIs for Nashorn?

It is straightforward to use Java classes in Nashorn scripts. Sometimes you may want to use Nashorn objects in Java code. You may pass Nashorn objects to Java code or Java code may evaluate a Nashorn script and retrieve the reference of Nashorn objects. When Nashorn objects cross the boundary (script-to-Java), they need to be represented as objects of a Java class and you should be able to use them like any other Java objects.

If your application uses only Nashorn, to take full advantage of the Nashorn engine you may want to use options and extensions available in Nashorn. You will need to instantiate the Nashorn engine in Java code, using the classes that are specific to the Nashorn engine, not using the classes in the Java Scripting API.

The Java APIs for Nashorn provide Java classes and interfaces that let you deal with the Nashorn scripting engine and Nashorn objects directly in Java code. Figure 12-1 depicts a class diagram of those classes and interfaces that you are supposed to use in the client code when you are dealing with the Nashorn engine. They are in the jdk.nashorn.api.scripting package.

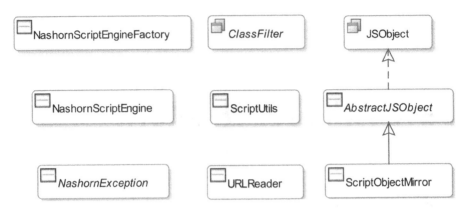

Figure 12-1. A class diagram of Java APIs for Nashorn in the jdk.nashorn.api.scripting package

Note that the Nashorn scripting engine internally uses a lot of other classes in other packages. However, you are not supposed to use them in your application directly, except for classes from the jdk.nashorn.api.scripting package. The webpage at https://wiki.openjdk.java.net/display/Nashorn/Nashorn+jsr223+engine+notes contains the links for the documentation for the jdk.nashorn.api.scripting package.

■ **Note**   The ClassFilter interface in the jdk.nashorn.api.scripting package has been added in JDK8u40, which is planned to be shipped at the end of the first quarter of 2015. If you want to use this interface earlier, you will need to download the early access build for JDK8u40.

I will discuss some Nashorn-specific Java classes and interfaces in detail in subsequent sections. Table 12-1 lists the classes and interfaces in the jdk.nashorn.api.scripting package with their descriptions.

Table 12-1. *The List of Java Classes/Interfaces to be Used with Nashorn Scripting Engine*

Class/Interface	Description
NashornScriptEngine Factory	This is a script engine factory implementation for the Nashorn engine. You need to instantiate this class when you want to create a Nashorn engine that uses Nashorn-specific options and extensions.
NashornScriptEngine	This is the script engine implementation class for the Nashorn engine. You do not instantiate this class directly. Its instance is obtained using the getScriptEngine() method of a NashornScriptEngineFactory object.
NashornException	This is the base exception class for all exceptions thrown from Nashorn scripts. When you use the Java Scripting API, your Java code receives an instance of the ScriptException class that will be a wrapper for the NashornException. An instance of the NashornException may be thrown directly in Java code if you access scripts directly from Java code such as by implementing a Java interface in scripts and using that interface's instance in Java code. This class contains many methods that give you access to the details of the script error such as line number, column number, the script's error object, and so on.
ClassFilter	ClassFilter is an interface. You can use its instance to restrict the availability of some or all Java classes in the Nashorn script. You will need to pass an instance of this interface when instantiating a NashornScriptEngine using a NashornScriptEngineFactory.
ScriptUtils	A utility class intended to be used in Nashorn scripts.
URLReader	Reads contents of a URL. It inherits from the java.io.Reader class.
JSObject	An instance of this interface represents a Nashorn object in Java code. If you want to pass a Java object to a Nashorn script that should be treated as a Nashorn object, you need to pass an instance of this interface. You can use the bracket notation in Nashorn scripts to access and set properties of such Java objects.
AbstractJSObject	This is an abstract class that implements the JSObject interface.
ScriptObjectMirror	This is a mirror object that wraps a Nashorn script object. It inherits from the AbstractJSObject class and implements the Bindings interface. When Java code receives a Nashorn object from scripts, the script object is wrapped in a ScriptObjectMirror instance before being passed to the Java code.

Instantiating the Nashorn Engine

In previous chapters, you have been instantiating the Nashorn engine in Java code using the standard Java Scripting API. The Nashorn engine provides several custom features. To take advantage of those features, you will need to instantiate the Nashorn engine directly. First, you will need to create an object of the NashornScriptEngineFactory class, and then call one of the overloaded versions of the getScriptEngine() method to create a Nashorn engine:

```
// Create a Nashorn engine factory
NashornScriptEngineFactory factory = new NashornScriptEngineFactory();

// Create a Nashorn engine with default options
ScriptEngine engine = factory.getScriptEngine();
```

By default, the Nashorn engine factory creates a Nashorn engine with the --dump-on-error option enabled. I will show you how to set other options for the Nashorn engine in the next example.

The following snippet of code creates a Nashorn engine with the --no-java and -strict options:

```
// Create a Nashorn engine factory
NashornScriptEngineFactory factory = new NashornScriptEngineFactory();

// Store the Nashorn options in a String array
String[] options = {"--no-java", "-strict"};

// Create the Nashorn engine with the options
ScriptEngine engine = factory.getScriptEngine(options);
```

Because of the --no-java option, you cannot use any Java classes inside the scripts executed by this engine. The -strict option will force the engine to execute all scripts in strict mode.

You can also pass options to the Nashorn engine using the nashorn.args system property on the command-line. The following command runs the com.jdojo.script. Test class, passing four options to the Nashorn engine:

```
java -Dnashorn.args="--global-per-engine -strict --no-java --language=es5"
com.jdojo.script.Test
```

Notice that options are separated by a space and they all are passed as one string. If you have only one option to pass, you can omit the double quotes around the option's value. The following command passes only one option, --no-java, to the engine:

```
java -Dnashorn.args=--no-java com.jdojo.script.Test
```

The following snippet of code creates a Nashorn engine using a class filter, which is an instance of the ClassFilter interface, to restrict the usage of any classes from the com.jdojo package and its subpackages. Notice that the ClassFilter interface was added in JDK8u40; it is not available in JDK8:

```
NashornScriptEngineFactory factory = new NashornScriptEngineFactory();
ScriptEngine engine = factory.getScriptEngine(clsName -> clsName.
startsWith("com.jdojo"));
```

ClassFilter is a functional interface. Its method is passed the fully qualified name of the Java class that the Nashorn script is trying to use. If the method returns true, the class can be used in the script; otherwise, the class cannot be used in the script.

■ **Tip** If you do not want any Java classes to be exposed in scripts, you can use clsName -> false as the lambda expression for the ClassFilter. Using a Java class in the script that is restricted by the ClassFilter throws a java.lang.ClassNotFound exception.

The following is a list of the overloaded versions of the getScriptEngine() method of the NashornScriptEngineFactory class:

- ScriptEngine getScriptEngine()

- ScriptEngine getScriptEngine(String... args)

- ScriptEngine getScriptEngine(ClassFilter classFilter)

- ScriptEngine getScriptEngine(ClassLoader appLoader)

- ScriptEngine getScriptEngine(String[] args, ClassLoader appLoader)

- ScriptEngine getScriptEngine(String[] args, ClassLoader appLoader, ClassFilter classFilter)

Sharing the Engine Globals

By default, the Nashorn engine maintains the global objects per script context. In this discussion, the term "globals" means the global variables and declarations stored in the global scope of the Nashorn script, which you refer to by this in the top-level scripts. Do not mix up the global scope bindings in the script context with the globals in the script. The script globals are searched first when you reference any variables or create variables in your script. If you reference a variable in a script that is not found in the script globals, the engine will search for it in the global scope bindings of the script context. For example, the script objects Object, Math, String, and so on are part of the script globals. Consider the program and its output in Listing 12-1.

Listing 12-1. Using Multiple Script Globals Per Nashron Engine

```java
// MultiGlobals.java
package com.jdojo.script;

import javax.script.ScriptContext;
import javax.script.ScriptEngine;
import javax.script.ScriptEngineManager;
import javax.script.SimpleScriptContext;

public class MultiGlobals {
public static void main(String[] args) {
                // Get the Nashorn script engine
                ScriptEngineManager manager = new ScriptEngineManager();
                ScriptEngine engine = manager.getEngineByName("JavaScript");

                try {
                        // Add a variable named msg to the script globals
                        engine.eval("var msg = 'Hello globals'");

                        // Print the value of the msg variable
                        engine.eval("print(this.msg);");

                        // Execute the same script as above, but using a new
                        // ScriptContext object. The engine will use a fresh
                        // copy of the globals and will not find this.msg that
                        // was created and associated with the default script
                        // context of the engine previously.
                        ScriptContext ctx = new SimpleScriptContext();
                        engine.eval("print(this.msg);", ctx);

                }
                catch (Exception e) {
                        e.printStackTrace();
                }
        }
}
```

```
Hello globals
undefined
```

The program performs the following steps:

- Creates a Nashorn engine with default options.

- Executes a script using the eval() method that uses the default script context of the engine. The script creates a global variable named msg that is stored in the script globals. You can refer to the variable using its simple name msg or this.msg in the global scope.

- Executes a script using the eval() method that uses the default script context of the engine that prints the value of the msg variable. The first line in the output confirms that the correct value of the msg variable is printed.

- Executes a script using the eval() method that uses a new script context. The script tries to print the value of the global variable msg. The second line in the output, by printing undefined, confirms that the variable named msg does not exist in the script globals.

This is the default behavior of the Nashorn engine. It creates a fresh copy of the globals per script context. If you want to use the globals of the default context (if you want to share globals), you can do so by copying the engine scope Bindings of the default context to your new script context. Listing 12-2 uses this approach to share the script globals between two script contexts.

Listing 12-2. Sharing Script Globals by Copying the Engine Scope Bindings of the Engine's Default Context

```
// CopyingGlobals.java
package com.jdojo.script;

import javax.script.Bindings;
import javax.script.ScriptContext;
import static javax.script.ScriptContext.ENGINE_SCOPE;
import javax.script.ScriptEngine;
import javax.script.ScriptEngineManager;
import javax.script.SimpleScriptContext;

public class CopyingGlobals {
        public static void main(String[] args) {
                // Get the Nashorn script engine
                ScriptEngineManager manager = new ScriptEngineManager();
                ScriptEngine engine = manager.getEngineByName("JavaScript");
```

```
        try {
                // Add a variable named msg to the global scope of
                // the script
                engine.eval("var msg = 'Hello globals'");

                // Print the value of the msg value
                engine.eval("print(this.msg);");

                // Create a ScriptContext and copy the ENGINE_SCOPE
                // Bindings of the default
                // script context to the new ScriptContext
                ScriptContext ctx = new SimpleScriptContext();
                ScriptContext defaultCtx = engine.getContext();
                Bindings engineBindings = defaultCtx.
                getBindings(ENGINE_SCOPE);
                ctx.setBindings(engineBindings, ENGINE_SCOPE);

                // Use the new ScriptContext to execute the script
                engine.eval("print(this.msg);", ctx);
        }
        catch (Exception e) {
                e.printStackTrace();
        }
    }
}
```

```
Hello globals
Hello globals
```

The `--global-per-engine` option for the Nashorn engine accomplishes the same things as in the previous example. It shares the script globals among all script contexts. Listing 12-3 shows how to set this option for the engine. The output confirms that the engine is using only one copy of globals to execute all scripts.

Listing 12-3. Sharing the Script Globals among All Script Contexts in a Nashorn Engine

```
// SharedGlobals.java
package com.jdojo.script;

import javax.script.Bindings;
import javax.script.ScriptContext;
import static javax.script.ScriptContext.ENGINE_SCOPE;
import javax.script.ScriptEngine;
import javax.script.ScriptEngineManager;
import javax.script.SimpleScriptContext;
import jdk.nashorn.api.scripting.NashornScriptEngineFactory;
```

```
public class SharedGlobals {
        public static void main(String[] args) {
                // Get the Nashorn script engine using the
                // --global-per_engine option
                NashornScriptEngineFactory factory = new
                NashornScriptEngineFactory();
                ScriptEngine engine = factory.getScriptEngine("--global-per-
                engine");

                try {
                        // Add a variable named msg to the global scope of
                        // the script
                        engine.eval("var msg = 'Hello globals'");

                        // Print the value of the msg value
                        engine.eval("print(this.msg);");

                        // Execute the same script, but using a new
                        // ScriptContext. Note that the script globals
                        // are shared and this script will find the
                        // this.msg variable created by the first
                        // script execution.
                        ScriptContext ctx = new SimpleScriptContext();
                        engine.eval("print(this.msg);", ctx);

                }
                catch (Exception e) {
                        e.printStackTrace();
                }
        }
}
```

```
Hello globals
Hello globals
```

Using Script Objects in Java Code

When objects and values from Nashorn cross the script-Java boundary to enter Java code, they need to be represented as Java objects and values. Table 12-2 lists the mapping of classes between script objects and their corresponding Java objects.

Table 12-2. *The List of Mapping Between Classes of Script Objects and Java Objects*

Script Object's Type	Java Object's Type
Undefined	`jdk.nashorn.internal.runtime.Undefined`
Null	`null`
Number	`java.lang.Number`
Boolean	`java.lang.Boolean`
Primitive String type	`java.lang.String`
Any script object	`jdk.nashorn.api.scripting.ScriptObjectMirror`
Any Java object	`The same as the Java object in the script`

Note that you are not supposed to use the classes and interfaces in the `jdk.nashorn.internal` package and its subpackages. They are listed in the table only for informational purposes. In this table, the mapping for the Nashorn Number type is shown as `java.lang.Number` type. Although Nashorn tries to pass `java.lang.Integer` and `java.lang.Double` objects for numeric value whenever possible, it is not reliable to depend on such specialized Java types. You should expect a `java.lang.Number` instance when a Nashorn Number is passed from a script to Java code. Whenever necessary, values of Number and Boolean types in Nashorn are converted to the corresponding Java primitive types, such as `int`, `double`, `boolean`, and so on.

In Nashorn, a script object is represented as an instance of the `jdk.nashorn.internal.runtime.ScriptObject` class. When the script object is passed to Java code, it is wrapped in a `ScriptObjectMirror` object. Before JDK8u40, if you passed a script object to a Java method that declared its parameter as `java.lang.Object` type, a `ScriptObject` was passed, not a `ScriptObjectMirror`. JDK8u40 has changed this behavior to pass a script object to Java code as a `ScriptObjectMirror` every time. If you had declared the method's parameter as `JSObject` or `ScriptObjectMirror` in Java, Nashorn always passed the script object to Java as a `ScriptObjectMirror`.

■ **Tip** It is possible for a script to pass the value `undefined` to Java code. You can check if a script object passed to Java is `undefined` using the `isUndefined(Object obj)` static method of the `ScriptObjectMirror` class. The method returns true if the specified `obj` is `undefined`; otherwise, it returns false.

The `ScriptObjectMirror` class implements the `JSObject` and `Bindings` interfaces. The class adds more methods to deal with script objects. You can store the reference of a script object in Java code in any of the three types of variables: `JSObject`, `Bindings`, or `ScriptObjectMirror`. What type you use depends on your needs. Using the `ScriptObjectMirror` type gives you more flexibility and access to all features of the script object. Table 12-3 contains the list of methods declared in the `JSObject` interface.

Table 12-3. *The List of Methods Declared in the JSObject Interface with Their Descriptions*

Method	Description
`Object call(Object thiz, Object... args)`	Calls this object as a function. You will use this method when the JSObject contains the reference of a Nashorn function or a method. The argument thiz is used as the value of this in the function invocation. The arguments in args are passed as the arguments to the called function. This method works in Java the same way as func.apply(thiz, args) works in Nashorn scripts.
`Object eval(String script)`	Evaluates the specified script.
`String getClassName()`	Returns the ECMAScript class name of the object. This is not the same as the class name in Java.
`Object getMember(String name)`	Returns the value of the named property of the script object.
`Object getSlot(int index)`	Returns the value of the indexed property of the script object.
`boolean hasMember(String name)`	Returns true if the script object has a named property; returns false otherwise.
`boolean hasSlot(int index)`	Returns true if the script object has an indexed property; returns false otherwise.
`boolean isArray()`	Returns true if the script object is an array object; returns false otherwise.
`boolean isFunction()`	Returns true if the script object is a function object; returns false otherwise.
`boolean isInstance(Object instance)`	Returns true if the specified instance is an instance of this object; returns false otherwise.
`boolean isInstanceOf(Object clazz)`	Returns true if this object is an instance of the specified clazz; returns false otherwise.
`boolean isStrictFunction()`	Returns true if this object is a strict function; returns false otherwise.
`Set<String> keySet()`	Returns the names of all properties of this object as a set of strings.
`Object newObject(Object... args)`	The object on which this method is invoked should be a constructor function object. Call this constructor to create a new object. This is equivalent to new func(arg1, arg2...) in Nashorn scripts.

(continued)

Table 12-3. (*continued*)

Method	Description
void removeMember(String name)	Removes the specified property from the object.
void setMember(String name, Object value)	Sets the specified value to the specified property name of this object. If the property name does not exist, a new property with the specified name is added.
void setSlot(int index, Object value)	Sets the specified value to the specified indexed property of this object. If the index does not exist, a new property with the specified index is added.
double toNumber()	Returns the object's numeric value. Typically, you will use this method if the script object is a wrapper for a numeric value such as a script object created in Nashorn using the expression new Object(234.90). On other script objects, it returns the value Double.NAN.
Collection<Object> values()	Returns all property values of this object in a Collection.

I will show how to use these methods and some methods of the ScriptObjectMirror class in the subsequent section. The JSObject interface can be implemented by any Java class. Objects of such a class can be used just as if they are script objects and can use the syntax obj.func(), obj[prop], delete obj.prop, and so on to work with their methods and properties in scripts.

Using Properties of Script Objects

The ScriptObjectMirror class implements JSObject and Bindings interfaces. You can use methods of both interfaces to access properties. You can use the getMember() and getSlot() methods of JSObject to read the named and indexed properties of the script object. You can use the get() method of Bindings to get the value of a property. You can use the setMember() and setSlot() methods of JSObject to add and update a property. The put() method of Bindings lets you do the same.

You can use the hasMember() and hasSlot() methods of JSObject to check whether a named property and an indexed property exist. At the same time, you can use the containsKey() method of the Bindings interface to check whether a property exists. You can think of the JSObject and Bindings interfaces implemented by the ScriptObjectMirror class providing two views of the same script object—the former as a simple object and the latter as a map.

Listing 12-4 contains a Nashorn script that creates two script objects and calls two methods of a Java class, as shown in Listing 12-5. The script passes the script objects to the Java methods. The Java methods print the properties of the passed objects and add a new property to both script objects. The script prints the properties after the method returns to confirm that the new properties added to script objects in Java code still exist.

Listing 12-4. A Nashorn Script That Calls Java Methods Passing Script Objects to Them

```javascript
// scriptobjectprop.js

// Create an object
var point = {x: 10, y: 20};

// Create an array
var empIds = [101, 102];

// Get the Java type
var ScriptObjectProperties = Java.type("com.jdojo.script.ScriptObjectProp");

// Pass the object to Java
ScriptObjectProperties.propTest(point);

// Print all properties of the point object
print("In script, after calling the Java method propTest()...");
for(var prop in point) {
        var value = point[prop];
        print(prop + " = " + value);
}

// Pass the array object to Java
ScriptObjectProperties.arrayTest(empIds);

// Print all elements of teh empIds array
print("In script, after calling the Java method arrayTest()...");
for(var i = 0, len = empIds.length; i < len; i++) {
        var value = empIds[i];
        print("empIds[" + i + "] = " + value);
}
```

Listing 12-5. A Java Class Whose Methods Access Properties of Script Objects

```java
// ScriptObjectProp.java
package com.jdojo.script;

import java.nio.file.Files;
import java.nio.file.Path;
import java.nio.file.Paths;
```

```java
import javax.script.ScriptEngine;
import javax.script.ScriptEngineManager;
import javax.script.ScriptException;
import jdk.nashorn.api.scripting.ScriptObjectMirror;

public class ScriptObjectProp {
    public static void main(String[] args) {
        // Construct the script file path
        String scriptFileName = "scriptobjectprop.js";
        Path scriptPath = Paths.get(scriptFileName);

        // Make sure the script file exists. If not, print the full
        // path of the script file and terminate the program.
        if (!Files.exists(scriptPath)) {
            System.out.println(scriptPath.toAbsolutePath()
                    + " does not exist.");
            return;
        }

        // Create a scripting engine manager
        ScriptEngineManager manager = new ScriptEngineManager();

        // Obtain a Nashorn scripting engine from the manager
        ScriptEngine engine = manager.getEngineByName("JavaScript");

        try {
            // Execute the script that will call the propTest() and
            // arrayTest() methods of this class
            engine.eval("load('" + scriptFileName + "')");
        }
        catch (ScriptException e) {
            e.printStackTrace();
        }
    }

    public static void propTest(ScriptObjectMirror point) {
        // List all properties
        System.out.println("Properties of point received in Java...");
        for (String prop : point.keySet()) {
            Object value = point.getMember(prop);
            System.out.println(prop + " = " + value);
        }
```

```
                // Let us add a property named z
                System.out.println("Adding z = 30 to point in Java... ");
                point.setMember("z", 30);
        }

        public static void arrayTest(ScriptObjectMirror empIds) {
                if (!empIds.isArray()) {
                        System.out.println("Passed in obejct is not an array.");
                        return;
                }

                // Get the length proeprty of teh array
                int length = ((Number) empIds.getMember("length")).intValue();

                System.out.println("empIds received in Java...");
                for (int i = 0; i < length; i++) {
                        int value = ((Number) empIds.getSlot(i)).intValue();
                        System.out.printf("empIds[%d] = %d%n", i, value);
                }

                // Let us add an element to the array
                System.out.println("Adding empIds[2] = 103 in Java... ");
                empIds.setSlot(length, 103);
        }
}
```

```
Properties of point received in Java...
x = 10
y = 20
Adding z = 30 to point in Java...
In script, after calling the Java method propTest()...
x = 10
y = 20
z = 30
empIds received in Java...
empIds[0] = 101
empIds[1] = 102
Adding empIds[2] = 103 in Java...
In script, after calling the Java method arrayTest()...
empIds[0] = 101
empIds[1] = 102
empIds[2] = 103
```

Creating Nashorn Objects in Java

You may have constructors in scripts and want to create objects in Java using those constructors. The newObject() method of the ScriptObjectMirror class lets you create script objects in Java. The method declaration is:

```
Object newObject(Object... args)
```

The arguments to the method are the arguments to be passed to the constructor. The method returns the new object reference. This method needs to be invoked on a constructor. First, you will need to get the reference of the constructor in Java as a ScriptObjectMirror object, and then call this method to create a new script object using that constructor.

You can call the methods of a script object using the callMember() method of the ScriptObjectMirror class. The method's declaration is:

```
Object callMember(String methodName, Object... args)
```

In Chapter 4, you created a constructor called Point. Its declaration is shown in Listing 12-6 for your reference. In this example, you will create objects of the Point type in Java.

Listing 12-6. The Declaration of a Constructor Named Point in Nashorn

```
// Point.js

// Define the Point constructor
function Point(x, y) {
    this.x = x;
    this.y = y;
}

// Override the toString() method in Object.prototype
Point.prototype.toString = function() {
    return "Point(" + this.x + ", " + this.y + ")";
};

// Define a new method called distance()
Point.prototype.distance = function(otherPoint) {
    var dx = this.x - otherPoint.x;
    var dy = this.y - otherPoint.y;
    var dist = Math.sqrt(dx * dx + dy * dy);
    return dist;
};
```

Listing 12-7 contains the Java program that performs the following steps:

- Loads the point.js script file that will load the definition of the Point constructor

- Gets the reference of the Point constructor by calling engine. get("Point")

- Creates two Point objects named p1 and p2 by calling the newObject() method on the Point constructor

- Invokes the callMember() method on p1 to invoke its distance() method to compute the distance between p1 and p2

- Invokes the callMember() method on p1 and p2 to get their string representation by calling their toString() method declared in the Point constructor

- Finally, prints the distance between the two points

Listing 12-7. Creating Nashorn Objects in Java Code

```java
// CreateScriptObject.java
package com.jdojo.script;

import java.nio.file.Files;
import java.nio.file.Path;
import java.nio.file.Paths;
import javax.script.ScriptEngine;
import javax.script.ScriptEngineManager;
import jdk.nashorn.api.scripting.ScriptObjectMirror;

public class CreateScriptObject {
        public static void main(String[] args) {

                // Construct the script file path
                String scriptFileName = "point.js";
                Path scriptPath = Paths.get(scriptFileName);

                // Make sure the script file exists. If not, print the full
                // path of the script file and terminate the program.
                if (! Files.exists(scriptPath) ) {
                        System.out.println(scriptPath.toAbsolutePath() +
                                " does not exist.");
                        return;
                }

                // Get the Nashorn script engine
                ScriptEngineManager manager = new ScriptEngineManager();
```

```
ScriptEngine engine = manager.getEngineByName("JavaScript");

try {

        // Execute the script in the file
        engine.eval("load('" + scriptFileName + "');");

        // Get the Point constructor as a ScriptObjectMirror
        // object
        ScriptObjectMirror pointFunc = (ScriptObjectMirror)
        engine.get("Point");

        // Create two Point objects. The following statements
        // are the same as var p1 = new Point(10, 20);
        // and var p2 = new Point(13, 24); in a Nashorn script
        ScriptObjectMirror p1 = (ScriptObjectMirror)
        pointFunc.newObject(10, 20);
        ScriptObjectMirror p2 = (ScriptObjectMirror)
        pointFunc.newObject(13, 24);

        // Compute the distance between p1 and p2 calling
        // the distance() method of the Point object
        Object result = p1.callMember("distance", p2);
        double dist = ((Number)result).doubleValue();

        // Get the string forms of p1 and p2 by calling
        // their toString() method
        String p1Str = (String)p1.callMember("toString");
        String p2Str = (String)p2.callMember("toString");
        System.out.printf("The distance between %s and %s is
        %.2f.%n",
                        p1Str, p2Str, dist);
    }
    catch (Exception e) {
        e.printStackTrace();
    }
  }
}
```

The distance between Point(10, 20) and Point(13, 24) is 5.00.

Invoking Script Functions From Java

You can invoke script functions from Java code. The Java code may be passed the script function object from the script or it may obtain the reference of the function object through the script engine. You can use the call() method on a ScriptObjectMirror that is the reference of the function object. The method's declaration is:

```
Object call(Object thiz, Object... args)
```

The first argument is the object reference that is used as this in the function invocation. The second argument is the list of arguments passed to the function. To invoke the function in the global scope, use null as the first argument.

In Chapter 4, you created a factorial() function to compute the factorial of a number. The declaration of this function is shown in Listing 12-8.

Listing 12-8. The Declaration of the factorial() Function

```
// factorial.js

// Returns true if n is an integer. Otherwise, returns false.
function isInteger(n) {
    return typeof n === "number" && isFinite(n) && n%1 === 0;
}


// Define a function that computes and returns the factorial of an integer
function factorial(n) {
    if (!isInteger(n)) {
        throw new TypeError("The number must be an integer. Found:" + n);
    }

    if(n < 0) {
        throw new RangeError("The number must be greater than 0. Found: " + n);
    }

    var fact = 1;
    for(var counter = n; counter > 1; fact *= counter--);

    return fact;
}
```

Listing 12-9 contains the Java program that loads the script from the factorial.js file, obtains the reference of the factorial() function in a ScriptObjectMirror, uses the call() method to call the factorial() function, and prints the result. At the end, the program calls the Array.prototype.join() function on a String object using the call() method of the ScriptObjectMirror class.

Listing 12-9. Calling a Script Function from Java Code

```java
// InvokeScriptFunctionInJava.java
package com.jdojo.script;

import java.nio.file.Files;
import java.nio.file.Path;
import java.nio.file.Paths;
import javax.script.ScriptEngine;
import javax.script.ScriptEngineManager;
import jdk.nashorn.api.scripting.ScriptObjectMirror;

public class InvokeScriptFunctionInJava {
    public static void main(String[] args) {
        // Construct the script file path
        String scriptFileName = "factorial.js";
        Path scriptPath = Paths.get(scriptFileName);

        // Make sure the script file exists. If not, print the full
        // path of the script file and terminate the program.
        if (!Files.exists(scriptPath)) {
            System.out.println(scriptPath.toAbsolutePath()
                    + " does not exist.");
            return;
        }

        // Get the Nashorn script engine
        ScriptEngineManager manager = new ScriptEngineManager();
        ScriptEngine engine = manager.getEngineByName("JavaScript");

        try {
            // Execute the script in the file, so teh
            // factorial() function is loaded
            engine.eval("load('" + scriptFileName + "');");

            // Get the reference of the factorial() script function
            ScriptObjectMirror factorialFunc =
                (ScriptObjectMirror)engine.get("factorial");

            // Invoke the factorial function and print the result
            Object result = factorialFunc.call(null, 5);
            double factorial = ((Number) result).doubleValue();
            System.out.println("Factorial of 5 is " + factorial);
```

```
                    /* Call the Array.prototype.join() function on a
                    String object */

                    // Get the reference of the Array.prototype.join method
                    ScriptObjectMirror arrayObject =
                            (ScriptObjectMirror)engine.eval(
                            "Array.prototype");
                    ScriptObjectMirror joinFunc =
                            (ScriptObjectMirror)arrayObject.
                            getMember("join");

                    // Call the join() function of Array.prototype on a
                    // string object passing a hyphen as a separator
                    String thisObject = "Hello";
                    String separator = "-";
                    String joinResult = (String)joinFunc.
                    call(thisObject, separator);
                    System.out.println(joinResult);
                }
                catch (Exception e) {
                    e.printStackTrace();
                }
        }
}
```

```
Factorial of 5 is 120.0
H-e-l-l-o
```

The ScriptObjectMirror class contains several other methods to deal with script objects in Java code. You can use the seal(), freeze(), and preventExtensions() methods to seal, freeze, and prevent extensions of the script object; they work the same as the Object.seal(), Object.freeze(), and Object.preventExtensions() methods in a Nashorn script. The class contains a utility method called to(), which is declared as follows:

```
<T> T to(Class<T> type)
```

You can use the to() method to convert a script object to the specified type.

Converting Script Dates to Java Dates

How will you create a date object in Java such as a java.time.LocalDate object from a script Date object? Converting a script date to a Java date is not straightforward. Both types of dates have one thing in common: they work with the same epoch, that is, midnight on January 1, 1970 UTC. You will need to get the milliseconds in the JavaScript date elapsed since the epoch, create an Instant, and create a ZonedDateTime from the Instant. Listing 12-10 contains a complete program to demonstrate the date conversion between JavaScript and Java. You may get a different output when you run this program. In the output, the string form of the JavaScript date does not contain milliseconds part, whereas the Java counterpart does. However, both dates internally represent the same instant.

Listing 12-10. Converting Script Dates to Java Dates

```
// ScriptDateToJavaDate.java
package com.jdojo.script;

import java.time.Instant;
import java.time.ZoneId;
import java.time.ZonedDateTime;
import javax.script.ScriptEngine;
import javax.script.ScriptEngineManager;
import jdk.nashorn.api.scripting.ScriptObjectMirror;

public class ScriptDateToJavaDate {
    public static void main(String[] args) {
        // Get the Nashorn script engine
        ScriptEngineManager manager = new ScriptEngineManager();
        ScriptEngine engine = manager.getEngineByName("JavaScript");

        try {
            // Create a Date object in script
            ScriptObjectMirror jsDt = (ScriptObjectMirror)
            engine.eval("new Date()");

            // Get the string representation of the script date
            String jsDtString = (String) jsDt.callMember("toString");

            System.out.println("JavaScript Date: " + jsDtString);

            // Get the epoch milliseconds from the script date
            long jsMillis = ((Number) jsDt.
            callMember("getTime")).longValue();

            // Convert the milliseconds from JavaScript date to
            // java Instant
            Instant instant = Instant.ofEpochMilli(jsMillis);
```

```
            // Get a ZonedDateTime for the system default zone id
            ZonedDateTime zdt =
                    ZonedDateTime.ofInstant(instant, ZoneId.
                    systemDefault());
            System.out.println("Java ZonedDateTime: " + zdt);
        }
        catch (Exception e) {
            e.printStackTrace();
        }
    }
}
```

```
JavaScript Date: Fri Oct 31 2014 18:17:02 GMT-0500 (CDT)
Java ZonedDateTime: 2014-10-31T18:17:02.489-05:00[America/Chicago]
```

Summary

The Java APIs for Nashorn provide Java classes and interfaces that let you deal with the Nashorn scripting engine and Nashorn objects directly in Java code. All classes for Java APIs for Nashorn are in the jdk.nashorn.api.scripting package. Notice that the Nashorn scripting engine internally uses a lot of other classes in other packages. However, you are not supposed to use them in your application directly, except for classes from the jdk.nashorn.api.scripting package.

A Nashorn script can use different types of values and objects such as Number, String, Boolean types of primitive values, and Object, String, Date, and custom objects. You can also create Java objects in scripts. The script values of type Number and Boolean are represented in Java as java.lang.Number and java.lang.Boolean. The Null type in a script is represented as null in Java. The String primitive type in a script is represented as java.lang.String in Java. A script object is represented as an object of the ScriptObjectMirror class in Java.

The NashornScriptEngineFactory and ScriptEngine classes in the jdk.nashorn. api.scripting package represent the Nashorn script engine factory and script engine, respectively. You will need to work with these classes directly if you want to pass options to the Nashorn engine. You can also pass options to the Nashorn engine using -Dnashorn.args="<options>" on the command-line. If you pass the --globals-per-engine, to a Nashorn engine, all script contexts will share the globals. By default, script contexts do not share globals.

The ScriptObjectMirror class contains several methods to add, update, and delete properties from the script object. The class implements the JSObject and Bindings interfaces. The JSObject interface lets you treat a script object as a simple Java class, whereas the Bindings interface lets you treat a script object as a map. You can use getMember(), getSlot(), and get() methods to get the value of the property of a script object. You can use setMember(), setSlot(), and put() methods to add or update the value of a property. You can use the callMember() method to call a method of the script object. The call() method lets you call a script function, allowing you to pass the this value for the function invocation. The ScriptObjectMirror class contains several other methods that let you work with script objects in Java programs.

■ ■ ■

CHAPTER 13

Debugging, Tracing, and Profiling Scripts

In this chapter, you will learn:

- How to debug standalone Nashorn scripts in the NetBeans IDE

- How to debug Nashorn scripts that are called from Java code in the NetBeans IDE

- How to trace and profile Nashorn scripts

NetBeans 8 with JDK 8 or later supports debugging, tracing, and profiling Nashorn scripts. You can run and debug standalone Nashorn scripts from within the NetBeans IDE. You can also debug Nashorn scripts when they are called from Java code. You can use all the debugging features for debugging scripts that you can use for debugging Java code; you can set breakpoints, display variables' values, add watches, monitor call stacks, and so on. When debugging Nashorn scripts, the debugger shows the Nashorn stack.

In NetBeans, all debugger-related panes can be opened using the menu item Windows ➤ Debugging. For a list of the complete debugging features in NetBeans, please refer to the help page in NetBeans. You can open the help page by pressing the F1 key while the NetBeans application is active. I will use the script in Listing 13-1 as an example of debugging scripts in this chapter.

Listing 13-1. A Test Script Containing an isPrime( ) Function and Calls to That Function

```
// primetest.js

function isPrime(n) {
        // Integers <= 2, floating-point numbers, and even numbers are not
        // primes
        if (n <= 2 || Math.floor(n) !== n || n % 2 === 0) {
                return false;
        }
```

```
        // Check if n is divisible by any odd integers between 3 and sqrt(n).
        var sqrt = Math.sqrt(n);
        for (var i = 3; i <= sqrt; i += 2) {
                if (n % i === 0) {
                        return false;
                }
        }
        return true; // If we get here, it is a prime number.
}

// Check few nubmers for being primes
var num = 8;
var isPrimeNum = isPrime(num);
print(num + " is a prime number: " + isPrimeNum);

debugger;
num = 37;
isPrimeNum = isPrime(num);
print(num + " is a prime number: " + isPrimeNum);
```

Debugging Standalone Scripts

To run or debug a standalone Nashorn script in NetBeans, first you need to open the script file in the NetBeans IDE. Figure 13-1 shows the script shown in Listing 13-1 open in NetBeans. To run the script, right click in the editor showing the script and select the Run File menu item. Alternatively, press Shift + F6 while the script pane is active.

Figure 13-1. *A Nashorn script opened in the NetBeans IDE*

To debug scripts, you need to add breakpoints using one of the following three methods:

- Place the cursor in the line where you want to set/unset the breakpoint. Right click and select the menu item Toggle Line Breakpoint to set and unset the breakpoint.

- Place the cursor in the line where you want to set/unset the breakpoint and press Ctrl + F8. Pressing this key combination for the first time sets the breakpoint. If the breakpoint is already set, pressing the same key combination unsets the breakpoint.

- Add the debugger statement in the script. The debugger statement acts like a breakpoint when a debugging session is active. Otherwise, it has no effect.

Figure 13-2 shows the same script with two breakpoints at lines 21 and 26.

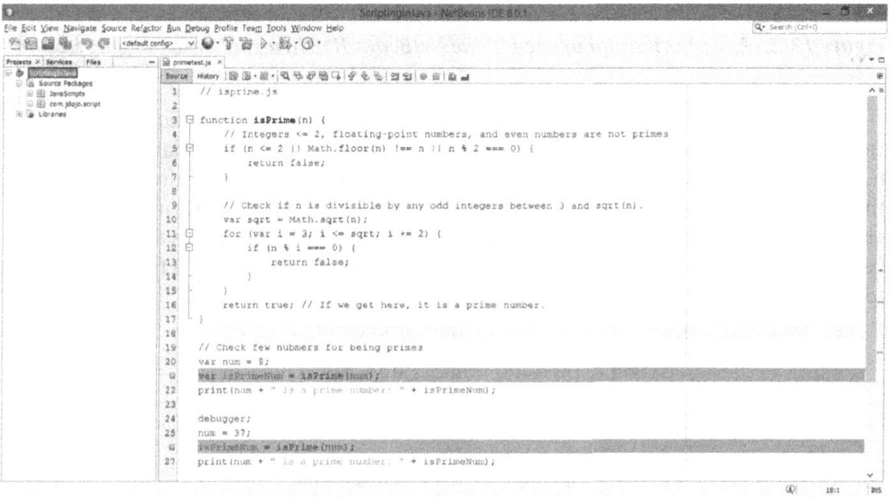

Figure 13-2. *A Nashorn script opened in the NetBeans IDE that has two breakpoints*

Now you are ready to debug the script. Right click in the script pane and select the Debug File menu item. Alternatively, press Ctrl + Shift + F5 when the script pane is active. It will start the debugging session as shown in Figure 13-3. The debugger stops at the first breakpoint, as shown in the figure. At the bottom, you see the Variables pane open that shows all the variables with their values in scope. If you want to view other details of the debugging session, use one of the menu items under the main menu Window ➤ Debugging. If you close any debugging panes such as the Variables pane, you can reopen them using the Window ➤ Debugging menu.

Figure 13-3. *A Nashorn script opened in the NetBeans IDE in an active debugging session*

When the debugger session is active, you can use the debugging actions such as step into, step over, step out, continue, and so on. These actions are available from the main menu item named Debug as well as from the debugger toolbar. Figure 13-4 shows the debugger toolbar. It appears by default when the debugger session is active. If it is not visible when the debugger session is active, right click in the toolbar area and select the Debug menu item to make it visible. Table 13-1 contains the debugging actions available for scripts with their shortcuts and descriptions.

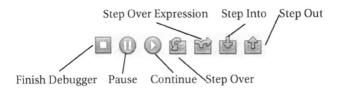

Figure 13-4. *The items in the debugger toolbar in NetBeans IDE*

Table 13-1. *The List of Debugger Actions in NetBeans*

Debug Action	Shortcut	Description
Finish Debugger	`Shift + F5`	Ends the debugging session.
Pause		Stops all threads in the current session.
Continue	`Ctrl + F5`	Resumes execution of the program until the next breakpoint.
Step Over	`F8`	Executes the current line and moves the program counter to the next line in the file. If the executed line is a call to a function, the code in the function is also executed.
Step Over Expression	`Shift + F8`	Enables you to proceed through each method call in an expression and view the input parameters as well as resulting output values of each method call. If there are no further method calls, it behaves like the Step Over action.
Step Into	`F7`	Executes the current line. If the line is a call to a function and there is source available for the called function, the program counter moves to the declaration of the function. Otherwise, the program counter moves to the next line in the script.
Step Out	`Ctrl + F7`	Executes the rest of the code in the current function and moves the program counter to the line after the caller of the function. Use this action if you have stepped into a function that you do not need to debug anymore.

Debugging Scripts from Java Code

Debugging scripts that are called from Java code work a little differently. Just setting breakpoints in the script file and starting a debugger or stepping into the script from Java code does not work. You will use the Java program shown in Listing 13-2 to debug the script shown in Listing 13-1. The Java program uses a Reader to execute the script from the primetest.js file. However, you can also use the load() function. In Listing 13-2, you can replace the code in the try-catch block with the following snippet of code and the program will work the same; you need to remove two import statements that imports classes from the java.io package:

```
try {
        // Execute the script in the file
        engine.eval("load('" + scriptFileName + "');"); // First time, add a
                                                         // breakpoint here
}
catch (ScriptException e) {
        e.printStackTrace();
}
```

Listing 13-2. Debugging Scripts That Are Called from Java Code

```java
// PrimeTest.java
package com.jdojo.script;

import java.io.IOException;
import java.io.Reader;
import java.nio.file.Files;
import java.nio.file.Path;
import java.nio.file.Paths;
import javax.script.ScriptEngine;
import javax.script.ScriptEngineManager;
import javax.script.ScriptException;

public class PrimeTest {
        public static void main(String[] args) {
                // Construct the script file path
                String scriptFileName = "primetest.js";
                Path scriptPath = Paths.get(scriptFileName);

                // Make sure the script file exists. If not, print the full
                // path of the script file and terminate the program.
                if (!Files.exists(scriptPath)) {
                        System.out.println(scriptPath.toAbsolutePath() +"
                                        "does not exist.");
                        return;
                }

                // Get the Nashorn script engine
                ScriptEngineManager manager = new ScriptEngineManager();
                ScriptEngine engine = manager.getEngineByName("JavaScript");
```

```
        try {
                // Get a Reader for the script file
                Reader scriptReader = Files.
                newBufferedReader(scriptPath);

                // Execute the script in the file
                engine.eval(scriptReader);  // First time, add a
                                            // breakpoint here
        }
        catch (IOException | ScriptException e) {
                e.printStackTrace();
        }
    }
}
```

As the first step in debugging the script, you need to set a breakpoint at the line of code that calls the eval() method of the script engine. Without performing this step, you will not be able to step into the script from the debugger. Figure 13-5 shows the code of the PrimeTest class with a breakpoint at line 35.

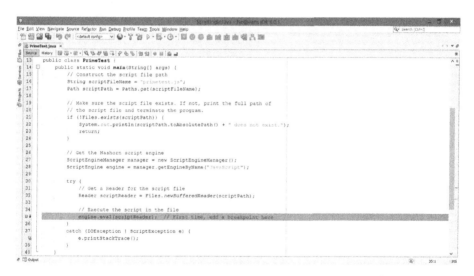

Figure 13-5. *The code of the PrimeTest class with a breakpint at line 35 in the NetBeans IDE*

The next step is to start the debugger. You can use Ctrl + Shift + F5 when the editor pane containing the PrimeTest class is active. The debugger will stop at the breakpoint at line 35. You need to step into the eval() method call by pressing F7; this will take you to the AbstractScriptEngine.java file, as shown in Figure 13-6.

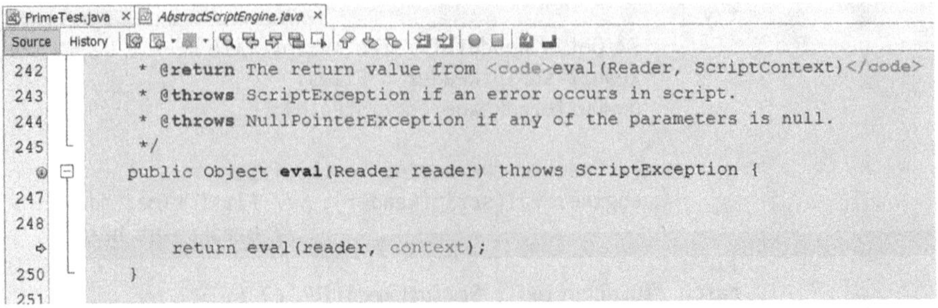

Figure 13-6. *The debugger window when the AbstractScriptEngine.java file is being debugged*

Step into the eval() method call by pressing F7. The debugger will open a file named <eval>.js that contains the script from the primetest.js file that you were trying to load through the Java code using a Reader. You can scroll through the script and set breakpoints in the <eval>.js file. Figure 13-7 shows the file with two breakpoints—one at line 21 and one at line 27.

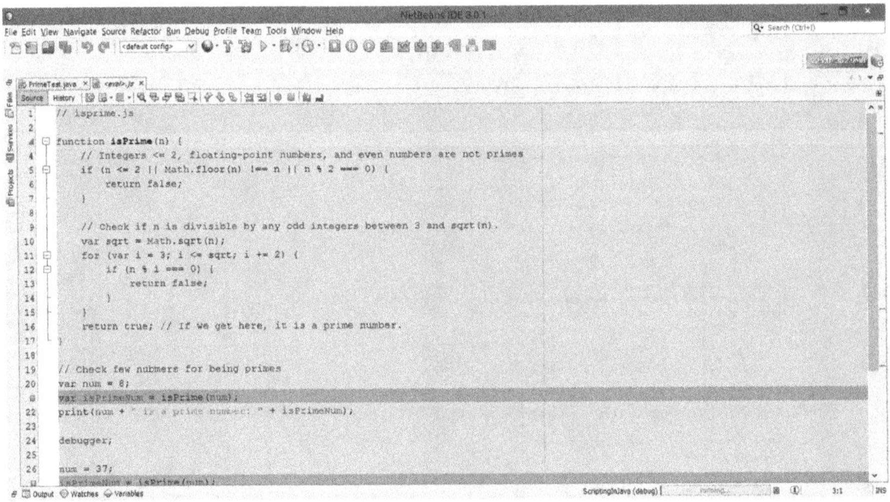

Figure 13-7. *The debugger window showing the loaded script in the <eval>.js file*

After you have set the breakpoints in the script in the <eval>.js file, you are ready to proceed with normal debugging actions. For example, the Continue debugging action (F5) will stop the execution at the next breakpoint.

When the debugger finishes, you can remove the breakpoints from the Java code that is the `PrimaTest.java` file in this example. If you start a new debugging session, the debugger will stop at the breakpoints you had set in the `<eval>.js` file previously. Notice that you had to step into the `<eval>.js` file only once. All subsequent debugging sessions remember the breakpoints from the previous sessions.

■ **Tip**   Even though the `debugger` statement is supported by Nashorn, the NetBeans IDE does not seem to recognize it as a breakpoint in Nashorn scripts. Adding the `debugger` statement in scripts does not suspend the execution when the debugger is active.

Tracing and Profiling Scripts

Nashorn supports callsite tracing and profiling. You can enable these options in the `jjs` command-line tool as well as in the embedded Nashorn engine. You can enable tracing and profiling for all scripts run by the engine or per script/function. The `-tcs` option enables callsite tracing for all scripts and prints the callsite tracing information on the standard output. The `-pcs` option enables callsite profiling for all scripts and prints the callsite profiling data in a file called `NashornProfile.txt` in the current directory.

You can use the following four Nashorn directives in the beginning of scripts or functions to selectively trace and profile the entire script or functions:

- `"nashorn callsite trace enterexit";`
  `// Equivalent to -tcs=enterexit`

- `"nashorn callsite trace miss";`
  `// Equivalent to -tcs=miss`

- `"nashorn callsite trace objects";`
  `// Equivalent to -tcs=objects`

- `"nashorn callsite profile";`
  `// Equivalent to -pcs`

■ **Tip**   The `-tcs` and `-pcs` options work on per script engine basis, whereas the four tracing and profiling directives work on per script and per function basis.

These Nashorn directives are enabled only in debug mode. You can enable Nashorn debug mode by setting the `nashorn.debug` system property to true. These directive are available in JDK8u40 and later. JDK8u40 is still in development at the time of writing of this book. Listing 13-3 shows a script with a Nashorn callsite profile option enabled for a function. The script has been saved in the file named `primeprofiler.js`.

Listing 13-3. A Script with a Nashorn Callsite Profile Directive Enabled for a Function

```
// primeprofiler.js

function isPrime(n) {
        // Profile this function only
        "nashorn callsite profile";

        // Integers <= 2, floating-point numbers, and even numbers are not primes
        if (n <= 2 || Math.floor(n) !== n || n % 2 === 0) {
                return false;
        }

        // Check if n is divisible by any odd integers between 3 and sqrt(n).
        var sqrt = Math.sqrt(n);
        for (var i = 3; i <= sqrt; i += 2) {
                if (n % i === 0) {
                        return false;
                }
        }
        return true; // If we get here, it is a prime number.
}

// Check few nubmers for being primes
var num = 8;
var isPrimeNum = isPrime(num);
print(num + " is a prime number: " + isPrimeNum);

num = 37;
isPrimeNum = isPrime(num);
print(num + " is a prime number: " + isPrimeNum);
```

The following command runs the script in the primeprofile.js file with Nashorn debug option enabled:

```
c:\>jjs -J-Dnashorn.debug=true primeprofile.js
8 is a prime number: false
37 is a prime number: true

C:\
```

The command will generate a file named NashornProfile.txt in the current directly that contains the profile data for the isPrime() function call. The contents of this file are shown in Listing 13-4.

Listing 13-4. The Contents of the NashornProfile.txt File

```
0        dyn:getProp|getElem|getMethod:Math      438462        2
1        dyn:getMethod|getProp|getElem:floor     433936        2
2        dyn:call                                650602        2
3        dyn:getProp|getElem|getMethod:Math      313834        1
4        dyn:getMethod|getProp|getElem:sqrt      283356        1
5        dyn:call                                     0        1
```

Listing 13-5 contains the Java program that sets the nashorn.debug system property and runs the script shown in Listing 13-3. Running the program will create a NashornProfile.txt file in the current directory, and the contents of the file will be the same as shown in Listing 13-2.

Listing 13-5. Setting the nashorn.debug System Property and Profiling Scripts

```java
// ProfilerTest.java
package com.jdojo.script;

import java.io.IOException;
import java.io.Reader;
import java.nio.file.Files;
import java.nio.file.Path;
import java.nio.file.Paths;
import javax.script.ScriptEngine;
import javax.script.ScriptEngineManager;
import javax.script.ScriptException;

public class ProfilerTest {
        public static void main(String[] args) {
                // Set the nashorn.debug system property, so the tracing and
                // profiling directives will be recognized
                System.setProperty("nashorn.debug", "true");

                // Construct the script file path
                String scriptFileName = "primeprofiler.js";
                Path scriptPath = Paths.get(scriptFileName);

                // Make sure the script file exists. If not, print the full
                // path of the script file and terminate the program.
                if (!Files.exists(scriptPath)) {
                        System.out.println(scriptPath.toAbsolutePath() +
                                        "does not exist.");
                        return;
                }
```

```
                    // Get the Nashorn script engine
                    ScriptEngineManager manager = new ScriptEngineManager();
                    ScriptEngine engine = manager.getEngineByName("JavaScript");

                    try {
                            // Get a Reader for the script file
                            Reader scriptReader = Files.
                            newBufferedReader(scriptPath);

                            // Execute the script in the file
                            engine.eval(scriptReader);
                    }
                    catch (IOException | ScriptException e) {
                            e.printStackTrace();
                    }
            }
}
```

```
8 is a prime number: false
37 is a prime number: true
```

Summary

NetBeans 8 with JDK 8 or later supports debugging Nashorn scripts in the NetBeans IDE. You can run and debug standalone Nashorn scripts from within the NetBeans IDE. You can also debug Nashorn scripts when they are called from Java code. The debugger jumps from Java code to Nashorn scripts seamlessly.

Nashorn supports callsite tracing and profiling. You can enable these options in the jjs command-line tool as well as in the embedded Nashorn engine. You can enable tracing and profiling for all scripts run by the engine or per script/function. The -tcs option enables callsite tracing for all scripts run by the engine. The -pcs option enables callsite profiling for all scripts run by the engine and prints the callsite profiling data in a file called NashornProfile.txt in the current directory. JDK8u40 adds four Nashorn directives: "nashorn callsite trace enterexit", "nashorn callsite trace miss", "nashorn callsite trace objects", and "nashorn callsite profile". These directives can be added in the beginning of scripts and functions to trace and profile scripts and functions selectively. They work only in debug mode, which can be enabled setting the system property nashorn.debug to true.

Index

Get the eBook for only $10!

Now you can take the weightless companion with you anywhere, anytime. Your purchase of this book entitles you to 3 electronic versions for only $10.

This Apress title will prove so indispensible that you'll want to carry it with you everywhere, which is why we are offering the eBook in 3 formats for only $10 if you have already purchased the print book.

Convenient and fully searchable, the PDF version enables you to easily find and copy code—or perform examples by quickly toggling between instructions and   applications. The MOBI format is ideal for your Kindle, while the ePUB can be utilized on a variety of mobile devices.

Go to www.apress.com/promo/tendollars to purchase your companion eBook.